FINDING STRONG

by CLAUDE COOPER

with Leigh Cooper Wallace

Also by Claude Cooper

Leavings: Honeycutt to Cooper Ridge

Copyright (©) 2016 by Claude Cooper

ISBN – 13: 978-1539537038

TABLE OF CONTENTS

INTRODUCTION

In December, 2012, teacher, coach, runner, mother, survivor and force of nature Leigh Cooper Wallace died of pneumonia, a complication resulting from a tragic case of what was probably a mistake. Leigh had become a local celebrity in the High Country of North Carolina, a pinnacle of emotional, mental, and physical strength. She was someone who not only personified courage but had an extraordinary way of finding that same strength and courage in others.

Leigh taught me how to run . . . *hard.* But in doing so, she provided me with a sense of endurance and personal empowerment that bled into every channel of my personal and professional life.

My last moments spent with Leigh were just two weeks before she died . . . and while I often replay that day in my mind, imagining an afternoon full of heartfelt truths, an endless trickle of wisdom that I had no idea would soon run dry, what we really did . . . was gossip. Fleeting romances (mine), impossibly perfect marriages (hers), and the amount of calories contained in our chicken tacos (decidedly, too many). When Leigh laughed, she used her whole body. And for someone who had faced terrifying challenges, she had a staggering sense of humor.

But then Leigh said something *really* funny. She told me that she worried that maybe she didn't have as much impact on the world as she could or should have . . . that she didn't touch enough people with her story and her strength . . . that she wasn't brave.

Then it was my turn to laugh. Hard enough maybe to have earned a second taco. And she smiled, knowingly, as I told her that I, among many, would not be the person I am if not for her inspirational and downright aggressive intervention. Leigh Wallace, I told her, is the bravest woman I know. And I could tell, by her fiery-eyed grin, that she knew that too.

It's been four years since Leigh's death, and like so many of those who knew and loved her, I've had to gossip without her, laugh without her, cry without her. Yet she always finds a way to remind me, as she did so many times in life, that I am much, much stronger than I think I am.

And because Leigh never sat still, and sought to inspire so many, I know I'm not the only one.

--Lauren Elle Smith

"Above all, be the heroine of your life, not the victim."

- Nora Ephron, Wellesley Commencement Address, 1969

PROLOGUE

CLAUDE

August 12, 2016

Now that we've sold the house, we don't go back as often. We still have rental property that we check on occasionally, but that's not why we were going this time. It was her birthday.

Louise has always felt a little guilty that we've left her up on the mountain all alone. When everyone else in the family left, we just didn't feel like we could remain out on Cooper Ridge in that big house by ourselves. We needed to be around people, people who cared about us. We needed to get on with our lives, as she surely would have wanted for us. But we both agreed that we at least had to be with our daughter on her birthday.

As always, the trip to Boone took exactly three hours and fifteen minutes. We drove up on Thursday, the day before her birthday. Our time would be very limited, as Louise had a mandatory teacher training session in Pickens, SC, starting at noon on Friday. Louise had booked a room at the Comfort Suites in Boone. We had friends who had kindly offered lodging for us, but we knew our schedule would be tight and, frankly, we wanted to be alone.

We checked into the hotel and changed into our exercise clothes. A few years ago, that would mean running gear; now it's walking. But it's anything but a stroll; it's all I can do to keep up with Louise when she's walking for exercise. We went to the Greenway Trail where Leigh spent so much of her time: racing during and after college and coaching her high school teams. She probably knew that trail as well as anyone in the county. One branch of the trail leads to the high school where she coached cross-country, track, and lacrosse. We took that branch and walked all the way to the school. As we made our way along the fence surrounding the lacrosse field, we were serenaded by the high school band practicing on the field. We continued around the field to the entrance where we used our phones to take pictures of the sign proclaiming, "Leigh Cooper Wallace Memorial Field." The stone pillars supporting the sign were beautiful and prompted Louise to comment, "I need to send a card to the mason who did this. He volunteered his labor."

I nodded in agreement, but another thought was running through my mind: "I wonder if any of those band members there on the field bearing her name know that tomorrow is her birthday." I didn't say it out loud, fearing I would break down.

We always run into people we know when we return to Boone. This time was no exception as we were stopped twice on the return to the car by old friends. We shared hugs and tears and updated them on our lives since leaving Boone. When we returned to the car, Louise reminded me that we needed to go by Michael's to get flowers. I waited in the car as she went in to pick out the flowers. She returned with gold flowers, blue flowers, white flowers and one red rose.

"The gold is for App State," she explained, "and the blue and white is for Watauga High School."

"And the red rose is for the love we have for her," I replied.

"Yes, and the love she shared with everyone she knew."

We discussed our dinner options. We were both sweaty from the walk and neither of us was emotionally ready for the likelihood of meeting other acquaintances.

"Let's just do what Leigh would do," suggested Louise.

"Well," I replied, knowing what Louise was thinking, "she'd probably order food to take back home and watch the Olympics on TV. Shall we order pizza?"

The next morning we were up early. We ate breakfast in the hotel and drove across town to Mount Lawn Cemetery.

"I really wish they would repave this road," Louise said as we negotiated the potholes on the main road into the cemetery. We drove to the old maple tree at the highest point in the cemetery. We had picked out this prime location many years ago for our own plots. When we came out with Leigh's husband, Chris, to pick out a plot for Leigh, all the good locations had been taken. Louise and I looked at each other with the same thought.

"Should we give him our plot?" she suggested. I readily agreed. We were so happy that the site overlooked the new high school Leigh loved so dearly; I could see the lights of the lacrosse field that had been named for her.

Louise, as she always does when we visit the grave, replaced the flowers and got down on her hands and knees to clean the marble slab. She brushed off all the dirt, picked the grass around it, and wiped it down with a wet towel. While she worked, I sat on the grass and pulled out the letter I had written. I read to myself, too choked with emotion to read aloud:

> Well, Leigh, it's been over three years now, and I don't think I'm any nearer to getting closure than I was the day you left us. I'm not even sure I'm supposed to get closure. Everyone says it will get better with time, but it's not getting better. Maybe it's the way you left us: so suddenly, when things seemed to be going so well for you and for all of us. You were like a rock star in Watauga County, loving everybody, and everybody loving you. It happened so quickly. We didn't know you were dying; I'm certain you never knew you were dying. By the time we realized how serious it was, the doctors had put you in a coma with tubes running into you everywhere. I guess that's the part that just tears me up and that I have such trouble coping with: you never said goodbye.
>
> So much has happened since you left us. Your death started a domino effect of changes. You know that Mom and I expected to live on Cooper Ridge until we died. You had always assured us you would care for us when we were old and dying. Even though I was getting tired of the rough winters and plowing the snow off the roads on those cold mornings, I expect we would have been there as long as you were. But you know,

11

driving by your house two or three times a day knowing you were not there and never would be again – that was so hard on us. And all the other little things we had grown to expect; like coming home from a trip and your insisting that we stop by your house or either your rushing up to our house to ask all about the trip, or you on the spur of the moment asking us to come down to your house for supper, or asking what we were having for supper and could you and your family join us. And now, there's a new family living in your dream house and a new family living in our dream house.

When everyone else in the family left the Boone area, your mom and I felt like we, too, had to make a change. After considerable thought and discussion, we decided to move to Clemson. We have many very close friends here, people who genuinely care about us, and we just felt like we needed to be around people more.

Leigh, you would love our house here in Clemson; you would love everything about Clemson, and especially our friends here. It's such a paradox. We love being here, but we'd give anything to be back on Cooper Ridge if you and your family were still there. And while I know you would love what we have in Clemson, the notion to leave Cooper Ridge wouldn't have even crossed our minds if you hadn't left us. And you never said goodbye.

You were so strong, Leigh. I've said many times that you were the strongest person I ever knew. Some people don't understand, thinking I'm just talking about physical strength. Of course, you had great physical strength: that finely chiseled body; the efficiency of your heart and lungs that gave you that incredible aerobic capacity; your extremely high pain threshold, allowing you to run through pain. But one would have to look much deeper to get the total package: the intensity with which you tackled anything you did, your character, the desire to make those around you better and stronger.

It took that total package to survive what you went through in 1989. You looked death squarely in the eye and you beat it. I don't know anyone else who could have done what you did then. Maybe you were put in that car for a reason. After that incident, and considering the amazing things you did with your life over the next 24 years, neither I nor anyone else expected you to leave us the way you finally did. I have a theory though. In 1989, you knew you were facing death. You had warning – not much warning – but enough to formulate a strategy, and you managed to escape. In December of 2012, death sneaked up on you. You never knew you were dying. I'll always believe that if you had known how serious your situation was, you would have beaten death again. I know you weren't ready to go. I know you would never leave without saying goodbye. You would want to ensure that everyone was going to be okay after you left, that we would be able to get on with our lives. That's the way you were in that car with Daniel Lee in 1989. When he had the gun to your head and you knew he was about to pull the trigger, you were thinking more about us than about yourself. You were concerned that we would never find your body, that we would never know what had happened to you. You were concerned that we would suffer terribly. Even when he pulled the trigger, and you realized the gun was not loaded and you would have to die a slow and very painful death, you worried more about us than yourself. Your biggest concern was how your death would affect your family.

I know it would have been terribly hard on you and on each of us to say a final goodbye. I don't know how any of us could have done it, especially me. But at least I wish I had heard you say that you were okay and that in time we would be okay. Leigh, I just wanted you to tell me goodbye.

You had finally started to write your story, a story to inspire others. I have vowed to finish it for you; perhaps this will be my way of saying good-bye.

When Louise was finally satisfied that the grave marker was perfectly clean, we stood. We embraced and cried together as we stared at the words:

Leigh Cooper Wallace, August 12, 1969 – December 17, 2012
You're Stronger Than You Think.

We took several pictures to send to family.

"Happy birthday, Leigh," said Louise as we turned to walk to the car.

Oh, how I wish it were a happy birthday. The tears continued to flow as we drove out of town and headed back down the mountain. I'm sure Leigh would say, and I'll just have to believe, it's okay for the strong to cry.

LEIGH

September 29, 1989

I was having a good run, thinking positive thoughts. Nearing the end of the run, I was thinking about my plans for that night. Chris and I planned to go out with his friends. About fifteen minutes from the end of my run, going downhill, I really started flying, and I loved to finish a run this way. It was the end of September and getting dark earlier, an overcast day and drizzling. I love this kind of run, not raining at first, but then during the run, when you're hot and you're feeling free, a light rain comes and splashes in your face and it just feels really good. You feel like you're an animal in its natural habitat, free of all concerns; you're running and water's dripping down on you and you're flying and feeling free.

I was coming down the left side of Meadowview Drive. No sidewalks here and, on the right, a steep drop-off with shops and a trailer park at the bottom. On the left, just woods and a steep, uphill bank, the only part of the run where people were not visible.

Looking ahead, I noticed a white car approaching. Rather than giving room as drivers typically do for runners, the car edged closer to my side of the road. My first thought: What a jerk; this guy is not going to give me any room to run on the road! He was slowing down so my next thought was maybe this is someone I know, though I didn't recognize the car. He edged closer, giving me even less room on the road. I slowed to a jog, realizing now that he was intentionally approaching me, possibly to ask for directions. From where I stood, I could not see the driver's face through the windshield; it was raining and the windshield wiper on the passenger side was sticking straight out and obviously not working.

I walked the few steps it took to get from the front of the car to the passenger door and had my first look at him. My heart jumped. I stepped back and took a deep breath, instantly scared and knowing I was in trouble. I expected a familiar or at least friendly face, but the man looked scary. He was dirty-looking, with greasy, scraggly long

15

hair, an unshaven face with a mustache and long, heavy sideburns. He wore a t-shirt, and he had eyes that I remember locking onto; they were emotionless. When I stepped back and took a deep breath, he said, "Get in the car." It's almost like you don't believe what you are hearing.

"Are you kidding?" I knew he wasn't kidding; I saw a gun in his lap. I said to myself, "Please tell me this isn't real. Is this actually happening?" I did not want to believe that a dirty-looking man with emotionless eyes and a gun had just told me to get in his car. I immediately started crying. I knew I was in trouble.

Suddenly, a pickup truck came from the direction I had been running. As the truck approached, I looked at its driver, who slowed down as if trying to figure out what was happening. I was already crying, but I was frozen with fear and couldn't say anything. I kept my eyes locked on the truck driver the whole time he drove by, my eyes pleading and begging for his help. He stared at me, then turned away.

"Get in the car or I'll shoot."

I looked in the car at the gun in his lap and knew the man was not kidding. I froze; running never entered my mind. I saw the gun and I did what I was told. As I sat down in the car and shut the door, I told myself, "I'm dead. I'm dead. I just made a deadly mistake. I should not have gotten into this car."

I was begging for a chance to make a different choice.

CHAPTER ONE

"SHE CAN PUT A WORM ON A HOOK"

LEIGH

As a child, my parents gave me great leeway to make my own choices. I don't know if it was because I was the oldest or just so bullheaded and insistent on doing things my way.

People have told me my whole life that I am a strong person. I remember when I was six years old and enrolled in gymnastics, a sport in which I competed until I was twelve. My greatest attribute in gymnastics was my physical strength. My best event was the uneven parallel bars because strength and courage were essential. What I lacked in gymnastics, the elements that kept me from being successful at a higher level, were grace, flexibility, and poise. But I was proud of my strength and courage and welcomed any chance to show both qualities.

Friends and family frequently challenged me to perform feats of strength, like demonstrating how many pushups I could do or arm-wrestling someone. In my 7th grade keyboarding class, the boys lined up to arm-wrestle me. Beating me in arm-wrestling became an unofficial rite of passage for the boys. Built very much like my dad with big thighs, muscle definition and a large and broad back, I looked strong. Later, as a teenager, my physique was not something I particularly liked; but as a young girl, I was always proud of my physique, looking and being strong and broad, but lean. My self-image early in life was clearly built around the notion that I was physically strong and could impress people with my strength.

CLAUDE

Louise and I met at a fraternity costume party at Clemson in February, 1967. I spotted Louise across the room and an inner voice told me to meet her. We chatted but made no plans to get together.

A month later, to my great fortune, my friend Rusty Adkins suggested he arrange a date for me with his friend, Louise Dickert, describing her as the perfect date for me. I remembered her name and face and eagerly agreed. "Sure," I said. "I met her at the costume party and spoke with her. I'm not sure I made much of an impression in my Viet Cong costume, but she definitely got my attention."

Louise and I had our first date at a fraternity party over spring break weekend and found a natural attraction. We dated every weekend during my final year at Clemson until I graduated in May, 1967. After I reenlisted in the Army to attend Officer Candidate School at Fort Benning, Georgia, we saw each other whenever possible and were married on June 8, 1968, five days after graduation from OCS. Except for a second tour in Vietnam in 1971-72, we haven't been apart since.

We began our married life in a small apartment in Oxen Hill, Maryland, as I attended the Army's Spanish language school in Alexandria, Virginia. Louise was the fourth of six children in her family, and I was the second of five in mine. Family was and still is the most important thing in both of our lives. We were eager to begin our own family.

After our six-month stay in the DC area, we moved to Fayetteville, NC, for a four-month assignment at the Special Forces Officer Course (SFOC) at Fort Bragg. We knew that my next assignment would be to 8th Special Forces Group in Panama, Canal Zone. We also learned our family life would change dramatically in Panama, as Louise discovered she was pregnant.

Leigh Martin Cooper was born at Coco Solo Hospital in the

Canal Zone on August 12, 1969. She was a beautiful baby at 9 pounds, 3 ounces. Sixteen months later, also at Coco Solo Hospital, Julie Louise Cooper was born. Life was great in Panama for a young couple with two infant children. With my promotion to First Lieutenant, my airborne pay, and living in government housing, we could afford a live-in maid, which gave Louise and me plenty of free time to pursue our athletic interests. Louise and I began bowling, and I played golf and fast-pitch softball whenever possible.

With the Vietnam war winding down, we hoped I might avoid being assigned for a second combat tour. I had served a one-year tour in 1963-64 prior to graduation from Clemson. Our hopes were dashed when after two years in Panama, I received orders for duty in Vietnam. Louise and the girls went back to South Carolina to live with her parents in Rock Hill while I served a year in Vietnam. Missing a year in the early development of Leigh and Julie troubled me. I wanted to impact their development, to be a major influence in their young lives. I never had a good relationship with my dad. He did not have a father figure in his life; and even though I bear some blame for our poor relationship, I always thought he just did not know how to be a father. I was determined to earn the love and respect of my children.

After my tour in Vietnam, we went to Fort Benning, Georgia, for the Infantry Officer Advanced Course. IOAC was primarily an academic assignment and a great relief from the rigors and stresses of combat. It also provided a wonderful family atmosphere, enabling Louise and me to build a solid, loving family foundation for Leigh and Julie. Louise began running for exercise, and her success in local races encouraged her to train more seriously. She had always been a good athlete, but now she had found a sport in which she could excel.

A year later found us at Fort Bragg, NC, assigned to the 82nd Airborne Division, where Louise and I became avid tennis players and developed better than average ability on the court. Louise also became pregnant again and, on July 14, 1975, cancelled a tennis game with her good friend, Maureen McNeill, to give birth that afternoon to our third daughter, Holley Elizabeth Cooper.

At the ages of six and five respectively, Leigh and Julie showed athletic potential. Each was clearly the fastest runner in her age group in fun runs at Fort Bragg, and Leigh was doing pushups and situps with me on the living room floor each night.

In August of 1976, we moved to Altoona, PA, where I was assigned as the Assistant Professor of Military Science at the Altoona Campus of Penn State University. Louise and I had often discussed our desire to have our children experience athletic competition and to help them discover their abilities and, if possible, find sports in which they could excel. Louise and I were good athletes, but we missed opportunities to compete in college-level varsity sports; therefore, we were determined to help our children discover whatever athletic ability they had at an early age and to do all we could to cultivate that ability and encourage competition at every level.

When Louise saw an ad for a youth gymnastics club in Altoona, we decided it would be the ideal sport for the girls. Leigh and Julie were excited about the opportunity to compete in an organized sport. Gymnastics is a great sport for young girls, requiring and developing confidence, flexibility, grace, speed, balance, strength, and courage. Leigh had the strength and courage, which were enough for her to become competitive.

As a result of the daily pushups and situps with me, Leigh had become quite proficient at both. She knew she was strong and she loved it. She also loved to "show off." She never bragged, but she loved to see the admiration or the astonished look on others as she accomplished some feat of strength or daring. She especially loved to please me. She never heard it from me, but she always knew I wanted a son. While she loved being a girl, she also wanted to be as boy-like as she could for my benefit. Being strong was important to her.

As a young girl living in Altoona, Pennsylvania, many of my friends were boys. My best friend was Billy Wyant. He lived a few houses down from us; we were too young to have a crush on each other, so it was just a platonic thing. We lived a couple of blocks from the college campus, and we rode our bikes to and around campus. There was also a creek that ran behind our houses, and our backyards went to the edge of the creek. One day a small child was swept downstream and drowned, so playing around that creek was always kind of eerie, knowing someone had died there.

I remember spending the night at Billy's house. Knowing that he accepted me as an equal and that my being a girl didn't bother him was very important to me. I've always felt like I live in a man's world, and I've always felt like every man dreams of having a son. While I knew that my dad loved me and my sisters tremendously and was a wonderful father, I always wondered if maybe he felt there was something missing. Although he never treated us that way and never gave us reason to believe that we were less important to him than a son would be, I felt sorry for him that he didn't have a son (at least not at that time). So, my being a strong female and perhaps impressing him in that way was, in my mind at least, the next best thing. Not that I was trying to be a boy; I knew I was a girl and had no problem with being a girl, but I was determined to do things a boy would do and make my dad proud. I liked being strong and hanging out with boys like Billy.

When I was ten years old, I had a birthday party and, of course, invited Billy. About this time I was starting to wonder if maybe I was developing a crush on him, and I feared our relationship might change. That year, for my birthday, he gave me a plaque I have always cherished. It was an unusual plaque, a ceramic one I could hang on the wall. It depicted a girl doing a one-hand handstand, which was the perfect gift for me as a gymnast. But the words on the plaque were so important to me: "Girls Can Do Anything." I consider that gift one of the greatest gifts I've ever received. And the fact that it came from a boy made it even more special. Looking back on it and knowing how boys are, I realize that his mom likely picked out the plaque and wrapped it for him, and that he might have had little or nothing to do with it; but in my mind it came from him, and that's what he was telling me he believed about me. When I thanked Billy and asked him if he really believed what it said on the plaque, he told me, "Shoot, Leigh, I was telling my dad just the other day that you could put a worm on a hook." It took me a while to understand that, in his mind at least, he was giving me a supreme compliment. That message was very powerful to me because it was the message I always got from my dad: I could do whatever I set my mind to do.

I have always tried to project myself as being courageous. I must admit that my entire life I have tried to impress people with my physical skills and I don't know why. Does it mean I'm lacking in self-esteem and am seeking that "pat on the back," that acknowledgement that I have impressed someone? In gymnastics, when trying a new skill with a higher degree of difficulty, I was usually nervous and maybe even a little fearful of it; but if the coach told me she thought I could do it, I wanted to show her I was courageous. I would try anything. If I was hurt or failed to complete the skill, I would jump up and try again.

We often went to Bent Tree, Georgia, to vacation when I was young, as my parents had bought land there. Bent Tree had a swimming pool with a high diving board, and I tried double front flips off it, using my gymnastics skills to impress people. I never became good at it but I wanted to demonstrate my courage. When doing a front one-and-a-half, it's easy to figure when to open up from a tucked position and reach for the water because you can see the water. But with a double, you're going into the water feet first, so you can't see the water; you're opening up blindly. And flipping fast enough to hit a double, you tend to lose the sense of where you are in the air. I frequently flipped a little shorter than necessary and landed flat on my back. The pain was excruciating, and of course I was embarrassed because a lot of people were watching. People would squirm and say, "Oh, that must have really hurt," but I would climb right back up the ladder, stand on the board for a time, knowing it was going to hurt, and try it again. I had to prove to myself and to others that I was tough. It seems that I have always done things to be noticed, to make people

24

believe that I am strong and tough and courageous. Sometimes I wonder if I ever completely believed it myself. I've always had a nagging fear that I might not be as powerful or as strong as others believe me to be.

CLAUDE

Leigh progressed nicely in gymnastics. Louise and I never thought she would be an elite gymnast, but we liked what she was doing and what the sport was doing for her. She was improving in all her weaker areas, such as confidence, flexibility, and balance, and she was getting even stronger physically. Julie, who was 16 months younger than Leigh, also joined the team. Julie had the same courage and willingness to try anything but wasn't quite as strong physically as Leigh. Louise, after working as a volunteer spotter for the girls, earned her coaching certification and became an assistant coach.

Louise and I were also active in sports. I continued to play tennis and also played on a highly competitive level softball team in Altoona. Louise was becoming a very competitive runner. She entered road races in Altoona and central Pennsylvania and finished first in her age group more often than not. Leigh, Julie, toddler Holley, and I became the support team for Louise, rushing from point to point along the course to cheer her on and give her water. She ran her first marathon in Johnstown, PA, in a time of 3 hours, 45 minutes, and a month later ran the Marine Corps Marathon in Washington, DC. I really believe that the girls seeing Louise and me as athletes helped them develop a love for competition. At an early age, each of our children showed a desire to be an athlete and a love of competition.

LEIGH

Looking back on my youth, I can see there was no way I, or any of my siblings, could grow up and not be athletes. Everything we did revolved around athletic competition, either us kids competing, or my mom or dad competing. When I was nine or ten years old, we went to Washington, DC. I was old enough to understand the significance of DC as our nation's capital and very excited to see the historic sites, but the trip actually revolved around my mom running in the Marine Corps Marathon. My dad had a map of the DC area with the marathon course plotted on it. He had circled all the historic sites along the course route.

We dropped Mom off at the start point at the Iwo Jima Memorial and rode to the 5-mile mark near one of the sites along the route. Dad, Julie, Holley, and I ran or jumped in the car and drove to the next site to cheer Mom on as she ran by. Holley was a toddler then, so Dad carried her if we had to hurry to the next point. I was more excited watching Mom run than I was seeing the historic sites in DC.

CLAUDE

After three years in Altoona, I received orders to report to 7th Special Forces Group at Fort Bragg, NC, a great assignment for me. I was especially eager to get back into special operations. My first year in 7th Group was as Commander of Company C, 1st Battalion. I had always been a runner; being in the Army I had little choice. But at Fort Bragg I began to run competitively, entering all the road races on post and some in surrounding areas. As a company commander I was determined to be the fittest and fastest man in my company. I was actually looking forward to turning 40, figuring I would be winning most of the local road races in the over-40 age group. Of course Louise was also still winning road races. It was natural then for Leigh and Julie to enter the fun runs that usually accompanied the big road races. They both started showing potential immediately. Both girls also continued their gymnastics while we were at Fort Bragg, as we found an excellent club in Fayetteville, Omega Gymnastics.

Louise gave birth to Graig Wilson Cooper on November 1, 1979, taking the onus off Leigh to be the son I always wanted. Graig's birth didn't slow Leigh's competitive spirit though. She wasn't winning gymnastics events, but she was hanging in there with some very highly skilled gymnasts. And in the fun races, usually one-mile events which preceded the longer races in which Louise and I were competing, she was finishing first among the girls and the boys in her age group.

I have the best parents in the world; I love my mom and my dad dearly. But at the age of eleven I developed an independent streak, or maybe I should call it an argumentative streak. I never argued with my dad. He was a very quiet man around the house, but when he did speak, he expected us kids to listen and heed his words. I was a little intimidated by him for awhile, until I realized that he was fun and interesting to talk to and that we could talk about anything. My mom, on the other hand, was very outgoing. I inherited my physical body and strength from my dad and my personality from my mom. My mom and I were very close and very much alike, and I guess that's why we occasionally clashed. My dad often said that neither of us ever let a thought go unspoken. So, while there was great love between Mom and me, we also quarreled and I would say or do things I later regretted. One afternoon while we were living at Fort Bragg, I made a mess in my room, and my mom asked me to straighten it up. We got into a loud argument. I stormed out of the house at about the time Dad was getting home from work. I yelled that I was leaving for good, words I regretted as soon as they left my mouth. I started walking down the street that led out of our neighborhood. About three blocks later, Dad rode up on my bicycle and suggested I take my bike if I were running away for good. We talked for awhile and I finally admitted that I had no plans and would be back home in a few minutes. He helped me to see how ridiculous I was acting.

"I expect she's back there fixing your supper," he said.

I came back home and apologized to Mom. Mom and I laid our emotions out for all to see. Julie was also emotional, but she tended to sit on her emotions and not vent them. Everyone could see she was boiling inside though. Holley, on the other hand, was very quiet; we rarely knew what was going on inside her head. Each of us sisters handled emotions differently.

One of the biggest thrills of my young life was when my brother

29

Graig was born. We were living at Fort Bragg and attended school on post. Julie and I were in the same school. The technology wasn't sophisticated then, so people did not learn the sex of the baby before the birth. I had hoped and prayed for a boy; I wanted a little brother so badly, and I knew my parents wanted a son. As the anticipated birth date neared, I became more nervous and excited. Each day I went to school thinking and hoping this would be the day.

On November 1ˢᵗ, 1979, I woke up to find a neighbor in the house and Mom and Dad gone. Mom had gone into labor at about four o'clock in the morning, so they called our neighbor over to get us ready for school while Mom and Dad went to the hospital. I couldn't concentrate on anything in school that morning, hoping to find out that I had a brother. I was in Ms. Gaddy's 5ᵗʰ grade class. She was very old and had arthritic hands, but I loved her, a really sweet lady and a great teacher. She knew I was excited that my mom was having a baby. At 10:15 the intercom came on. As soon as I heard the speaker click, I became very excited. I just knew it was an announcement for me. And, sure enough, the office receptionist asked Ms. Gaddy to please send Leigh Cooper to the office. My classroom was the farthest down the hall from the office, while Julie's was only about two doors from the office. But I was so excited, I dashed down the hall and beat her to the office. When I walked in, my dad stood there smiling.

"Is it a boy?" I asked.

"Wait until Julie gets here and I'll tell you both," he replied. I just couldn't understand why Julie was taking her time getting there. Finally, she walked into the office and my dad said, "Girls, you have a brother."

"YES!" I shouted, and my classmates heard me all the way down the hall. I was so happy. And it wasn't that I was tired of trying to be the boy that I knew Dad wanted; I was thrilled to have a brother ten years younger whom I could mentor. I looked forward to watching him play football and baseball, or whatever sport he chose, and growing up to be a man.

Strong and Brave on the High Dive

CHAPTER TWO

"WITH ALL DUE RESPECT, SIR, SHE'S A RUNNER"

CLAUDE

I was reassigned to Readiness Group, Puerto Rico at Fort Buchanan, reporting there in January, 1982. Fort Buchanan was a lovely little Army post in San Juan, and we moved into a very nice three-bedroom tropical house on post. The house had a large sunroom that I partitioned to create an additional bedroom, which became Leigh's room.

LEIGH

I was 11 years old when we moved to Puerto Rico. One of the first things we did was search for a competitive gymnastics school. The nearest school we found was close to an hour and a half away through heavy traffic. When we visited the school, I was asked to perform some exercises to show them what I could do and at what level I might compete. The language barrier was a problem. Most of the gymnasts spoke only Spanish, and the coaches spoke very little English. From the start, I felt uncomfortable and out of place. This gym was nothing like my old gym, and I had a feeling I wouldn't like it. At one point, I was told to do a tumbling pass. I thought the coach understood I would do a round-off, back hand-spring, back flip, a skill I performed routinely, but normally with a spotter. The coach thought I was just going to do a round-off, back flip; so when I started my back hand-spring, the coach tried to throw me, thinking I was not getting the height needed for the back flip. Of course, my balance and timing were thrown off, which made for an awkward performance of a skill I had mastered. I was not hurt, just somewhat embarrassed. My mom and I discussed gymnastics all the way home.

"What do you want to do?" she asked.

I decided to discontinue gymnastics altogether and begin swimming. I had not swum competitively in the States, but Julie and I grew up spending our summers at the pool, so we were already good swimmers. I joined the Antilles High School swim team, which trained only during the fall; and I thought that if I was going to really get competitive, I should probably train year-round. A coach for one of the other schools in our conference, an all-boys school, was also the head coach of what was, in effect, a Puerto Rican national team. Sponsored by Caparra Country Club in San Juan, the team was very competitive and trained year round. I watched this coach, Coach Myers, at swim meets. A very intimidating man, he reminded me of my grandfather, my dad's dad. He was short and stocky and didn't speak much at all, but when he did speak, he was gruff. He looked mad, never smiled. He had *a very loud whistle, and when one of his swimmers was in a race, he would give a shrill whistle every time the swimmer came up for a breath. His presence at a swim meet was always very noticeable. Even though he frightened me, I wanted to join his team and swim for him. In order to join the Caparra team, at some point I had to talk to him, a frightening prospect at the time.*

One day, on the way home from a swim meet with my school team, we stopped at McDonald's, and Coach Myers' boys' team was also in the restaurant. Seeing this intimidating man sitting at a table by himself, I conjured up the courage to approach him. Scared to death, I walked over to his table and sat across from him. When he looked at me, I said, "Coach Myers, my name is Leigh Cooper. I swim for Antilles High School, but I would like to join your club team. I'd like to join Caparra."

His expression seemed to say "So what? What are you doing here bothering me?" He stared at me for two or three seconds, and said, "Well, are you ready to work?"

"Yes, Sir." I've never been one to say 'Yes, Sir' or 'Yes, Ma'am' very much. But to this man, it was "Yes, Sir."

"Well okay, if you're ready to work, you can swim on my team."

I returned to my teammates, proud of myself for conquering my fear and making a choice by myself without help or guidance from my parents. At home, I told my mom I had talked to Coach Myers and I wanted to join the Caparra swim team. Shortly afterwards, I became a member of the Caparra Swim Team during the fall of my freshman year in high school.

Not only was the team's pool an Olympic size pool, the athletes on this team were Olympic caliber swimmers, so I was way out of my element. My strength, though, got me through. Most of the athletes on this team, including the boys, were not nearly as strong as I, but they were better swimmers because of their technique. Their strokes were perfect. The practices were the hardest, most grueling thing I've ever done as an athlete in any sport. I came home from every practice

36

completely exhausted, with muscles so tired and so worked that it was almost like a state of complete relaxation and calm. Frequently, I fell asleep on the way home.

In practice, we were assigned lanes depending on how fast we were. I swam in the third lane, one of the slower lanes of an 8-lane pool. Each day, before we got in the water, we would loosen up by running laps around the pool area. The other swimmers ran at an easy pace. I ran this warm-up hard, like it was a race, to prove to the others that I was good at something. We also did strength exercises: pushups, sit-ups, and weight lifting. I worked very hard on these exercises, trying to stand out in some way since I wasn't the same caliber swimmer as the others. In the water, I was blown away by the other swimmers in every exercise except doing laps with the kick board. The other swimmers would usually take it easy and converse with each other during the kick board laps, but I would be way out in front of everyone else, really motoring and working as hard as I could. These laps on the kick board gave me the one exercise in the water in which I felt like I was better than everyone else. Of course, I wasn't actually better; I was just trying a lot harder. The swimming was exhausting. We did 10 X 100 meters intervals with a minimum time within which to complete the interval followed by a short rest interval. I rarely finished the 100 meters in the required time; and by the time I finished, the rest interval was over, and I had to go right into the next 100. I rarely got a rest. From the time I entered the pool until the practice was over, normally two hours, I was swimming non-stop, as hard as I could go.

.   .   .   .   .

I think I started running with my dad in the 8th grade. He ran every day on Fort Buchanan and also ran in most of the local 5K and 10K races. I soon realized that I might be a good runner. Occasionally I ran alone at night. I'm a night person, and in the evening hours I get a lot done. My body works best in the evenings, not in the mornings, so I am most active at night. I loved to run in the dark of the evening. It was liberating; no one could see me, and I ran faster at night. Living *on an Army base, I felt secure and wasn't concerned about whether it was safe to run outside at night. One night I ran by a big bush and I remember thinking, "What would I do, how would I react if a man jumped from behind this bush to attack and rape me?" At that age I wasn't sexually experienced, but I was old enough to know that rape happened to women. I knew it was a horrible thing, terrifying and awful. I remember thinking I hope it never happens to me.*

Leigh

Julie   Holley

Graig

CLAUDE

In Puerto Rico, I learned two things about Leigh before she competed in any high school sport. First, she had a very high pain threshold. Second, and related to the first revelation, Leigh had the ability and determination to push her aerobic threshold to the very limit, far beyond what most people were able or willing to do. Learning these two things about Leigh was exciting and convinced me she had tremendous potential as an athlete; but I was also concerned, even scared, that disregarding her body's signals could result in adverse consequences. Leigh would occasionally run with me on Fort Buchanan. From those runs, I recognized she had exceptional ability, but my big revelation came in a 10-K race that the post sponsored when she was in the 8th grade. Leigh wanted to run the race; not only run it, she wanted to attempt a 6-minute per mile pace. She knew 6-minute miles was my normal 10-K race pace, and she felt that since she could keep up with me on my training pace, she could probably match my race pace. Reluctantly, I agreed to help her.

In training sessions prior to the race, we did some higher intensity runs to give her a feel for a 6-minute pace; and I agreed not to race but instead ride my bike ahead of the race to give her the split times at each mile mark. The temperature on race day was typical Puerto Rico, above 90 degrees and muggy. Leigh started very strong, running the first mile in well under a 6-minute pace. She held that pace through three miles and still looked comfortable. At the 5-mile point, she had slowed a little but was still well under the 6-minute pace. I told her to ease up and coast in for the last mile, that she was going to easily make her goal. I then pedaled to the finish line to wait for her. There was an uphill portion beginning a little over a quarter-mile from the finish, then it leveled off for the last 100 yards across a large parking lot into the finish chute. When she came into view cresting the hill, my heart jumped. She was staggering back and forth, and she stumbled and fell at the beginning of the parking lot. I ran to her and started yelling for a medic. Fortunately, there was an EMT vehicle at the finish line, and they reached her shortly after I did. Leigh was incoherent, and my first thought was heat stroke. I was relieved to feel that her skin was not especially hot to the touch. The medics checked her out thoroughly, took her to the emergency room, and gave her IV fluids. She was suffering from heat exhaustion, just short of heat stroke. The bottom line, though, was she had ignored the pain and had run through her aerobic threshold. She admitted later that she had disregarded my advice and not slowed down at the 5-mile point. She wasn't content to meet her goal; she wanted to shatter it.

As with most girls, my self-image changed as I entered high school. Before my freshman year of high school, I put on a couple of extra pounds, the kind of weight that any young girl puts on as she develops as a woman. But at that time, it bothered me that my body was getting a little rounder and fatty tissue was obscuring my muscle definition. I didn't like my larger upper arms. I had always had short hair, which never really concerned me as a kid. My mom was always in charge of our hairstyles, and she had convinced Julie and me we looked great with short hair. Of course, short hair was appropriate for a gymnast, but I've always joked that Mom also wanted us to look like her; she has had a short hair style for as long as I can remember. She loved the Dorothy Hamill style from the 70's. But now, my hairstyle was an issue.

As I entered high school, my interest in boys was growing. I wanted to be attractive to them, yet I felt like I was anything but attractive to the opposite sex. I was stocky, muscular, flat-chested, had short hair, and thought I looked too much like a boy to be a girl that boys would notice. I had several boys who were friends. They liked my sense of humor; they liked that I could relate to them, and I knew that looks weren't everything. I had personality; I could make guys laugh. My school had a very large Puerto Rican student body, and being one of a few stateside students was enough to make me interesting and popular.

When I was in 9th grade at Fort Buchanan, Puerto Rico, my dad entered me in a 5-K race on post just before Thanksgiving, the annual Turkey Trot. I ran it with my dad, and I was the first female finisher, beating the star runner from the Antilles High School cross-country team. Distance running was not really her strength; she was a 400-meter runner. Nonetheless, she was the top runner on the cross-country team. Mr. Weidlein, the head football and wrestling coach, and husband of the high school cross-country coach, was at the race. He came to my dad and me after the race and said to me, "You need to run track and cross country."

My dad said, "Well, she can run, but as of now, swimming is her number one priority as a sport."

Coach Weidlein said, "She may be a good swimmer, but with all due respect, sir, she's a runner. I'll talk with my wife and see if we can work something out."

When spring track season came around, Mrs. Weidlein agreed to let me continue to practice with the Caparra Swim Team but compete at the track meets on the few days when the track team had meets. With very little actual running training during my freshman year, I ran the 1500 and the 3,000 meters races and also ran a leg on the 4 x 400 relay. My first race was the 3,000, and my only serious competition in that race was two girls from the same team who were considered to be the premier high school distance runners in Puerto Rico. To save time, boys and girls ran together for this race. I had actually never run on a track before, so I decided to keep pace with the two girls who were supposed to be the best in Puerto Rico. I felt like I could run a faster pace but opted to stay with them for the first mile or so. They kept glancing back to see if I was still with them and were obviously a little surprised when I tried to pass them at about the one-mile point. They had been running side by side, and as I pulled out to go around, the girl on the outside drifted wider. I dropped back to the inside, but she also dropped back slightly to my outside, boxing me in. I finally passed them at about a mile and a half and pulled away to win comfortably. A few minutes later, the announcer told the crowd that I had just broken the Puerto Rico High School Athletic Alliance record for the girls' 3,000 meters. Later that night, in the 1500 meters race, the same two girls, who knew a little more about me this time, again boxed me in for a good portion of the race. When I finally got to the outside, it was too near the end of the race, and they both out-kicked me. With each race after that first 3000, I lowered my state record by a few seconds, also winning the state championship meet in the 3,000.

Although I was running well, my left knee bothered me, a carry-over condition from gymnastics. My parents took me to see several doctors and we decided knee surgery would help. The surgeon performed a lateral release, realigning my kneecap, a surgery that is somewhat frowned upon today. Coming out of that surgery, I was different. I often cried. I don't cry much and it was strange to me that I could not control my crying. I learned later that it is common for people coming out of anesthesia to be very emotional. Also, I did not have an appetite. My mom was feeding me a plate of spaghetti, and I fell asleep while she was feeding me. When I woke up, I had remnants of the spaghetti in my mouth, and I was disgusted by the taste and feel of food in my mouth. I don't know why the spaghetti episode seems significant, except that maybe it was a trigger that influenced me to eat less. In my first few days of recovery, of course, I wasn't eating a lot, so I lost some weight. I liked getting thinner and smaller, and I particularly liked being able to control my size. I was very self-conscious of my upper body, an upper body that many women today try to achieve: a muscular back and well-defined arms. Today, other people often comment and compliment me on the way my upper body looks, but in the 80's, as a 9th and 10th grader, I did not like to wear tank tops or other clothes that showed my upper arms. I felt ridiculous wearing dresses, like a football player in a dress. I was too broad, and my waist wasn't very narrow. My muscularity, which had always made me proud, was evolving into something I no longer took pride in, and the change affected my self image. When I lost weight from the surgery, I also lost muscle tone. Losing weight and muscle definition appealed to me because I felt more feminine as a result.

My parents weren't aware that, as I recovered from the surgery, I ate very little. I kept a chart on the wall in my room, a yellow piece of poster board. I marked how many calories I ate each day. A good day in my mind was a day of 200 calories or fewer, maybe a couple pieces of bread and one or two pieces of fruit. A bad day was 800 or more calories.

My knee prevented me from my usual running and swimming, so I did push-ups and sit-ups in my room. Every night, while listening to both sides of a tape by the group, Chicago, I did two hours of abdominal exercises. I calculated the calories I burned each day. By the end of summer, I had added leg raises, other stomach exercises and jumps to my routine. My weight had dropped from 115 to 104 pounds. On my frame, the eleven-pound weight loss was significant. I also lost quite a bit of muscle tone, and I looked different, including a bad leg

44

smaller than the good leg. Returning to school after that summer to begin my sophomore year, I expected my classmates to react positively to my new, smaller physique from the weight I had lost. I hoped I looked more feminine.

When I rejoined the Caparra team about a month after school started, one of the first reactions was from a guy. He was a Puerto Rican teammate, and he said in Spanish, "Que chumba," but I did not know what that meant. I had to ask another friend who spoke Spanish.

She said, "Chumba has several meanings, but in your case, he's saying you don't have much butt."

In fact, most of the remarks from guys were negative. The boys told me I looked better before losing the weight. They certainly weren't impressed that I had lost muscle tone, my butt was flat, and my legs didn't look as good. The negative comments did not bother me so much. I liked eating less and losing weight. What did bother me was my loss of strength. I wanted to be thinner but not at the expense of losing strength.

I watched my weight and continued to limit the food I ate, but I was losing needed energy and calories. My loss of strength triggered me to hit the gym and begin lifting weights. I liked being one of the few females in the gym, this being a time when you didn't see many females lifting weights. Men gave me lots of looks, not flirtatious looks, but looks from men who were obviously impressed that I was a strong female who knew what she was doing. I developed an obsession with personal fitness and took great pride in knowing about the body and how to train the body. For a high school sophomore, I really knew a lot about the body; I learned the muscles of the body and how the muscles functioned. In every high school research paper, I wrote about the human body or running and conditioning. If asked to write about the biggest influence in my life, the paper would be about running. Although my English teacher made nice comments about all she was learning about running, I'm sure she must have been completely bored. I knew much more than my high school students today know.

During the first semester of my sophomore year, one boy always seemed to be standing around as I walked to the school bus. Each day

45

he said, "Leigh, go home and eat; you're too skinny." I didn't reply, but his words made me angry. I didn't think he had any right to say that, and when I finally did start eating again, I blamed him for putting that idea in my head. A person who is not eating enough is still obsessed with food, and I was clearly obsessed with food. I was not eating; I felt a tremendous sense of control, and I was terrified of losing that control and getting fat. And that's what happened to me. Once I allowed myself to eat again, partly because I needed strength for my sport, I sensed that I was losing my ability to control my eating. Not eating to the point of almost starving yourself is very difficult to do; very few people can eat so little, and my doing that gave me a false sense of strength. I also had a sense of power in that very few people knew what I was doing.

I started eating again and very quickly spiraled out of control. I came home from school and had about an hour or so before swim practice. One of my favorite things to eat was bread. My mom did not keep junk food around the house, so I would peel the crust off the bread and roll the remainder into a dough ball and pop the whole slice of bread in my mouth. Many days I would eat an entire loaf of bread and go to swim practice feeling completely sick and bloated from having all the grain and carbs in my stomach. I tried to swim it off, feeling terrible throughout practice. Of course, any time I was around junk food or at a banquet, I totally pigged out. I quickly went from complete control and eating very little to the point where I was completely out of control and eating too much. This overeating eventually affected my self-image. I felt that I was weak and doing something that was terribly bad for me and making me unhappy, but I was helpless to control it.

Food became one of the most important things in my life. The pleasure I got from eating food was more important than the dissatisfaction and unhappiness that followed with my feeling bad physically and gaining weight. I couldn't understand: why did it mean so much to me to eat when it was clearly bad for me and was self-destructive? I had never been a big drinker; I have never done drugs or other things that were bad for me except eating to excess. I knew I was being self-destructive, and it destroyed my positive self-image. Rather than seeing myself as a strong person, I felt weak and helpless to stop doing something I knew I should not do. I knew I could be a really good runner or swimmer, but I wasn't allowing myself a chance to reach my potential. I knew I was not allowing myself to be as good as I could be, and I could not understand why.

.　　　.　　　.　　　.　　　.

As in my freshman year, I did not run cross-country in my sophomore year. I'm not sure why, unless it was that I still considered swimming as my primary sport and therefore swam year-round. When track season started that spring, my track coach insisted I begin training with the team and not just running the races. Rather than choosing between running or swimming, I decided to do both. I practiced with the track team immediately after school, then ran home and had maybe twenty or thirty minutes to eat as much food as I could gorge on and then went to Caparra for swim practice. Even with all this activity, I was still gaining weight. I wasn't obese, but I had gained about fifteen or twenty pounds and was much bigger than necessary to be a distance runner, and, of course, I wasn't eating in a way that helped me be competitive at the level at which I should have been competitive. Despite the weight gain during my sophomore year, I was still quite successful in track. I was the Puerto Rican champion again in the 3,000, lowering my record to 10:59, and I finished second in the 1500.

CLAUDE

I wasn't sure how fast 10:59 for 3000 meters was for a high school female. I knew it was pretty good, but Leigh had not improved as much as I thought she should have in her sophomore year. It never dawned on me or Louise that Leigh had an eating problem. The fact that her weight went down for a few months after her surgery and then went up higher than it was before the surgery did not seem out of the ordinary. As for not lowering her time as much as I thought she would, I rationalized she was still swimming more than running.

I had just received reassignment orders sending us to Fort Leavenworth in Kansas. I figured leaving Caparra would shift her emphasis from swimming to running, and with year-round training in running, she would surely see great improvement.

CHAPTER THREE

STRESS FRACTURES AND OREOS

CLAUDE

Fort Leavenworth was a great place to live and a great place to raise a family. Although I knew we would only be there for three years, four at the most, I was excited about Leigh and Julie going to high school in Leavenworth and Holley and Graig going to the schools on post. I knew that Leigh and Julie would get competition in running at the high school level in the state of Kansas, and if they did well, they would get noticed by college coaches. I was absolutely confident that Leigh would be a star at the state level and that Julie also had the potential for success.

Louise and I suggested that it might be time for Leigh to concentrate on running and consider training year-round. Leigh readily agreed and was excited about finding her best competitive sport. We read a Kansas City newspaper ad about a running club in Kansas City that was affiliated with a fitness center operating as Health Plus. I phoned the number listed and spoke to Tom Dowling. Tom seemed impressed when I told him Leigh's 3000 meter times as a sophomore, and he invited us to come over one afternoon and check out the facility and perhaps have Leigh go on a training run with his elite group of runners. School had not yet started, so Leigh and I visited Health Plus the next day. Leigh went on about a five-mile run with Tom and a few other runners, mostly boys of high school and college age, while I looked over the facilities. I was impressed; it was clearly a first-class fitness center, with a 50-meter indoor pool, an indoor track, and a well-equipped strength room.

After the run, Tom invited us into his office. He was very excited about the prospect of working with Leigh. He explained that he had previously trained Cathy Schiro when she was in high school. Cathy was one of the top runners in the nation as a high schooler and later competed in the Olympics as a marathoner. Tom expressed the opinion that Leigh had very similar potential as Cathy. He was amazed that she was running the times she was running with very little training mileage (less than 20 miles per week at the time).

We joined Health Plus, and Tom set up a training schedule for Leigh, initially upping her mileage to 45 miles per week, with an eventual goal (within a year to eighteen months) of 60 miles per week. He felt, and we agreed, that Leigh was ready for 45 miles per week. I had now noticed that she was carrying about 10-15 pounds more than she should as a distance runner, and I felt that her increased mileage would quickly bring her weight back down to an optimal level. We drove over to the fitness center two or three times per week, including every Saturday, for Leigh to run with Tom and some of his other elite runners and for Leigh to work out in the strength room.

Leigh had no trouble handling the increased mileage from a cardiovascular standpoint. She had the stamina to do much more. But her weight was not coming down; as a matter of fact, she was still gaining weight. I didn't understand how the continued weight gain could be possible with all the running she was doing. It wasn't long before her legs started breaking down; a combination of the extra mileage and the extra weight. At first it was shin splints; then stress fractures cropped up. As a result, she was unable to run cross-country at Leavenworth High that first year, her junior year.

We moved to Kansas my junior year, and I still had short hair. I decided that no longer would my mom be in charge of my hair, so I let it grow out. Most of the boys I had a crush on had first been friends or acquaintances from cross-country or track. I didn't really date a lot in high school. I would go out with a guy a time or two, and then he would get on my nerves and I would realize that this relationship just would not work out.

My eating problem didn't really have much impact on my running until we moved to Kansas. Carrying too much weight caused shin splints in Puerto Rico but not to the point of having to stop running. Clearly, I was not running to my potential, but I was a two-time Puerto Rico champion and a record holder. By the time we moved to Fort Leavenworth for my junior and senior years of high school, I had made the decision that swimming was no longer my primary sport. There was no question in my mind I was a distance runner. I knew running was where I needed to spend my training time, and if I were going to go to college as an athlete, it would be as a runner.

I continued to feel powerless to control my eating, but I ran more, and I ran harder to try to burn those calories. It wasn't long before I developed injuries. As I ran through the minor pain of shin splints, I would begin to feel a much sharper pain, more localized to specific areas of the shin. Knowing that this was worse than shin splints, I still ran through this pain, resulting in a series of stress fractures that haunted me my last two years of high school and into college. As a result of these stress fractures, probably nine over a three-year period, I could not train as I needed to and could not race to my potential. I learned then that I had a pretty high tolerance for pain and was able to run through stress fractures, often more than one at a time. Because of these injuries, I began doing something that later would become very popular but wasn't very common at the time: cross-training. At times when I was physically unable to run, I would spend hours at the pool, swimming, or running in the water, or biking on a stationary bike. I knew the benefits of training in the water, and I had the ability and experience to conduct hard water workouts. There was also a small Catholic college in Leavenworth that had a small gym with an exercise bike. I would go to that room most days of the week and bike. I soon realized that I had very strong cardiovascular endurance. I remember days when I rode that bike for three hours or more. I would get on the bike thinking I would bike for 45 minutes. I would get to 45 minutes and say "Well, I'll just make it an hour." Then when I got to an hour, I would think wouldn't it be crazy if I biked for two solid hours. And a couple of times when I got to two hours, I told myself, "People will not believe me if I told them I rode this bike for three hours," and I would do it.

During my last two years of high school, I was really doing very little actual running but still entering the races and relying mostly on my cross training. Because of my injuries, I did not run in any cross-country races in my junior year, so my first competitive running in Kansas was in outdoor track in spring semester of my junior year.

CLAUDE

Louise and I were very frustrated that Leigh could not compete in cross-country her junior year. I knew Leigh's junior year was the year college coaches would be closely watching for possible scholarship consideration. She worked out with the team doing minimal mileage, but she exercised long hours on the exercise bike and in the pool. I became concerned she might have a metabolism problem.

Leavenworth High was a 6A school, the highest classification in Kansas, so I knew Leigh would have good competition during her final two years of high school. High school outdoor track in Kansas has the 1600 and the 3200 as its distance events rather than the 1500 and 3000 as in Puerto Rico. Leigh was a competitive miler but not a great one. The mile was more of a speed event as opposed to an endurance event like the two-mile. Leigh needed that extra distance beyond a mile to burn the speed out of her competitors. She could hold a blistering pace, running at almost her top speed throughout a two-mile race, thus taking the kick out of her opponents who weren't willing or able to endure the pain Leigh could endure. And she certainly endured pain; running with shin splints or stress fractures or both, the pain had to be excruciating.

It was exciting finally to see Leigh go to the starting line in track season for her first race at Leavenworth High. The race was the 3200 meters at the Shawnee Mission South Relays in Kansas City. She did not run her best race, but she definitely got everyone's attention. She left the pack early, ran by herself most of the race, and beat her nearest competitor by over 200 meters, shattering the Leavenworth High record by almost a minute with a time of 11:52. But I knew she had much faster times in her.

The next week, at the Washington Relays, she met Mary Powell of Lawrence, Kansas, who was the reigning cross-country state champion. Leigh was a newcomer to the Kansas City running scene, but her performance the week before created a buzz about the showdown between the established star and the rising newcomer. They did not disappoint anyone. Leigh set the pace for the entire race with

Mary one or two strides behind. No one else was able to stay near them. Leigh pushed the pace, trying to break away from her, but Mary was an outstanding distance runner. As they pounded down the final stretch, Mary had just enough kick left to edge Leigh by one second. She ran an 11:35.2 to Leigh's 11:36.2, which lowered the school record she had set the week before. Julie, who was a sophomore, was also running track and improving each week. She was more competitive in the 1600, finishing fifth in the Washington Relays.

At the Leavenworth Invitational, Leigh cruised to a 12:00.8 finish in the 3200, winning easily, while Julie broke 6:00 in the 1600 for the first time. Then at the Sunflower League Championship meet, Leigh finished second to Mary Powell again in the 3200, with Julie also helping the team win the league championship with a 6th place finish in the 3200.

At the outdoor track state championship at the end of her junior year, Leigh weighed about 135 pounds. At her height, and with all the training (mostly biking and water training), she should have weighed no more than 110-115. She had been dealing with two stress fractures during the year but was probably as strong as she had been all year in terms of less pain. She had qualified in the two-mile event. Leigh ran the best race of her high school career that day, finishing third in the state of Kansas with a time of 11:35, again, a new school record for Leavenworth High School.

College coaches throughout Kansas contacted Leigh to visit their campuses. During the summer, I began a search of potential colleges for best fits for Leigh. Clemson, my alma mater, was my first choice for her. She, like me, liked the idea of a university in a small-town environment with excellent support of athletics and a solid academic reputation. Clemson certainly met all those requirements. But I knew she would have to get her weight under control and get her times down in order for schools like Clemson to have enough interest to offer scholarship aid.

During that track season, I was very self-conscious at the starting line of a race. I would look around at the other runners on the starting line and see all these skinny girls. Being one of the highest seeded (if not the top seed) in all of my races, I was placed in lane 1, and being so stocky, I felt out of place. For years, I had this notion that not being built like a distance runner held me back as a competitive runner. Years later I realized that none of that really mattered. I eventually learned I was going to win races because of the way I prepared to race and because of the discomfort I was willing to endure, not because of how I looked.

Mary Powell, a girl from Lawrence, Kansas, was the dominant distance runner in track during my junior year. She won the 6A State Championship in cross-country. She was in our conference, so I faced her several times that year. I never beat her in high school. She always outkicked me in the last 100-200 meters, usually beating me by only one or two seconds. Each time we raced, my dad came up with different strategies for how I could beat her. The bottom line was that I had to blow her away early in the race. Because she had a tremendous kick, I had to set an all-out pace in the hopes she would burn the life out of her legs and have little or nothing left for a kick at the end. If we were close near the end of the race, she was going to beat me at the finish. So I would essentially run all-out from the start of the race. Running all-out was very painful; my legs would be burning, my lungs were burning the whole time I ran, so I really did not enjoy racing. In fact, I hated it. Of course, my excess weight and my injured legs just exacerbated my feelings. At some point, I began to rationalize, telling myself at the start of each race, "Okay, this is going to hurt. I'm not going to be comfortable, but it's only going to last about fifteen minutes. Can I do it? Is it worth it?" I would always tell myself that it was worth it and I could do it.

I was struggling physically with all the injuries and the pain, but I knew that I was a runner and a good one. I always considered myself an elite runner even though my times weren't quite at an elite level while I was in high school.   I always thought that someday, somehow, I would figure it out , take control of my eating and start blowing people away.

My dad always talked to me about race strategy; I respected his ideas and suggestions and listened intently to what he had to say, but I was developing my own racing philosophy.   My greatest fear stepping on the starting line of a race was not whether I would run the time I wanted or expected to run and not whether I would win the race.   What I knew would disappoint me was giving up at any point during the race. And, of course, I would be the only one who would know.   Giving in to the pain and discomfort and settling for less than my capabilities was the part of racing that scared me the most.   If I backed down from the pain, if I slowed down and did not challenge my aerobic threshold, I would not be happy with my race, and it would be hard to face myself. When I crossed the finish line feeling like I had given it everything I had and did not give in to the pain, I was proud of myself, even if I didn't win the race.   And usually if I followed this strategy, the results would take care of themselves.   I've always carried that philosophy with me, both as a runner and as a coach.   People get so caught up in tactics, in the pace they think they have to run or in the place they should finish, and I believe that's the wrong approach to coaching and to running. The most important thing for a distance runner is how to talk yourself through the discomfort; how not to give up or settle or give in to the pain and discomfort.   This philosophy enabled me to finish 3rd in the 2-mile race at the Kansas 6A state championships in my junior year in spite of being overweight and injury-riddled.

Certainly by my senior year of high school, my self-image was seriously damaged due to my over-eating and the way I was treating my body.   I knew that if I were not twenty pounds heavier than I should be, I could run amazing times.   I knew I could beat the best runners in Kansas and surrounding states.   I was invited to all the top invitational races in the state, and I always qualified for the state championships. And I was always close enough to the winner that it was clear to me that if I were a little lighter, I would be winning these elite races. Watching videos of my races was discouraging.   My parents taped many of my races, but I hated to watch them because I was reminded of how much bigger I was than anyone out there.   My arms were much

58

bigger than anyone else's. Our uniform included a tank top, which I hated because it showed how big my arms were. Before the race I wouldn't strip out of my tee shirt until just as we were moving to the start line, and immediately after the race I would put my tee shirt back on. And since I wasn't using my arms as much as I did in gymnastics or swimming, most of the muscle definition was gone.

.   .   .   .   .

Because I was so competitive at the highest levels of high school racing in Kansas in spite of my self-destructive actions, I really struggled with myself and asked myself why I was so self-defeating. The solution was so simple: I had to control my food intake, eat healthy, lose weight, and race well. But, in fact, I was powerless to stop my over-eating. During my senior year, I went to extreme methods. At one point I had heard that after gorging, some people purged themselves of food by taking laxatives. I began abusing laxatives, taking five or six at a time, sometimes as many as ten, and I would take them several times a day. I was basically losing water weight, and just putting it right back on whenever I drank anything. Eventually I stopped taking laxatives, realizing that it was very dangerous and was not giving me the results that I wanted.

The summer before my senior year, I told myself, "I've got to have a good season." But I had gained more weight over the summer and knew that I was going to look even worse in my track uniform. Also, a new runner enrolled in school who was really good, a girl named Suyong Jenerette. When we did our summer training, it was evident that I might not be the #1 runner on my team. And I had always identified myself as the best runner at Leavenworth High School and one of the best runners in the state. Now, to have someone on my own team who was probably going to beat me was not easy to accept.

My gorging took a different form that summer. After eating the wonderfully nutritious meals that my mom would cook, I would drive to a gas station and buy and eat gobs of junk food, food that was almost total sugar: Little Debbie Fudge Rounds, Oatmeal Creme Pies, any type of cake or pastry that had chocolate and was sweet and was known to

59

be bad for you. And I couldn't stop at eating just one; I would eat a Fudge Round, and it was so good that I would go back to the store and buy another one. Or, if I had the money, I bought several at a time. I ate them and stored the wrappers under the seat of my car and then felt tremendous guilt that I was a disgusting person. I looked at my arms after eating this junk, and in my mind they had already gotten bigger. At these times, I often asked myself, "Am I sabotaging my efforts? Am I trying not to be as good as I could be because maybe it wouldn't be good enough?" Since I knew the solution was so simple, I thought I must be subconsciously sabotaging any chance at excellence. Eventually, I started trying to throw up. I would go to the basement of our house trying to throw up, sticking my fingers or a spoon down my throat; anything to cause a gag reflex. I was never successful at throwing up the food I had just gorged on. My trying so hard to throw up was even causing blood vessels in my eyes and face to pop, leaving red spots on my cheeks and around my eyes that I would try to cover with makeup. One time my mom noticed and made a comment at the dinner table about the red dots on my face. I brushed it off, saying it was just some kind of rash and was no big deal. But I knew what it was. I tried regurgitating for about three weeks but did not have any weight loss. I was simply eating too much. I was not a good example of bulimia; I continued to be overweight because I couldn't stop eating.

.   .   .   .   .

At the beginning of cross-country season my senior year, the team voted for team captains. I considered myself the leader of that team and thought I had proven myself, and should and would be elected captain by my teammates. When the votes were counted, both Suyong and I tied and were made co-captains. I thought some of the team members knew or suspected that my eating habits were negatively affecting my potential and the team's potential as well. I was initially disappointed not to receive the support to be sole captain, but I accepted the outcome. Suyong was a great runner and we became good friends, racing side by side most of the time. Of course, each of us knew that cross-country is a team sport, and you want every member of *the team to do well, but at the same time, you want to win the race. She knew that if she were with me at the end of the race, she would probably outkick me and win the race, so her strategy was to just try to stay with my pace throughout the race and hope she had enough left at the end for a kick. She didn't win every race, but most of the time she beat me. Not being the fastest runner on my team was very frustrating. I knew the reason: I was carrying too much weight.*

.　　　　.　　　　.　　　　.　　　　.

At the cross-country state championship meet my senior year, I set a goal to finish in the top three in the state. I ran very, very hard throughout that race. In distance racing, there is a line for each runner that can't be crossed too soon, one's aerobic threshold. It's basically the fastest pace one can run and reasonably expect to be in control to finish the race. One can cross that threshold, but it had better be near enough to the finish that he or she still has enough control to finish the race. If a runner crosses the threshold too soon, he or she will "die," a term often used when a runner gives out, or "hits the wall," a marathoner's term. Whenever I race, my intent is to run as hard as I possibly can without crossing that threshold or getting into the "danger zone" until 100-200 meters from the finish line. I wanted to do well in the state championships, for myself and for the team. I pushed my threshold throughout the race and was right there with the leaders until near the finish line. The course was over uneven terrain, which is not unusual for cross-country, and with about 200 meters to go, I stepped in a bit of a dip in the terrain. The dip was not anything dangerous that shouldn't have been on the course, but it was just enough to jolt me and cause me to lose my balance. In effect, though, I had crossed my aerobic threshold. I was essentially in a semi-conscious state on the course. Even though I was still staggering toward the finish line, I knew that I had slowed considerably, was moving from side to side not really knowing where I was, as other runners blew by me. I finished in 11th place, collapsing at the finish line. I had run myself into the ground. Not only did I not achieve my goal of finishing in the top three, I wasn't even in the top ten, so did not make All-State.

CLAUDE

Between cross-country season in the fall and track season in the spring of her senior year, Leigh did very little actual running. She spent hours on the exercise bike and working out in the pool. When track season began, she was in fairly good shape in terms of injuries. She still wasn't running anywhere near her potential due to her weight and the low mileage she was putting in on the track.

She began the track season her senior year by winning the 3200 meters at Shawnee Mission South Relays in a respectable time of 11:37. Two weeks later, at the Seaman Relays, a very competitive meet with the top schools in the state at all class levels, she doubled for the first time, finishing 3rd in the 3200 and 4th in the 1600. Neither time was impressive: 12:06 in the 3200 and 5:35 in the 1600. She then ran in an even more competitive race, the KU Relays at Kansas University. This meet had the best runners in Kansas from all classifications, plus top runners from neighboring states. Leigh ran an 11:42, finishing in sixth place, one second behind her nemesis Mary Powell. Finishing in 6th place in such a quality race was no disgrace, but her time was nowhere near her potential. She should have been running much lower times at that point in her career.

Leigh again finished second to Mary Powell at the Sunflower League Championships, running the 3200 in a slow time (for her) of 11:52. She also ran the 1600, in an equally unimpressive time of 5:35, finishing in fifth place. Julie was 24 seconds behind her in sixth place.

Leigh qualified to run in the 3200 meter race at the Regional Championships, but she almost missed the race altogether. Just prior to the start of the race, she had to go to the bathroom. Julie had also qualified for the 3200, so Julie marched down to the start line with the Clerk of Course for the start. He turned them over to the starter, who started his instructions for the conduct of the race. Julie became very nervous that Leigh had not come out of the bathroom. As the starter told the runners to take their positions, Julie boldly took another stride down the track to stall for time. She slowly walked back to the annoyance of the starter. The starter repeated, "Take your positions please." Julie knelt down and began slowly retying her shoes. Finally, she saw Leigh come out of the building and begin to run toward the start line. "Wait for my sister; here she comes," pleaded Julie. As soon as Leigh reached her position, the starter went into the commands to begin the race. Julie ran the first two laps with tears streaming down her face. Leigh had another classic duel with Mary Powell, finishing a close second to her again in another school record time of 11:35. In the final sprint down the home stretch, Leigh felt a sharp, severe pain in her right thigh as Mary eased ahead of her. Julie recovered from her scare for her sister to run a very respectable 12:21 for sixth place. She later that evening ran a 5:47 in the 1600 for fifth place.

Two days later, still in great pain, Leigh met with an orthopedic surgeon, who told us she had a stress fracture of the femur. We assumed there was no way she could run at the State Championships, which were two weeks away. During those two weeks, she did no running at all. She worked out exclusively in the pool, swimming and doing strides in the water. The doctor examined her again two days prior to the state meet. He told Leigh that he did not recommend her running at State, but he would not forbid it. He advised that if she could stand the pain, she probably would not damage it further; and if it did break further, she had the summer to rehab.

Toward the end of my last season of high school running, I experienced severe pain in both legs. The orthopedic surgeon at Fort Leavenworth told me I had stress fractures in each leg, including the femur of my right leg. The stress fracture of the femur, the large bone in the thigh, was very serious. Most of my training in the second half of that season had been cross training in the pool. Going into the state meet, I prepared to run the 3200 with stress fractures in each leg. The doctor had warned me that running the state meet could cause one or both to break deeper into the bone, possibly breaking through, and that if either broke through, I would feel excruciating pain immediately. He said the pain I was already feeling probably wouldn't get any worse unless either bone did break, so he gave me clearance to run my last high school race, knowing that I would have an entire summer to rest and treat my injuries after the race.

The state meet was in Topeka, Kansas. Our team travelled the day before and we stayed in a hotel the night before the meet. That night we were able to do pretty much what we wanted; we just had a certain time that we had to be in our rooms and a certain time that we had to be in bed. We had a team meeting in the hotel lobby, talking about our goals, and getting motivational talks by the coaches.

The biggest thing on my mind, though, was food. The first thing I did after our meeting was find the vending machines. One of my favorite kinds of cookies was Oreo cookies. Well, the hotel vending machine had these huge Oreo cookies. They were about four inches in diameter with ½ inch of cream inside. Later studies have found that Oreo cream is one of the worst things you can put in your body. But I got very excited when I saw these cookies. I tried to talk myself out of getting one, telling myself that the state meet was tomorrow; people were counting on me to perform at my best; I was counting on myself to do well at this meet. My dad had spent time analyzing the way I should run the race. He and my mom were very much invested in this race. They never missed a race, and a great part of my racing was to please them. College recruiters were talking to me and my dad about running for their schools. All these thoughts were going through my mind as I pondered whether I should buy the Oreo cookie. I considered buying it and eating it after the race. I allowed myself to buy it; and once I had it in my hand, I had to eat it. I went off by myself and I ate the cookie as quickly as I could so I wouldn't get caught. After I ate the cookie, I went back to my room, got more money, and went back to the vending machine to buy another one. It was easier to allow myself to eat this next one because I rationalized that by now I had pretty much sabotaged my race. Of course, as soon as I ate that second cookie, I knew that there was no way I was going to do well; I knew I was gaining weight as I stood there and was going to be heavier on the starting line than I was right then. That night, I went on to eat four of those huge cookies. I went to sleep feeling ashamed of myself; my stomach hurt and I was disgusted with myself.

The next day, just before the race, my dad did what he always did; he pulled me aside and talked to me about the best strategy for running the race; how to set a torrid pace and take the kick out of the other runners. He talked about what my splits should be and at what point I should pull away from runners who were still with me. I couldn't look my dad in the eye. I couldn't tell him that none of these things were going to happen because I was a fat pig and I had already taken myself out of this race. I didn't even deserve to be at this race, I didn't deserve to win, and I was not going to run well. I knew my dad would be disappointed; and that was so sad to me. I finished fifth in that race in a slower time than I had run in my junior year. I came the closest I had ever come to quitting in the middle of a race and had to really dig down deep to get fifth place. My right leg was hurting in the warmups as I hobbled around the track. For about the first five laps, I was running dead last. I was thinking "Three laps to go and I'm losing ground; this is ridiculous." But the pain was not getting worse, or maybe I had just tuned out the pain. I had run with pain throughout my high school career and had learned to ignore it, to concentrate on other things. I picked up my pace as I glanced at my mom and dad, still cheering for me and urging me to hang in there. I took my mind off the pain and concentrated on the runners in front of me. I guess I was in a zone as I gained on the back of the pack and then passed runners one by one. I was the fastest runner on the track on the last lap, but I had allowed the lead pack to get too far ahead.

Actually, finishing fifth in the state of Kansas was pretty amazing considering my condition. But I was very disappointed with that finish, knowing that I should have easily beaten most of the other runners.

I was capable of running a much faster time if I had not been overweight and injured. I felt very weak, like someone who just would not allow herself to be successful. I often asked myself, "Why can't I stop this; why can't I control my obsession with food?" The answer was simple, or so it seemed. I was very knowledgeable about fitness and was very proud of what I knew about fitness. I also knew about nutrition; I knew what I should be eating and how I should be eating. Knowledge was not the issue; I knew what I was doing was all wrong, but I could do nothing to stop it.

CLAUDE

During Leigh's senior year, several colleges in Kansas and Missouri invited her for official visits. Leigh and I visited a couple of schools but were not really interested in them. I had become intrigued by Appalachian State University. It seemed a good fit for her: a small college town like Clemson, a good running program, though not at the same competitive level as most of the Atlantic Coast Conference schools, and in North Carolina, a state I was considering for retirement. Leigh wrote to Coach John Weaver, the women's coach at ASU, and he invited Leigh to come for a campus visit. I could not take time off my job at Fort Leavenworth at the time, so Louise drove to North Carolina with Leigh. They visited family in Rock Hill and spent a couple of days in Boone looking at the ASU campus and talking to Coach Weaver.

Leigh immediately fell in love with the campus and thought she would be happy attending college there and running for Coach Weaver, even though he told Leigh he had a very tight budget and could not offer her a scholarship. While Louise and Leigh were in the Carolinas, they also visited Wake Forest and Clemson to gauge any interest in Leigh the coaches of those schools might have. Both coaches welcomed Leigh to enroll in their respective schools, but they made clear their opinion that she would not be competitive in their programs. Immediately after returning to Fort Leavenworth, Leigh applied to ASU. She was thrilled when her acceptance letter arrived a couple of months later.

CHAPTER FOUR

FOOD EVERYWHERE

My eating issues went to college with me and became worse. I was on my own now and could buy my own food. I often went to the Sweet Shop with my roommate, who was not an athlete so not as concerned with keeping her body in top shape. Trips to the Sweet Shop with my roommate were fun because I didn't feel so guilty when we ate together. Of course, I never let my teammates see me gorging on sweets.

I began my college career on crutches, not from stress fractures, but from a second knee surgery. My right knee had begun hurting severely, and my orthopedic surgeon recommended surgery to remove a piece of calcified cartilege. This surgery shortly before my freshman year forced me to redshirt, which meant I could practice but not compete with the team. Even though I was on the team, I didn't feel a part of the team. I did not practice with the team every day because I went to the training room each day to rehabilitate my knee and strengthen my leg. Not running hard every day and not competing with the team made gaining weight easy. And, in college, food was everywhere. My roommate and I ordered Chinese food or pizza at midnight. Although I felt a little guilty, I loved the food and I loved the company. And actually, I was eating much more of the sweet stuff than my roommate. I knew I had a serious problem eating junk food; and I'm not talking about things like fried chicken. Junk food for me was M & M's, chocolate peanut clusters, Oreo's, marshmallows, things that were almost pure sugar. I guess it went back to my growing up with a mom who kept no junk food in our house.

CLAUDE

During spring semester of Leigh's freshman year, Louise and I began to discuss my retirement from the Army. I thought my chances of getting a battalion command were slim, so I began to think of other possible careers. Julie had been accepted for a three-year Army ROTC scholarship and had decided to follow in her sister's footsteps and attend ASU; she would enroll the next fall.

I took ten days of leave and drove to the Carolinas to do some networking. I visited several fraternity brothers who were in business, mainly just to get the feel for what opportunities might be available and to put the word out that I would soon be in the market for a job. While in the Carolinas, I drove to Duke University in Durham to watch ASU in a track meet. Leigh had told me she would run in a two-mile exhibition race. She had not fully recovered from her surgery, but I was anxious to evaluate how well she competed at the college level. I immediately noticed she had put on a few more pounds. I assumed the weght gain resulted from several weeks on crutches during fall semester, and the resulting decrease in training. Leigh did not run well, finishing well back in a rather slow race.

Watching her struggle around the track, I felt sad for her, knowing how embarrassed she must be feeling at performing poorly in front of me. I tried to encourage her and assure her that there would be much better days ahead if she kept working hard. Unfortunately, she would have to wait for those better days, as she was soon hobbled with another stress fracture.

LEIGH

I did not run many races in track my freshman year. I was still sluggish from the knee surgery and not very competitive. I was scheduled to run a two-mile exhibition race at Duke on a weekend when my dad was in North Carolina. He came to North Carolina to look for a retirement job. My family had not yet seen me race in college because they were in Kansas, but for the first time in several months my dad would see me race. Not many people entered the race, and the distance was just two miles instead of the usual 5K. My performance in this race was one of the most humiliating experiences of my life. I was thirty pounds overweight, and as Dad talked to me before the race, I was embarrassed. During the race, I could think only about how fat I must look to my dad and how disappointed he must be. Here he is, someone who believes in me and believes in my potential, and he's looking at me struggling to get around the track. With every lap he shouted, "Come on, Leigh, you can do it, you can do it," and I wanted to run off the track and run away.

Back then we didn't have e-mail and texting, but during my freshman year, I received letters from Dad each week. His letters were always about motivating me. He knew the difficulties I was having with my weight and with my injuries; he knew I still wanted to be a runner. His letters were full of motivating words: "Here's how you can lose weight, believe in yourself, and only surround yourself with good food, and when you want to eat something bad, remind yourself of your goals;" and he would end his letters with, "I believe in you, you have the potential, you can do this." These letters meant a lot to me but they also reminded me how much of a letdown I was. He had sent me these letters and he finally saw me race and I ran a slower time than I ran in my 9th grade year of high school. My shorts rode up in the front because my legs were so thick, my legs rubbed together, my arms were big and I didn't have any muscle tone.

I was humiliated.

CLAUDE

Toward the end of that spring semester, Leigh phoned home, as she normally did about once a week. During the call, she mentioned that the Professor of Military Science (PMS) at ASU would retire during the fall semester of the next year. Leigh was not on an ROTC scholarship, but she was in the ROTC program. From our separate phones, Louise and I looked at each other, obviously with the same thought in mind.

"Is this something you might have a shot at getting?" Louise asked.

I told her I should have as good a chance as anyone, assuming a replacement PMS had yet to be selected.

Louise asked Leigh if she would have a problem with her parents living in the same town where she attended college.

"I would love it," Leigh replied. "I would have a place to do my laundry!"

I was especially encouraged when Leigh said she thought the PMS's retirement date was in December. Retiring in December meant his replacement would be outside the normal replacement cycle and might not go through the normal selection process. After getting assurances from both Leigh and Julie that they would have no problem with us living in the same town where they were going to college, I decided to follow up on the prospect. A co-worker at Command and General Staff College had previously been assigned to Officer Personnel Branch in Washington, and he knew the civilian who handled all ROTC officer assignments. The three of us conferred by phone the next day. I was assured that the job was wide open and that if Officer Personnel Branch received a by-name request for me from the university and from the ROTC Region headquarters at Fort Bragg, the job was mine.

I explained the situation to my boss at Ft Leavenworth and asked for a five-day leave to visit the campus and talk to the outgoing PMS.

LTC Charlie Michael, the retiring PMS, introduced me to ASU Chancellor John Thomas, a former marine and strong supporter of ROTC on campus. The Chancellor assured me he would put in the request for me, and Charlie Michael informed me the Deputy Commander at 1st ROTC Region was Colonel Jim Lloyd, a Clemson graduate. I drove from Boone to Ft Bragg the next day. COL Lloyd and I hit it off very well. The Commanding General was out of town, but COL Lloyd promised to request me by name for the ASU job. So, Julie and I began our tours at ASU together that year, she in August as a student and ROTC cadet, and me three months later, taking over as the Professor of Military Science and Battalion Commander of the Mountaineer Battalion.

Louise, Holley and Graig stayed at Fort Leavenworth until the end of the school year the following May.

LEIGH

I trained hard over the summer before Julie and I came to ASU that fall for my sophomore year and her freshman year. I was still overweight, but my work ethic resulted in some success. I ran third on the team for about the first three meets of that season, and then my weight and injuries caught up with me. I had stress fractures again, and my season was over. I again started cross training. I remember when that season ended, my coach, John Weaver, very tactfully suggested I try to lose weight. I was very disappointed in myself. I knew that if I could be the #3 runner on ASU's cross-country team while carrying thirty extra pounds, just imagine what I could do if I weren't carrying all that extra weight. I was very down on myself and even hated myself at times, knowing that I was sabotaging my efforts and I couldn't figure out why. I was in a downward spiral. I felt a compulsion to eat to excess. After binge eating, I was disgusted with and mad at myself; I hated myself and wanted to give up on myself. But binging felt really good during the binging. Only afterwards did I hate myself. So I binged to feel better only to feel worse about myself which led to more binging followed by more self-hatred – a downward spiral.

I did not complete that track season either. I was injured because I was too big; I was frustrated because people told me that I was overweight and I wanted to tell them, "I know I'm overweight! I know I have to lose weight; I just don't know how to do it." At one point my mom made an appointment for me with a nutritionist. I kept the appointment but I knew it was a complete waste of time. I knew about nutrition; I'm not an expert but I know a lot and have always known a lot about nutrition and fitness because it's always been my passion. I've always known I would live a life of fitness and it would be my career. I knew what I should be eating; I could easily write down a plan of what would be a perfect way for me to eat and for me to lose weight safely. I didn't need someone to tell me; I needed someone to tell me and to help me deal with and figure out why I was self-destructing.

76

CLAUDE

At the time, I did not fully understand the problems Leigh was having with her weight. When I learned later that she had an eating disorder, I was reminded of my first two years of college. I was depressed over my relationship with my dad, my family moving to Texas during my freshman year, and a long-distance romance that went sour. Like Leigh, I had serious control issues: eating too much, drinking too much, and skipping too many classes. I did things that were very reckless and dangerous and was subconciously on a self-destruct path. I knew what I was doing was wrong but did not have the willpower or the control to stop it.

I eventually reached a low point and realized I had to make changes in my life. I dropped out of school and enlisted in the Army. Ironically, while I may have been the least gung-ho ROTC student at Clemson, I thrived on Army life. After three years of service, including a one-year tour in Vietnam, I returned to Clemson as a changed, more focused person. Meeting Louise in my senior year at Clemson was the final impetus I needed to get my life on track.

LEIGH

I met Chris Wallace in spring semester of my sophomore year. We were both PE majors and had a class together. He was two years ahead of me in the progam, and the class was a methods course for our major. We spent five weeks learning field hockey and how to teach field hockey, then five weeks of tennis, and five weeks of basketball. The first time I laid eyes on Chris, we were downstairs in Broome-Kirk Gym standing in line to get measured for our hockey sticks. What attracted me to him was his physique. Being an athlete myself, muscular and strong men have always been attractive to me. Also, since I am rather muscular, I am more comfortable around a male who looks stronger than I. Chris definitely fit that bill. He had rugged good looks, maybe not "gorgeous," but there was something about his face, a rugged seriousness. His athleticism also struck me; he was one of the best athletes in the class. From the first time I saw him, I was immediately attracted. Right off the bat, I wanted to date him. His side of the story of how we got together is interesting. Chris told me he saw me standing in line and was immediately attracted by my muscular legs, and later he told his roommate he had seen the girl he was going to marry. We started dating regularly.

My addiction to junk food continued. I drove a Mustang at the time, and one of my weaknesses was still Little Debbie Fudge Rounds. Driving to school, I sometimes stopped at a gas station on Highway 321 that sold individual packages of Fudge Rounds for 25 cents. I would buy one and eat it before reaching campus. On the road back to campus I would finish that Fudge Round. The taste would linger in my mouth and I had to have another one, so I would turn around and drive to get another one. Sometimes I would turn around three or four times. I would stuff the candy wrappers underneath the front seat of my car.

One day Chris surprised me by washing my car for me, and I immediately panicked. If he washed my car, then he vacuumed it, and if he vacuumed it, he's found the forty or so Little Debbie wrappers underneath the seat in my car. He asked me, "Why are there so many wrappers under your seat?" I said the wrappers had been there for years after some friends and I bought a bunch of them and my friends ate them. He probably knew I was lying, but I could not admit that all those Little Debbies were consumed by me.

CLAUDE

Leigh and Julie were both doing well in the ROTC program, Leigh as an MS II (second year) cadet and Julie as an MS I (first year). I spent my summers working at the ROTC Advanced Camp, where the third year ROTC cadets spent the summer training in tactics. ASU also often had an opportunity to send some of its cadets to other Army schools, such as Airborne School or Ranger School. This particular summer, ASU received a slot to send one cadet to the Army's Master Fitness Trainer School at Fort Harrison in Indianapolis. I had attended this school myself during my tour at Fort Leavenworth and knew it to be an outstanding program. The school existed to teach selected individuals how to organize and conduct fitness programs in Army units and included all aspects of fitness and healthful living, including nutrition. I had no doubt that Leigh was the best student at ASU to send to the Master Fitness Trainer School. Except for weighing too much for her height, Leigh was the most fit person in ASU's ROTC program. And having considered every possible reason for her weight gains and resulting injuries, I had more than a suspicion that Leigh had an eating problem. I hoped that she could come back from a summer at the school and help me set up and run the best possible fitness program for the ASU Mountaineer Battalion while also gaining control of her own eating habits. Leigh attended the Master Fitness Trainer course and performed very well. She lost about five pounds, but more importantly, she seemed to feel more positive about herself.

My belief that Leigh could be a national class runner never wavered. I had no doubt that if she had maintained her weight at about 115-120 pounds, which she could have done without losing her power, she would not have had all the injuries and would have beaten every runner she had ever raced. I hoped Leigh would return from the Master Fitness Trainer School believing in herself and ready to validate my belief in her.

LEIGH

At the Army Master Fitness Trainer School, which my dad arranged for me to attend, I made it into the top running group. I was really proud. I lost a little weight there because we were exercising so much, but I was still eating poorly. I won a 10K road race there, and my prize was a long-sleeved shirt with "Run for Life" across the back. We ran first thing every morning, then we went to class and learned about exercise, anatomy, exercise physiology. It was exactly what I loved to learn and talk about. We worked out again in the afternoon, and we learned different ways of working out: circuit training, boxing, different types of weight-lifting routines, different ways of running intervals. We learned so much, for the purpose of returning to our respective units and teaching our officers and soldiers about cross training: how to be fit in many ways, not just in running.

The school was perfect for me, but I was miserable the entire six weeks. Chris and I had been dating pretty seriously, so I counted down the days until I could see him again. I missed him terribly. I knew he probably didn't miss me as much as I missed him. I wrote him every single day and he wrote me maybe once a week. He must have been drinking while writing one of his letters, or it might have been at a time when he was missing me. In this letter, he talked about how one day he and I would get married, and he imagined the kids that we would have because we were both so athletic. He wrote, "If the kids have the best of us, they will have your quads, my speed, your endurance, my eyes, your skin." That letter meant so much for me. He was actually picturing our getting married and having kids. Spending my life with him had been my dream ever since we began to date. If I could attend the Fitness School again while secure in our relationship, I would truly love the experience, but I did not take full advantage of the opportunity because I felt sorry for myself and missed Chris.

Still struggling with my weight and injuries, I decided to sit out that next season, not because of injuries, but by choice. I had to get control of my eating and my running. I had no specific plan in mind, but I was so tired of being a disappointment to Coach Weaver. He had pretty much given up on me. I was tired of repeating the pattern of starting a season running well, building his expectations for me, and then ending my season with injuries and seeing his disappointment. I don't know if I knew at the time that I would come back, but I knew I needed to stop torturing myself. That fall, when school started, I was completely on my own for training.   I wasn't even reporting my workouts to Coach Weaver; I was just training and running on my own, but I knew how to train myself to get in shape.   I ran somewhere between four and seven or eight miles most days of the week. Not every day was a hard workout. I was smart enough about training to know that I had to have occasional easy days for recovery. But for the most part, I ran hard, and even though the actual running was painful, I knew that I had to do it. Running was and would be a big part of my life. I identified myself as a runner first and foremost. It's a label I've always carried proudly, and no obstacles I might have to overcome would stand in my way.   I was going to be a runner.

During these self-planned runs, I pictured myself coming back to the team, getting stronger, and convincing myself that I could compete. I gave myself pep talks: "You can do this, let's do this," and "Wow, I'm running really well today."   I told myself that if I could continue training well and without injury, I might be able to come back and be competitive.   But in the back of my mind, I knew I had to get control of my eating, and for the first time in years, I felt like I was gaining on that issue. Maybe not having the pressure of competition was a factor.

CHAPTER FIVE

MISSING

Chris and I struggled in our relationship. We started the relationship very strongly, very attracted to each other, and we enjoyed the time we spent together. We broke up for the first time after two months. Before meeting me, Chris had dated a girl for 2 ½ years, and she had broken it off with him the summer before I met him. She had broken his heart. When she found out that he was in a relationship with me, she called him and said she had made a mistake and wanted to get back with him. I guess Chris was still feeling hurt by that breakup and wanted to give it another chance, so he broke up with me. I was devastated. I knew he was the man I would marry, and I didn't understand how that could happen if he broke up with me. I knew he was meant to be my husband, and I was meant to have his children. It was devastating to think that he might not feel the same, but we were only broken up for a couple of days before he apologized profusely, said he made a mistake, and we got back together.

Chris was wonderful to me, he always treated me well, and I have no doubt that he was faithful to me; but I always sensed that he was holding back a little bit. I think he was afraid that he was about to graduate from college and that his life was going to change. He had always had a girlfriend throughout school, and maybe he felt like he owed it to himself to experience some freedom after he graduated, to know what it would be like not to be committed to a girl. Consequently, I felt he was not as committed to our relationship as I was. For a while we followed a pattern: he would break up with me; I would react very emotionally; then after a day or two, he would apologize and say he made a mistake; and we would be back together. By the fall, though, when he left to do his student teaching, our relationship had improved. I felt more comfortable in the relationship and felt that he was beyond the pattern of breaking up and getting back together. I believed he wanted to be with me, but I still felt like I loved him more than he loved me. I wasn't completely confident that we had the same level of affection for each other. While he treated me very well, I could sense a hesitation on his part to let go of any fears he had and to invest himself fully in the relationship.

CLAUDE

Boone, North Carolina is a wonderful place to live. Two of its biggest assets are Appalachian State University and tourism. It's a small town with the university campus contiguous to downtown Boone. It is just as close for a student to walk from his/her dorm to the heart of downtown as it is to most classrooms. King Street, which is Boone's main street, is lined with quaint shops, typical of most small college towns. Tourism is a year-round attraction as people flock to the High Country in the spring and summer to avoid the heat, in the fall to observe the beauty of the changing leaves, and in the winter for the numerous ski slopes in the area. The beauty of the surrounding mountains and the cool temperatures makes Boone a great place to walk, run or bike. Students, faculty, and local residents have never had any reason to feel unsafe doing those activities. Well, at least not until September of 1989.

The serenity of Boone and surrounding areas was initially altered on Friday, September 22nd, when the remnants of Hurricane Hugo blew through. Normally, hurricanes have little effect in the High Country other than heavy rains. Hugo was different. After striking land on the South Carolina coast, it continued to cut a wide swath as it drove inland toward Charlotte. After delivering a significant blow to Charlotte, it turned northeast eventually reaching Maine. Most of Boone and Watauga County received very heavy winds and had considerable damage from flooding and downed trees and limbs.

LEIGH

Chris chose to do his student teaching at Garringer High School in Charlotte because it was close to his home. He lived with his parents in Mint Hill while student teaching. On Thursday, September 21st, I planned to drive down to Mint Hill to see him. We all knew that Hurricane Hugo was about to hit the coast of South Carolina and its projected path was expected to take it directly toward Charlotte. Of course, my parents were concerned about the approaching hurricane and encouraged me not to make the trip, but I desperately wanted to see Chris.

Mom finally said, "Well, go now, so you can at least get there before the hurricane reaches Charlotte."

I left after my Thursday afternoon class and drove down I-77 in a hard rain. I finally made it to Chris's house and learned I had arrived just ahead of the hurricane. When we woke up the next morning, the damage was unbelievable. Huge trees were down everywhere, and those still standing had lost limbs. Chris's parents had an above-ground pool, and a massive tree had fallen into the pool, barely missing the house. Several large trees in the yard had fallen. Everyone in the neighborhood was outside walking around, surveying the damage, assessing what to do. Chris's family and I spent the entire weekend cutting up fallen trees and picking up debris, trying to figure how we were going to get through the weekend without electricity. We had no running water, so we bought jugs of water. Soon, the stores ran out of water, and the lines at gas stations were very long; we spent over an hour waiting in line to buy gas. Sunday afternoon, September 24th, was my last day at Chris's home, and by then we were sweaty and completely filthy. Chris and I, along with his brother and some of the other young people in the neighborhood, jumped into a neighbor's pool to wash off. We had soap and shampoo and took a bath in the neighbor's pool, laughing at the ridiculousness of our situation, bathing in filthy water. But we felt cleaner when we finished and glad to have the stickiness and scum washed off.

I left on Sunday and was relieved to get back to Boone but was surprised to see so much hurricane damage in Boone. Trees and limbs were down, but the situation was not as bad as in Charlotte. Life in Boone soon returned to normal. We had power, and I felt bad for Chris that for the rest of that week he was still without power and had little prospects of getting it restored soon. Schools in Charlotte were closed that entire week. I kept asking him to come to Boone. We normally alternated weekends going to see each other, and I suggested that, since it was unlikely that he would have school that week, he could come on up to see me. When Chris and I were apart, I always worried that I missed him more than he missed me.

CLAUDE

On Sunday morning, September 24th, Jim Gray drove from his home in Asheville to attend church with his daughter, Jeni, and then have lunch together. Jeni was a former ASU student who was working for the ASU News Bureau. When Jeni never showed up, Jim filed a missing person report with the Boone Police Department. Later that day, her car was found parked at the Lois Harrill Senior Center in downtown Boone. Suspecting foul play, an intensive search began.

The news of her disappearance traveled quickly in this normally quiet community. It was front-page news in the local print media and the subject of constant updates on the radio. Unfortunately, the updates reported the same result; after five days, there was no trace of her or of what might have happened to her. The Boone police did have a suspect. The police received reports of a man making inappropriate remarks and harassing young women in town. The Boone police picked up the man and learned that he was from a nearby town in Tennessee. He took and failed a polygraph test, but insufficient evidence forced his release from custody. The police kept him under surveillance. It was later learned that this man was not responsible for Jeni Gray's disappearance.

On Friday morning, September 29th, when he confirmed that Charlotte schools were still cancelled, Chris called and told me that he was coming to see me. He arrived in Boone around 10 o'clock. I was busy in class until noon, when my last class ended. He had let me know that he would probably go directly to the Quinn Center (the ASU fitness facility) to lift weights. When he finished lifting, around noon, we met at my apartment. We had dated for eight months, and we had a very strong attraction for each other, emotionally and physically. We hung out at my apartment for a couple of hours; we had sex, watched TV, and made plans for that night to go hang out with some of his former college roommates.

At some point, Chris realized he had left his sweatshirt at the Quinn Center, so we drove over to the Quinn Center on campus. When we drove up the hill by the Duck Pond, we noticed a big crowd of people standing around looking at the pond. It was normal for a few people to be at the pond, watching the ducks, but this crowd was unusually large, about 100 students or more. And it was not a pretty day; it was overcast and dreary, not a great day for watching or feeding ducks; and we also noticed three or four swimmers with SCUBA gear on. When Chris came out of the Quinn Center with his shirt, he said someone inside told him divers were searching for the body of Jeni Gray in the pond. This, of course, was very scary. I had told Chris earlier that week about the disappearance of Jeni Gray, a reporter for the Appalachian State University news bureau; how she had gone for a walk the previous Sunday morning, the 24th, and had never returned. The newspaper articles became more and more ominous, and it had become pretty evident that something bad had happened to her, that she had probably been kidnapped. The police chief, Zane Tester, reported that he had officers working up to 18 hours a day and that many off-duty officers were joining the search on their own time.

As we quietly drove past the Duck Pond that second time, I commented to Chris, "Could she possibly be in that pond, and if she is, who would do such a thing?"

It scared me to think I lived in a community where someone could take an innocent person off the street and dump her body in a pond. I imagined her body in that pond, realizing that if it was there, it had been there for five days, and what a horrible thing. We were both very quiet driving back with just a sick feeling in our guts. While he was in the Quinn Center, Chris had picked up a copy of The Appalachian, the student newspaper. When we got back to my apartment, we both sat down and read it; the story about Jeni's disappearance was front page news with big headlines. Her father had come from Asheville to attend church with her, but she hadn't shown up. Chris and I both got an eerie feeling reading the news of her disappearance. Later that afternoon, Chris left to visit friends, and I prepared for my daily run.

I love to run. Running has always been a way for me to feel powerful and exhilarated. I've always known I was a good runner, and it has always given me such a sense of freedom, strength and power. Even on my training runs, I try to set a pace that few people can do; and I, mentally, will my body to go beyond the limits of the normal human body. Running on my terms feels so good. Many times after a difficult run, I feel triumphant, like I have really accomplished a difficult task. Running has always served as a form of meditation for me: a time when I can escape my thoughts, or a time when I can think through my thoughts. But either way, when I finish my run, whether I was worried about something or stressed about something, the physical exertion helps me either to let go of some of that tension, or the thinking that I did on the run helps me to work through whatever it was I needed to work through. The thoughts most on my mind during this September 29, 1989, run were the status my running at that time and what I needed to do to make my running productive once again and become a competitive runner at the college level.

I don't consider myself a particularly talented or natural runner; I don't have great sprint speed. Looking at my legs, one might think I would be a good sprinter. I have powerful legs and hips like a sprinter, but I just don't have the fast turnover required of a sprinter. But when it came to running distance races, the talent and pure speed became less important. I found that determination and hard work can help one become very successful. I had determination and loved to *work hard at what I loved.. I thrived on the training. When I'm on a run and everything feels right and is clicking without pain and I'm running really fast, I know I'm doing something that is helping me. One of my favorite places to run is on the beach. There, you have an audience with so many people sitting around sunning or whatever, and I just go a little faster there. I don't deny I crave approval, and I want people to admire me. Maybe that sounds cocky, or maybe it shows a lack of self-esteem on my part, but I felt that when I ran hard, other people were impressed. Running gave me a feeling of strength; and finishing a run always gave me a feeling of total relaxation, physically and mentally.*

I was planning to go about six miles on this run. I dressed to run; I put on dark blue pants and the long-sleeve shirt I had won at the Master Fitness Course, the one that said "Run for Life" on the back. I took out a pad of paper to leave Chris a note, knowing he would probably get back to my apartment before I finished my run. I wrote, "Chris, I'm out running; be back around 6:30." I knew a six-mile run would take about 45 minutes. I generally base the length of my runs on time rather than miles, and I wanted to run for about 45 minutes. I hesitated before signing the note, not sure just how I wanted to sign it. It certainly seems ridiculous now, and it did at the time too, the way girls overthink things in a relationship. I wanted to write, "Love ya," because I did love him, and I wanted him to know it. But, I thought, "That's crazy." I was just going on a run; I saw him a couple of hours ago and was going to see him again in a little bit; and I didn't want it to appear I was trying too hard with the relationship. I figured it best to just keep things casual, so as not to scare him into thinking the relationship was more serious than it was or than he was comfortable with. I felt like maybe I should just say, "See ya." I thought about it for a couple of minutes, and finally talked myself out of saying 'Love ya', and finally wrote, "See ya, Leigh."

I left my apartment to go on a run, not knowing that within the next 30 minutes, my life would change forever.

CHAPTER SIX

"DO YOU WANT TO DIE A SLOW DEATH OR A FAST DEATH?"

"Get in the car or I'll shoot."

I looked in the car at the gun in his lap and knew the man was not kidding. I froze; running never entered my mind. I saw the gun and did what I was told. As I sat down in the car and shut the door, I told myself, "I'm dead. I'm dead. I just made a deadly mistake. I should not have gotten into this car."

He had a gun resting on his lap. I knew without a shadow of a doubt that I was going to die. It was such a sad feeling, an overwhelming sadness. It's almost like before you die, you are dealing with your own death. Sadness and loneliness are the two words that best describe the feeling, a sadness and loneliness that are almost unimaginable. When I try to recall how I actually felt, it's hard to remember the true depth of those emotions.

I saw he had a clock mounted to the side of his dash; the radio in his car didn't work, so he had a radio that was mounted between the two seats. The clock was on the radio. It was 6:10. I was due back from my run at 6:30, and I thought, "No one even knows that there's something wrong with me. Even if Chris is at the apartment, he's not worried about me; I'm not supposed to be back to the apartment for twenty more minutes." The fact that my life had completely flipped upside down and that the people I loved and who loved me had no idea I was in trouble was a completely lonely feeling. Loneliness that no one can help me, and no one is even worried about me.

He drove toward Highway 321, where a left turn would take us back toward town, campus and my apartment, but a right turn would go away from town. He took a right turn. As we drove away, I didn't look so much at him. I was shocked and numb, but I took a quick assessment of my situation: I had made a mistake and had a terrible feeling of regret - regret in the worst sense of the word. Sure, I had done plenty of things that I regretted, but this was different. I knew I had made a choice that would directly cost me my life, and this realization was very sad for me. I kept saying to myself, "Let me just start this day over, and I promise I won't get in the car, I won't go on this run."

I thought about my parents: "Where are they? Mom and Dad are probably at their house getting ready for dinner, and they have no idea that I'm in this situation, no idea of the danger I'm in." It was odd to me that while my life was being turned completely upside down and I had the worst feeling of horror ever, the people who love me could not feel anything. I thought surely my parents would sense that I'm in trouble, and it was weird to me that they probably wouldn't. They would be going about their normal routine as if nothing were different for them; nothing has changed for them, and absolutely everything has changed for me.

I thought about Chris, probably still with his friends, having a good time, and with no sense that something horrible was happening. From 6:10 to 6:30 when I was expected to be back from my run, I was painfully lonely. I wondered how anyone would find me; it would be a couple of days before my picture appeared on posters. I had a crazy thought: what picture of me are my parents going to use for the missing-girl poster? I also knew there was a witness to my kidnapping but I figured the passing motorist probably didn't know he had witnessed a kidnapping, and he won't know it until days later when my picture appears. Will he recognize me or realize it was a kidnapping? The police reports won't mention a kidnapping on Meadowview Drive. No one will know where I was kidnapped. I hoped that in a couple of days this witness would realize that I was the person he saw. I was also thinking that he probably never looked at the man in the car. The witness and I had our eyes locked on each other the whole time as he drove by.

All these thoughts were going through my head: the missing-girl poster picture, the passing motorist, my being taken against my will, and the realization that the trail would be cold for searchers. At least my family would know if the motorist comes forward; they would know I was kidnapped and was taken against my will, that I didn't run away. "Ran away" is often a theory when a college student disappears; they disappear because they wanted to get away for a couple of days. Mom and Dad would know I went against my will, but they wouldn't know where to look for me.

My thoughts were abruptly interrupted when my abductor asked, "What's your name?"

I answered, "Leigh."

"What's your last name?"

I knew it would not be good for me to tell him my last name. The quickest lie I could come up with - because when someone asks you your name you can't hesitate or it's obvious you are lying - the quickest lie I could come up with was my middle name. Growing up, I never liked my middle name; I am named after my father's mom; her maiden name is Martin, and quite a few people in my family have Martin somewhere in their name. It's a name that I take great pride in now. I appreciate it more now as an adult, but as a child I was embarrassed when people asked for my middle name and the answer was Martin. I saw it as a guy's name, not as a family name.

"Martin," I replied.

Somehow I knew right away that this man was the man who kidnapped Jeni Gray and that I would receive the same fate. I pictured him making me kneel in the woods and he would have a gun to the back of my head. He would shoot me in that position with me upright on my knees - shoot me in the back of my head. When I pictured that scene, I cried even more. I was already crying but it wasn't a sobbing out loud cry; it was more like a whimper, and I realized that I was grieving my own death. I was so sad about the prospect of dying; I pictured him shooting me in the back of the head and I cried even more.

"Why are you crying?" he asked.

"I don't want to die."

"If you do what I ask you to do, I won't kill you."

I told myself, "Just do what he says and he'll let you go." I tried to convince myself I would return to my normal life, but in the back of my mind, I knew that wasn't true, that he was just trying to keep me calm; and when he was done with me, he would shoot me in the back of the head.

I knew I was going to be raped before he told me. I think it's every woman's worst fear. I remembered the time when we were in Puerto Rico and I worried about a man jumping out from a bush and attacking and raping me and wondering how I would react.

After I stepped into the car, rape was one of my first thoughts. I had a huge sense of dread in the car. I dreaded the rape itself, but I told myself that's not the worst thing that's going to happen to me; the worst thing is I'm going to be killed. And I'm going to have to do what this man tells me to do. I'm going to have to endure the rape in order to survive, even for awhile; that if I fight the rape, he will kill me right away. I had been sexually active before, so I was thinking at least that part won't hurt. I tried to tell myself, "Just get through it, just zone it out, be calm, and you're gonna have to do it." But a horrible sense of dread and a devastating sense of regret remained.

The car smelled bad, not of body odor, but of stale, long absorbed tobacco smoke. I have always detested the smell of a tobacco smoker. In addition to the fear, regret, and loneliness: an oppressive smell.

As we drove down Hwy 321 toward Blowing Rock, he asked me how old I was. I told him the truth, that I was twenty.

He said, "Huh, I thought you were older than that."

He kinda said it like, 'Man that's too bad;' at least that's what I thought he was thinking, that I was going to have to die at the age of 20. I kept thinking to myself: "I can't believe this is happening to me," and it brought back the fear I had as a young girl of being grabbed and raped while running; and now it was actually about to happen. I even had a fleeting thought that as a young girl I had somehow known this would happen to me. Of course, I didn't believe that, but I just kept repeating to myself, "I can't believe that I'm in this car with this man, and that I'm going to be raped and die at the age of 20, actually be murdered." I was shaking, crying, and deep in my thoughts. Then he would interrupt with a question.

"Are you an ASU student?"

When I nodded, he said "Good, I wanted an ASU student."

I looked out of the car at the other cars passing us. It seemed so strange that normal daily life continued all around me; people were driving home or running errands; and in the next car over, everything was okay, and they were so close to me where horrible things were happening. It seemed strange that no one else knew what I was feeling. The windows started getting foggy, and I don't have any other memories of seeing anyone or any cars going by. I don't know if it was because of the fog that I couldn't see them, or if perhaps I was already tuning out and my mind was in a fog.

My body was very tense. As I sat in the front seat of the car, my legs barely touched the seat; my hip flexor muscles, my abs, and my arms were all so tight. I had my hands on my lap in front of me, one hand over the other, and rubbing my hands together over and over. Everything inside me was shaking. There have been times since then, at least within the first ten years, when I try to go back and think about what happened to me, when my whole body, inside and out, starts shaking, and I have no control over the shaking.

He turned off 321, taking a left onto Aho Road. I noticed a sign that read, "Road Closed." The sign actually was partially blocking the road. At that time, there were several roads in the vicinity of Boone and Blowing Rock that were closed due to downed trees and power lines from Hurricane Hugo. He cursed, turned around in a driveway, and headed back up 321 toward Blowing Rock. He then turned onto the road leading to the Blue Ridge Parkway and turned north onto the Parkway. I knew we were traveling away from the Lynn Cove Viaduct, so we were headed north. At that time, I wasn't familiar with the rural roads around Boone, so I really didn't know where I was.

As we were on the access road that took us up to the Parkway, he said to me, "You know why I got you, don't you?"

I didn't say anything.

It was then that he unzipped his pants and pulled out his penis and said, "This is going in your ass."

99

I was terrified. I had convinced myself when I realized I was going to be raped, that even though it would be horrible, at least it wouldn't hurt because I had had sex before. But now, I became very, very frightened of the rape because I had never had sex in that way and I knew it would be painful. I knew that it was going to be more horrible than I had imagined. He asked me if I had ever had sex before. I lied and said no. It felt good to lie to him; the less he knew about me, the better. But also, I thought to myself, "If he thinks I've never done any of this, maybe he'll be easier on me. If he thinks I've had sex, he might do more things to make it hurt." If his intent was to hurt me, I wanted him to think that he could accomplish that with simple intercourse. I just wanted to appear as innocent as possible.

He then pushed me over toward the door and told me to lean forward so he could "See what I got." He was looking at my bottom.

He also told me to "Go ahead and take off your underwear."

I was wearing running pants, so I took them off and removed my underwear. He told me to put my pants on the floor. He took my underwear and put them in the glove compartment. Just before he shut the glove compartment, I noticed an envelope facing away from me. I could see that in cursive handwriting was the name Daniel. I knew more information was on the envelope, but he shut the glove compartment before I could read it. He didn't know that I had looked at the envelope, so he wasn't shutting it quickly so I couldn't see anything. He just casually put the underwear in and shut it. Then he said he wanted me to take off my bra. I wasn't sure if he also wanted me to take off my shirt, which would make me completely naked, or to take my bra off underneath my shirt. He said to take it off from under my shirt.

He said, "I wanna keep this too," and he opened the glove compartment and put in my bra.

When he opened the glove compartment, I saw more of the envelope; "Daniel Lee" was written on it. I realized there was information in the car that could tell me more about this person. The more information I had, the more likely he would be caught if I could eventually get away. At the time, I really had no sense that I would get away, but I told myself that if I could, I wanted to have as much

100

information as possible. I did not want to be one of those victims who don't have enough information or evidence to get a conviction. I made a conscious effort to look around the car and notice things. The first thing I noticed was a piece of paper clipped to the sun visor on the driver's side with the name Daniel on it. Having now seen that name twice, I realized his name was most likely Daniel Lee. Obviously, his name was a great piece of information. Having his name (and his not knowing I knew his name) somehow gave me a fleeting sense of power.

I looked around at the dash and on the steering wheel for a logo or something that would indicate the make of car, but I couldn't find anything I recognized. I knew it was a white car, and that by its size could be something like a Honda or Toyota, and I had noticed when I was first outside the car that the paint job was not shiny as on late models; it was a very dull white paint. Even though I preferred to have the make and model, I felt confident I could adequately describe the car.

While we were still riding on the Parkway, he occasionally reached over and touched me; he would feel my bottom and feel my breasts from underneath my shirt. Sitting there while a stranger touched me was disgusting. He became aroused, and he asked if I had ever given anyone a blowjob.

I froze. "No."

"Well, you're going to do it right now."

He told me to bend over and put my mouth on him. Realizing now that the rape was actually starting, and I wasn't prepared, and I was going to have to do something so revolting to a man who was dirty and stunk of cigarette smoke, and I could only imagine what poor hygiene he had, I barely put my mouth on him. He was telling me that I needed to do more, to be more active, and he put the gun to my head.

He said, "Don't even think about biting me. If you bite me, I'll blow your head off."

I sat up and pleaded, "Could you please put the gun away? I promise I won't hurt you, but that gun against my head is scaring me. Please put it away."

101

"Okay, I'll put it right here." He put in the door pocket.

"Don't do anything stupid. If you do, the gun's right here and I'll blow your head off." He told me to put my mouth on him again, but in a short time, he asked me to sit up. I don't know if he was getting frustrated that he wasn't getting much stimulation, or perhaps it was because he was about to pull off the Parkway. He pulled off onto a gravel road and pulled over just off the road, saying that he needed to stop for a minute and get something out of the trunk.

"Before I do that, though, I need to tie your hands." He reached behind me into the back seat and grabbed a red bandana, and he tied my hands in front of me. The bandana wasn't long enough to get a good double knot, and I noticed that the second knot was kinda loose. I thought then that if he gets back from going to the trunk and sees his knot coming unraveled, he might think that I'm trying to untie it to escape, and he'll get very angry. I decided my only chance to survive my situation was to convince this man that he could trust me, so I began to build trust.

I stopped him as he was getting out of the car and said, "Wait a minute, wait a minute; you need to tie this knot tighter; it's coming undone." He stopped and looked back at me. I was looking down at the knot, but I could tell he was looking at me as if to say, 'What a strange request.'

"All right," he said, and he tied the knot again very tight. It wasn't uncomfortable or hurting, but it was tight.

He got something out of the trunk, then got back in the car and drove off again. He then took out some marijuana and started smoking it through a small pipe.

He asked me if I had ever smoked marijuana, and I shook my head, no.

He asked me if I had ever drunk alcohol, and I said, "No."

"Well, you've just led a sheltered life, haven't you?" The truth was that I had never smoked marijuana, but I had drunk alcohol. I was never a big drinker, even as a college student, but I had drunk alcohol.

Being very health conscious, in spite of my eating problems, I had always made a conscious choice not to do drugs. Also, as the oldest of four children, I felt a great responsibility to my younger siblings. I was very fearful of what drugs can do to a person, and I feared that if I made the wrong choices and became a drug addict, I would set a terrible example for my sisters and my brother. I wanted to be a leader to them, and I wanted to lead them in the right direction. He told me that he wanted me to smoke the marijuana. I had stayed away from drugs for good reasons, and I certainly did not want my first experience with drugs, if I were ever going to have a first experience, to be in the kind of situation I was in. I knew that my best hope for survival was for me to keep my wits and make the best choices possible. But I also did not want to anger him by refusing what he was asking. He handed me the pipe; it had a hole where I was supposed to inhale. I put my tongue over the hole and inhaled rather shallowly, not really inhaling any marijuana. I knew that if I were actually inhaling marijuana, it would make me cough, so I faked a cough.

He laughed and said, "Yeah, it'll really get ya the first few times you do it. It takes a while to get used to it."

I told him I didn't like it, and he took it back and smoked some. He gave it to me one more time and I faked it again, but he didn't ask me to do it anymore after the second time. He then asked me if I was hungry. I told him that I was never hungry right after a run.

"Well, believe me, this stuff will make you hungry."

He continued to smoke as he drove down the road. Several miles or minutes later, I realized he wasn't completely sure where we were. I guess not being able to go down Aho Road threw him off a little.

6:31: I remember saying to myself, "I'm a minute late." I still didn't feel like anyone would be worried about me, because I'm notoriously late. But I thought every minute that went by increased the chances that Chris or my mom or dad would begin to worry, and I found some comfort in that knowledge. I knew I would never be found. I knew I was going to die and no one was going to save me, but I felt better knowing that people who love me were probably thinking about

103

me. That helped, to know that they were thinking about me, and later, 7:00 – 7:30, I became more and more convinced that Chris and my parents were probably worried about me by now. I took some comfort in the fact that they had moved to Boone and were no longer halfway across the country. It made me feel less alone in my fear.

Eventually I saw that he was relieved to find the road he was looking for, and he pulled onto a gravel road. He drove down this very narrow, very bumpy road, which obviously was not well-travelled at all. I knew we were getting close to where we were going. Just before we drove into thick woods, I saw off to the left on a hill a large white barn with a red roof. The image of that barn stuck in my mind. We went down that road for about a half mile, to a point where we couldn't go any further because of a tree across the road. I didn't know about the tree across the road, but he did. This wasn't his first time down this road. Knowing he couldn't go any further, he turned the car around. Turning the car around was a task, for the road was so narrow, it took several back and forth maneuvers to get the car facing back the way we came in. Even though the road was narrow, he pulled over as much to the driver's side as he could, so that there was an embankment on his side and just trees on my side. He then untied my hands and put away the pipe. I knew what was about to happen.

He told me to take off my shirt. My shirt ended up in the seat later; I guess that's where I put it. He took off his pants and his boxers; I think he kept his shirt on. He reached over and reclined my seat and pushed it back, and he crawled on top of me. I was lying back in the seat, and he started to rape me, not saying anything other than "This is going to hurt a little." I cried harder and acted like I was in a lot of pain because I had told him I had never done this. The rape continued for a while without anything being said.

"Now I want you to turn over." I turned over, facing the back of the car. I noticed that it was dark outside, and I guess it had been dark pretty much the whole time we were out there. I couldn't see anything in the back of the car. There was a lot of stuff in the back, but I don't remember any specific items. I was just staring into the darkness.

"Now this is gonna hurt," and he started to rape me anally.

104

The pain was excruciating. I felt like I was being stabbed. It felt horribly painful inside my body, so I screamed and leaped toward the back seat. When I leaped, he was no longer in me, but he grabbed my hips and pulled me back and entered me again. The second time was just as painful as the first time, and I screamed again and jumped away, begging him not to do it again.

I was screaming, "THIS HURTS! YOU'RE HURTING ME!! Please don't do this!" That happened probably two or three more times. I was trying to tell myself to calm down, that I was being too tense and was making it worse. And I told myself, "He's not going to stop, and the only way to get through this is to try to relax." I tried as hard as I could to bear it and not to jump away. Eventually, after about two or three minutes, I became almost numb. I think some of the numbness was mental and some maybe physical as a result of my effort to relax, but I was trying not to focus on the pain. I was actually using some of my running experience. I've always told myself that you can't focus on the pain, you can't lose to the pain.

I realized I had no control over the pain he was inflicting on me. I had to relax and not focus on the pain; I had to put my thoughts somewhere else. It occurred to me that I had never experienced this type of pain before, a pain inflicted on me by someone else. This person knew he was inflicting severe pain on me, but he didn't care, and in fact, he was probably getting pleasure that he was hurting me. I felt even more alone; the situation seemed so much darker. No matter how much I might scream or beg him to stop, he would not care. I was scared, realizing that if he doesn't care that he's hurting me, what else is he capable of doing and how much worse is this going to get?

I was with a man who was not going to let me go and who also had a gun. I didn't know anything about guns. My dad is in the Army but he always made a point not to bring the military home with him. He doesn't tell war stories to us, nor does he talk about his job at home. I was never interested in guns and didn't seek to learn about them. During ROTC at ASU, I had probably fired one or two rounds in the indoor rifle range in the basement of the ROTC building, but that was my only experience seeing, touching, or firing a weapon. But I knew that Daniel Lee had a gun, and that was enough for me. And really, once I got in the car, the threat to me was Daniel Lee himself.

Knowing I was in for more pain, I tried to put the pain out of my mind and relax as much as I could. I had always told myself, and my dad had taught me, to push through the pain and the reward would come later. Of course, there was to be no reward in this situation, but I still knew I had to calm down. I tried to focus elsewhere, and I was able about this time to get lost in my thoughts. I almost felt like I was in a trance, and every time Daniel Lee would speak to me, I had to break myself out of my trance to understand what he was saying. There were a few minutes when I was calm, not screaming or yelling any more, before Daniel Lee broke the silence.

"Have you heard of Jeni Gray?"

His question upset me. Everything was so dark in my mind, being in his car in these surroundings, and never seeing myself get out of this situation. I knew he abducted Jeni Gray, but to give myself a small glimmer of hope, I tried to convince myself he was not Jeni Gray's abductor, so the fear wouldn't be so overwhelming that I would lose control. When he asked that question, I couldn't deny it any more. It was clear that he was the guy who got Jeni.

"Yes," nodding my head.

"Well, I'm the one that got her. She's right down the road there."

"Is she alive?" I asked him. When I asked that question, I pictured her farther down this road in a small wooden shack, tied to a chair in the middle of the room, battered and bruised, mentally exhausted. In my mind, she was alive. In that moment, I had a glimmer of hope. I knew if he kept her alive for five days, then he would also keep me alive in that shack. I remember thinking, what a relief it will be for Jeni Gray to see someone else, to see a normal person and know that together, we're going to survive. I'm going to save her, and it's going to be okay. All these thoughts went through my head in half a second. But as soon as I asked, "Is she alive?" with a little hope in my voice, he said,

"No, I killed her. She ran from me."

106

I became even more defeated and deflated. The little bit of hope that I had allowed myself to nurture was gone. I wanted her to be alive; I wanted to be the one to save her; but I knew if he was telling me he killed her, there's no way he will let me live. He must kill me to keep me silent. I know something this whole town wants to know; I have the answer. But I'm going to die with the answer. I'm going to die with all this information that could lead to this man's capture. What I know doesn't matter now because I'm going to die.

"Do you know the sheriff?"

I didn't understand why he asked me that question, and I shook my head, no.

"Well, Jeni knew the sheriff, and I was just wondering if you knew him, too."

"No, I've never met the sheriff."

All of this conversation was happening as he continued to rape me anally.

"Do you wanta know how I killed her?" I didn't answer.

"I beat her with a stick," he said, "a large stick. And then I kicked her in the throat about 12 good times. And you know what? That girl was still alive. So I turned her over, and I stood on her back and wrapped her sweater around her neck and pulled up on it until she died. Her body is about a half mile from here. Do you want to go see it?"

I shook my head no, despair mounting.

"It was a slow and painful death." Then everything was quiet for a while. I was even more in shock and still saying over and over to myself, "I can't believe this is happening to me. I can't believe this is happening to me. I'm not supposed to be here. This is not the way my life is supposed to end."

He again broke the silence.

"So you know I have to kill you too, don't you?"

I didn't answer.

"Do you want to die a slow death or a fast death? Because Jeni died a very slow and painful death."

I still didn't answer.

"Nod your head once for a fast death, and twice for a slow death." I dropped my head slightly.

"So, you want a fast death?"

And I was able to say, "Yes," and nod my head again.

"Do you want to die with your clothes on or clothes off? Jeni died in the nude."

I didn't answer.

So again he asked, "Do you want to die with your clothes on?" I nodded my head, yes.

At some point, he put the gun to my head, between my eyes. I shut my eyes.

"Tell me that you love me," he demanded.

I mumbled it weakly.

"TELL ME LIKE YOU MEAN IT!"

I tried to picture Chris in my mind and said "I love you" with more emphasis.

"Open your eyes," he said. "Do you see where my finger is?" I saw that his finger was on the trigger.

"Do you have one final request?" he asked.

"I want to see my mom and dad," I whimpered.

"Sorry, I can't do that."

He pulled the trigger. CLICK. "I'm not dead," I thought. It didn't go off. "Is he going to play Russian Roulette with me?" I wondered. I decided if he shot me and I didn't die right away, I would try to stay alive but play dead. But the image of my body as a corpse came into my mind. I pictured myself floating over my dead body.

"Look right here."

I looked where he was pointing at the gun. It said "BB Gun."

"So, this is not a real gun?" I asked.

"No, you could have run from the start and even if I had shot you, it wouldn't have killed you."

The notion that I should have run was distressing. But also, I had hoped to use the gun eventually to kill him, which was no longer an option. And probably the most upsetting thought was that the quick death option had been removed. I knew then that I would die a slow and painful death, just as Jeni did.

"So you know you won't die a fast death now, don't you?" He confirmed what I was thinking. "You're going to die anyway, you know, because I have AIDS."

I thought how much my death would hurt. He would have to beat me to death. I figured my best option was to keep my hands and arms to my side when he started beating me. If I did not block the blows, it might be quicker and less painful. I felt overwhelmingly sad.

I grieved my own death. I went through every stage of grief. I went through denial, trying to tell myself "This is not happening. This can't be happening to me." I bargained with God, telling him that if He would let me start this day over, I promise I won't get in the car. Please, God, give me a do-over, and I won't even go running today. Or give me the same situation and I'll do it differently. I just felt tremendous sadness and grief.

I thought how Mom would be destroyed. If my body is ever found, it will be months or years, and Mom will go that whole time not knowing what happened to her daughter. Not knowing would be unbearable for her. I also thought about Dad. I knew Dad would *grieve in his way, but I saw him trying to be more of a support for Mom. I knew the entire family would be devastated with grief, but I pictured them trying to hold Mom up. Mom and I were very close. I knew that losing any of her children would be difficult. I could picture her sitting in our living room. We had a sectional couch, and Mom always sat on the right side of that couch. To her right was Dad's recliner where he always sat. I pictured her sitting in her usual seat on that sectional couch with Dad and my sisters and brother all sitting around her and each of them comforting her.*

I thought of each person in the family and how each would handle my death. "What would this do to my dad? Will he show his grief or try to hide it? Will he be able to hold my mom up?"

I thought about Julie. Julie and I are 16 months apart, and we've gone through times when we've fought and times when we've been best friends. Usually the times when we're best friends are when we first move to a new place. With my dad being in the military, we moved about every three years. Whenever we moved, we initially had no friends, so we counted on each other for company and friendship. Once we had established our own friends outside the family, we didn't get along as well. And I guess part of that was because we spent so much time together and got on each other's nerves. She wasn't always easy to get along with, and surely sometimes I would provoke her. We had our ups and downs, and I was just hoping Julie would remember all the good times we had. We had lots of good times together, and I wanted her to remember those good times.

I thought of my other sister, Holley, who was six years younger than I. Being that much younger, Holley was a kid when I was a teenager. There was enough of an age gap that we couldn't really relate. She was always my little sister. Later, we became very close because, as we got older, six years wasn't so much of a gap. Holley was just starting to get into running herself and was showing potential, so we shared an interest and a talent, and I could see us coming closer together. But I was sad about Holley because I knew the two of us needed more time, that our connection, our bond, was just starting to get tighter. I hadn't had enough time with Holley and wasn't as close to her as I wanted to be. I felt really bad about that, and I hoped that she

110

would have enough good memories of me not to forget me.

I thought of my brother, Graig. In our relationship, the age gap was really something that was special to us. He was ten years younger than I and was my only brother. I had always wanted a brother; I spoiled him. My mom says once, when he was a few months old, I got jealous of all the attention he was getting, and I had a bit of a tantrum. But other than that, I had always adored my brother. When I was a teenager, he was a toddler, and I loved to show him off to my friends. He was adorable, and my friends would say that he was going to be so good-looking when he got older, and he was going to break some hearts. I loved to watch him and Dad wrestling in the living room. He was very funny, and all boy, and he did silly things. Julie admitted that some of his antics would irritate her, but in my eyes he could do no wrong. In spite of the age gap, I was really close to Graig; I felt like a second mom. I was especially sad that I was going to die when he was so young, only nine years old. His memories of me would fade as he aged, and the impact I had on his life would be much less than the impact he had on my life. I was saddened thinking I would not see my brother grow up. Even at the age of nine, he was showing the potential to be a great athlete, especially a great wrestler, and I knew there would be fun days ahead watching him compete; and I was sad I would miss all that.

I thought about Chris and how I had been so sure when we started dating that we would someday get married, and now it could not happen. I wondered how long Chris would grieve over me. We had been dating about eight months. How long would he grieve before he would get over me and start dating again? I wanted that for him. I realized that there will be someone else out there for him; and I hoped that whomever he does end up with will help him get over me, and that she won't be jealous if he has a picture of me. I wondered if he even had a picture of me and what kind of picture it was. Of course, all these were just fleeting thoughts, wondering about his future without me. How hard would this be for him?

I thought how my death would affect each family member. I was feeling sorry for myself, and I thought about all the things I was going to miss. The thoughts kept repeating in my mind: I can't believe

I'm going to die at the age of 20; I can't believe I'm going to be murdered. I'm supposed to get married, be a mom. I always looked forward to having kids. But now I'm going to die when there is so much more that I thought I would get to do.

I also went through a bit of an angry stage, although I didn't visually show it. This man doesn't even know me. He doesn't know that there are a lot of people who love me. He doesn't know how sad it will be for them if I die. And who is he to decide whether I live or die? It just seemed so unfair, and I wanted to tell him, "Who are you to decide what happens to me? You just don't know how much pain you're about to cause so many people, and you don't even care."

While all these thoughts were going through my mind as I was being raped, Daniel Lee might have been saying things; I don't remember. I was lost in my thoughts, staring into the back seat, into complete darkness, and my head was still, as if I was trying to look at something.

All of a sudden Daniel Lee said, "Don't even think about it," and he reached across me and grabbed something that was in the back seat and moved it over to the driver's side of the back seat.

I had actually not seen anything in the back seat, but as I looked to my right, I saw he had moved an empty six-pack of beer bottles. I realized he thought I would try to use one of the bottles to hit him. It jolted me out of my thoughts and actually gave me the idea: How am I going to get out of this; Is there any way? So, as I looked at the beer bottles, I pictured myself grabbing a bottle with my right hand and swinging the bottle behind me over my left shoulder at his head, thinking that I could hit him in the head with the bottle. Maybe I could knock him out, or daze him enough to continue attacking him. I had no doubt I could kill him if given the chance. I figured that one of us was going to die this night, most likely me, but I knew the only way to get away would be to kill him. I kept telling myself to grab the bottle, but I was frozen; I couldn't move my body. I tried to find the courage to grab the bottle and swing, and I worried that if I didn't try, I would regret another missed opportunity. I thought, "He will beat me in the woods, and I will regret it if I don't take this opportunity and grab this bottle." I already had so much regret, and I was going to blow another opportunity. But I just couldn't bring myself to do it; I knew that once I made a move, once I grabbed that bottle and hit him, he would become furious. I knew that as a rapist, his power was in controlling me, which was part of the thrill of the rape. And I knew that once I hit him, we were going to fight until one of us was dead.

I kept rationalizing, 'He's a man, he's on top of me, he's got rage in him; most likely if there's a fight, I'm going to be the one to die.'

I also told myself, "I'm alive and breathing right now, but within five minutes I could be dead!" And the thought of being dead so soon was horrifying. It was just so difficult to believe that I could be alive right now and dead in a couple of minutes. The fear of starting this fight kept me from grabbing the bottle. I just wasn't quite ready for that final moment. But I was mad at myself; I felt like I was giving up.

I was reminded of childhood attempts to perform double flips off the high dive in Bent Tree, Georgia. The diving board was empty and I stood on the high dive for the longest time talking to myself. "You're never going to learn it if you quit right now; don't let a little bit of pain stop you." I could not walk to the end of the board, my legs froze. Next I said to myself, "1, 2, 3, Go," and my foot started to take a step and I froze. After several false starts, I got so mad at myself I said, "This is it; don't even count, just GO!" And I did it.

In the car, I used the same self-instructions. I counted to three in my head and said "Go." But I could not grab the bottle. I told myself that not grabbing the bottle would just be one more regret. I asked God to forgive me of my sins.

I don't know how long he raped me with me lost in my thoughts, seemingly disengaged from my body. Eventually, he stopped. He briefly tried to penetrate me with one of the bottles – just one more power trip for him. I guess he wasn't getting much sexual gratification, because he got off me and told me to sit back in my seat. He sat back behind the wheel and lit a cigarette. Then he started talking as if we were boyfriend and girlfriend who had just finished having sex.

"Hey, I was just kidding about having AIDS," he said. "You know, it would be neat if I could take you somewhere."

113

The slightest glimmer of hope blinked in my head. If I could somehow get him to take me somewhere else, or to decide to kill me later, I might have a chance. I knew that in that car, in that desolate location, I was in a killing area.

"Yeah, maybe you could take me to a bar or something."

"That might be a problem, 'cause you're underage."

"Oh, I think they'd let me in."

He then started looking around in the glove compartment. "I don't even know if I have anything in the car to prove my age." As he was shuffling papers around looking for proof of his age, I saw another paper with his name on it. He took out his wallet and showed me some pictures in it. I acted interested.

I was confused. I asked myself, "How is this going to happen? He doesn't look angry enough to kill me." That glimmer of hope began slowly to brighten.

Then. . .

"When will people realize you're missing?"

I started crying then. Mainly because I knew my family must already know I was missing, which made me sad. But I also knew I could play that sadness as despair by lying to him.

"I don't think anyone will know I'm missing until Monday morning when my roommate comes back."

"What about your parents?"

"They live in Kansas, and they usually call once a week. I just talked to them last night," I said, not trying to stifle the tears. I felt the lie about my parents living in Kansas might support the glimmer of hope that was developing in my mind.

"How about friends? Will anyone come by your apartment?"

"Probably not. I haven't made any plans for this weekend."

114

"So, no one will know you're missing until Monday when your roommate comes back. I think I'll just take you home with me and kill you tomorrow."

'Oh my' I'm thinking, 'there may be a light at the end of the tunnel after all.' I was so excited, but trying desperately not to appear so.

"You were right about that marijuana, I am getting hungry. Do you think you could stop and get me something to eat?"

"I need to get gas, I'll get you something at the gas station."

I pictured a gas station with a hundred people milling around. 'Surely I can escape there.' My heart was pounding with excitement now.

"I'll have to tie your hands in front of you again." As he did so, he asked, "Is that too tight?"

"No, that's fine," I replied. I was brimming with excitement as he started the car. 'I WILL survive this,' I told myself; 'I WILL SURVIVE!' I still had no delusions about his intentions. He planned to kill me. I just started to believe at this point that somehow I would find a way to beat him.

As he drove back onto a paved road, I paid more attention to where we were going so I would be ready at the first opportunity to jump out and run. It was hard to see because the windshield wiper on my side did not work well. I even went over in my head the way I would jump out of the car: jump as far as I could away from the car and tuck and roll. With my hands tied together, I was concerned how I would unbuckle my seat belt without him noticing. When I saw the headlights of the first car to approach us, I thought about jumping out then, but we were still in a pretty isolated area, so I decided to wait until we reached a more populated area.

I soon recognized we had turned onto Highway 421. To my disappointment we were heading east, away from Boone. We had only gone a mile or two on 421 when he pulled into a gas station with a convenience store. Unfortunately, the gas station was nothing like I

115

imagined and hoped it would be. No other cars were in sight, and when I looked inside the store, I saw only the clerk behind the counter.

"You won't try to escape, will you?" Daniel Lee asked.

"No," I replied rather emphatically.

"Why not?"

"I'm too scared. I won't try anything." I could sense that he was watching me closely as he pumped the gas. I was thinking to myself, is this guy that vain or naïve as to believe that I really like him now, or is he just stupid?' He actually trusts that I'm not going to attempt to get away.

"Can I go into the store with you?" I asked, figuring I might make a scene inside and the clerk would rescue me.

"No, you stay in the car. I'll get you something to eat."

As he walked toward the store, I was praying, "Please God, make somebody come." His car was still the only car at the station. Then, as he walked inside, a car drove up with one man in it. The driver did not stop at a pump for gas but just parked and went inside. I watched him intently as he picked up something and walked to the counter to pay. Daniel Lee was near the rear of the store, still looking over the food racks. "Please come out before Daniel," I pleaded. As soon as the stranger turned and headed for the door, I reached over, unbuckled my seat belt and opened my car door. I sprinted around the front of the car and ran to the stranger's car. I opened the passenger door, jumped in, and scrunched down as low as I could in the floor. I was certain the stranger saw me jump in his car and for a moment feared that he might panic and go back inside the store. I had never taken off my shirt, but it was the only thing I was wearing. At this point, though, modesty was the furthest thing from my mind.

When he opened his door, I screamed, "PLEASE HURRY; GET OUT OF HERE; THE MAN INSIDE MURDERED JENI GRAY AND HE RAPED ME!" I was surprised and concerned that he said nothing. He rather calmly started the car and slowly backed out and turned toward the road.

"HURRY, HURRY, PLEASE TAKE ME HOME!" I yelled.

But to my dismay he turned east, away from Boone. "Am I going from one rapist to another?'"I wondered. "Or is he perhaps a friend of Daniel Lee?"

"I'm not going to hurt you," he said. "My wife and I are staying with friends near here. I'm taking you there."

He drove less than a half-mile and turned into a driveway. As soon as he stopped the car, I jumped out and ran into the house at the end of the drive. I saw a man and woman in the living room, but I bolted past them and ran into the kitchen. I sat on the floor of the kitchen in a fetal position and started sobbing uncontrollably. Meanwhile, the man who drove the car was explaining to the couple in the living room how I had jumped into his car and claimed to have been raped. The lady came into the kitchen and put her arm around my shoulder.

"I'm Crystal Adams; it's okay now, tell me what happened." She turned toward the living room. "Call 911."

I tried to compose myself enough to tell her I had been abducted and raped by the man who killed Jeni Gray.

Then I asked her for the phone. "I have to call my parents." She handed me the phone and I called home. My dad answered the phone and I broke down crying again. I'm sure I was totally incoherent. Crystal took the phone from my hand.

117

CLAUDE

Having experienced one winter in Boone, I didn't want to tackle another without a 4-wheel drive vehicle. On Friday, September 29th, I proudly drove off the lot of Norman Cheek Toyota with a brand new black 4-wheel drive Toyota truck. When I drove into our driveway with the new truck, Louise was preparing to take Holley to the Watauga High football game. She decided to test drive the truck by taking Holley to the game and then driving over to Leigh's apartment to show her the truck. Leigh lived in App South Apartments that semester, and Julie lived in the dorms. When Louise arrived at Leigh's apartment, her boyfriend, Chris, was pacing on the balcony outside the apartment. He was obviously worried. Leigh had left him a note that she was going for a run and would return around 6:30 PM. It was now a little past 7; for Leigh to be thirty minutes late was not surprising. She was rarely at any place less than thirty minutes after she said she would be there, so we weren't too concerned initially. Louise told Chris to call us when Leigh got back, and Louise returned home. About 20 or 30 minutes later, having heard nothing from Chris, Louise began to worry. She was reading the newspaper, and of course no one could pick up a local paper at that time without reading about the disappearance of Jeni Gray. She called Leigh's apartment number, and Chris said he still had heard nothing. He was very concerned. Louise hung up the phone and said, "Claude, I have a sick feeling about this. I think something bad has happened."

We decided that she should go back to the apartment and wait with Chris, and I would stay at the house in case Leigh phoned or came by. Louise and Chris drove around checking out the most likely routes Leigh might have run. They saw no signs of her, so they went back to the apartment and phoned the hospital, the campus pool where she sometimes worked, and the fitness center where she worked out. For Louise and Chris, I guess time was going by pretty fast because they were busy; for me, just waiting, time was crawling. Graig was with me, but I didn't say anything to him about why I was worried. He was only nine years old. Louise called me at about 8:45 asking if I had heard anything. My initial thoughts had been that Leigh might have sprained an ankle or suffered a knee injury and had just stopped somewhere to rest, but I knew she would surely have phoned someone by now. I was seriously concerned at this point. Finally, at 9:30 the phone rang. When I picked it up, I could hear crying in the background.

"Mr Cooper?"

"Yes."

"Mr Cooper, my name is ------ (I rarely hear names the first time on the phone). Your daughter is here with us …."

I could hear Leigh's voice yelling into the phone, "DAD, HE HURT ME!!"

The woman spoke again, "Your daughter was abducted and has been raped, but she's alive and appears to be okay. The sheriff and emergency personnel are on their way here."

She gave me directions to her house and repeated her name, "Crystal Adams."

I then dialed the number of my apartment, and when Mom answered the phone, Crystal gave her the same information as she had given Dad. Mom later said she heard me crying in the background and told herself, "That's Leigh crying, so she's alive. We can deal with anything else."

Jamie, my rescuer's wife, then brought me some clothes: a sweat shirt and sweat pants. Crystal went back into the living room, I guess to wait for the sheriff.

I desperately wanted to take a shower. I felt like I just had to get the smell of Daniel Lee off me. I asked Jamie where the bathroom was, and she took me to it. I turned on the shower and started undressing. Just as I was about to step into the shower, Crystal ran into the bathroom.

"No, no, no, you can't take a shower now!" she said.

"I know I'm not supposed to, but I must get the scent of that man off me," I pleaded.

"I know you want to, but you simply can't. You'll be washing away critical evidence. Just put these clean clothes on for now and you'll be okay."

A few minutes later, a sheriff's deputy came in with a couple of investigators.

"Can you tell me anything at all about the man who abducted you tonight?" one of the investigators asked me.

"Yes. His name is Daniel Lee; he is 24 years old; he lives in Triplett; he drives a small white car with a chain hanging from the mirror." I went on to describe his clothing down to his underwear.

The investigator immediately said, "I know who he is. We've arrested him before on drug charges."

At that point, the front door opened, and Mom and Dad and Chris rushed into the living room. I ran to them as the investigator spoke to the sheriff's deputy. I collapsed into my dad's arms and again began sobbing uncontrollably. I held onto my dad for a minute or two, then hugged my mom while the sheriff, Red Lyons, introduced himself to Dad, and they talked briefly. An ambulance had arrived by then, and the medics asked Mom if she wanted to ride in the ambulance with me to the hospital. My mom suggested that Chris ride with me, and she and Dad would meet us at the hospital. In the ambulance, Chris sat beside me with his head in his hands.

"Please don't leave me," I sobbed several times during the ride to the hospital.

My mom and dad followed the ambulance, and when we arrived at the hospital, Mom went in with me to the examination room while Chris and my dad stayed in the waiting room. During the rape kit examination, Mom held my hand and we talked. She was even able to make me laugh a couple of times. I don't know how long the examination lasted; it must have been about an hour. After I dressed, an investigator (it may have been a sheriff's deputy) walked in.

"Leigh, is this your watch?" he asked.

I was surprised to see my watch in his hand. I recalled that Daniel Lee had seen my watch on my wrist and had said, "Oh, I'm going to have to take that from you." He had taken three things from me: my watch, my underwear, and my bra.

"YES, THAT'S IT!" I exclaimed. "SO, YOU GOT HIM??"

"Yes, we've got him," he answered. "We drove up to his house and saw the car facing out. The first thing I noticed was the chain hanging from the mirror like you said. We knocked on his door and his dad let us in. When we told him we needed to see Daniel, his dad went upstairs and got him. We could see that he had on the same underwear that you described and the same glasses. I told him to empty his pockets, and that's when we saw the watch. I asked him where he got the watch, and he said his girlfriend gave it to him. But when I told him to show me how the stopwatch function works, he couldn't do it. We

121

then put him under arrest. His car is being towed in to the Boone Police Station where it will be impounded."

Special Agent Steve Wilson of the State Bureau of Investigation entered the room and introduced himself and asked if I would go down to the police station to provide a statement. It was very late, so my mom suggested that Chris go get some sleep and that she and Dad would go to the station with me. Steve Wilson explained to me and to Dad that he and other detectives had to ask for a very detailed account of everything that happened to me. He wanted to ensure that I would be comfortable giving a detailed account in front of my parents and that they, especially Dad, would be okay listening to it. I wanted Mom and Dad to know what I had been through and to know I had their support. Dad assured him they could handle anything they might hear.

The statement and interview at the police station lasted over three hours. They seemed impressed with the detail I recalled. I could sense that even the investigators were a little uncomfortable as I described the way Daniel Lee said he had killed Jeni Gray. They all knew Jeni, and they were hearing things about what happened to her that I'm sure they didn't want to hear. At some point about an hour into the statement, a sheriff's deputy came in with a photo lineup he had assembled. He placed several photos in front of me and asked me if I saw the man I knew as Daniel Lee. I picked him out immediately. "That's him," I said without hesitation. They confirmed I had picked out the same Daniel Lee they suspected.

After I finished my statement and answered all their questions, Steve Wilson asked if I thought I could take them to the spot where Daniel Lee had taken me. My mom protested briefly, as it was close to three o'clock in the morning by this time. Steve explained that it was very important to search for the location while events were fresh in my memory, and also that the sooner they could initiate their search for Jeni Gray in that area, the better.

"Mom, I need to go ahead and do it now," I said.

Steve suggested that my parents go home and assured them they would bring me home as soon as they found the spot. We drove around for over an hour, but I was lost. I explained that Daniel Lee took too

122

many turns and reversals of our route due to detours. I suggested we start at the gas station where I escaped and backtrack from there. There were fewer turns this way and I had been paying more attention during this part of the drive with Daniel Lee. Eventually, I saw the big barn.

"THIS IS IT!" I yelled. "Turn down this road." I took them to the exact spot where Lee turned around and parked. There were cigarette butts on the ground, as well as my clothes which he had thrown out the window.

"Jeni Gray is within one-half mile of here!" I exclaimed. "I know she's here!"

CHAPTER SEVEN

THE SEARCH FOR JENI GRAY

Louise and I stayed up the rest of that night, talking and crying. We were thankful, of course, that Leigh was alive, but it just tore our hearts out to think of what she had been through. We both wondered how she would be affected. Would she recover? Would she be the same outgoing and happy person she had been? Would she be afraid to step outside? Would she ever trust a man again? Would she ever run again? I was also beating myself up for not protecting her, as if there might have been something I could or should have done to prevent this tragedy. If I had only taught her more about guns so that she could have recognized the type of gun he was pointing at her; if I had only been there to tell her to just run. I felt I had failed her as a father.

Finally, at about 5:45 AM, Lieutenant Watson and Detective Harrison brought Leigh home. As soon as she came in the front door, she said excitedly, "WE FOUND IT! It's called Jake's Mountain Road. They're going to start searching for Jeni's body as soon as it gets light."

She broke down crying as Louise and I both went to her and just held her for several minutes.

Finally, Leigh said, "Mom, I've got to take a shower. I have to wash him off me." Louise went back to our bathroom with her as I sat in the living room. After showering for about 30 or 45 minutes, Louise sat with Leigh talking with her until Leigh finally dropped off to sleep. I continued to beat myself up.

The next afternoon, which was Saturday, we had been up for about an hour when the doorbell rang. Louise was in the kitchen, I was in the living room, and Leigh was out of bed but still in the bedroom. Louise went to the door, and I was a few steps behind her.

"Good afternoon, Mrs Cooper, and Colonel. My name is Tom Rusher (he pronounced it as 'Roosher'); I'm the District Attorney for Watauga County. I'm sorry to intrude, but may I come in for just a moment?"

"Of course, please come in," replied Louise, as I shook his hand.

"Would it be possible for me to have a word with Leigh, and of course, I want you two also to hear what I have to say?"

As Louise turned to get Leigh, who was already coming out of her room, Mr. Rusher said, "Colonel Cooper, I'm terribly sorry for what your daughter went through last night. She's a very courageous young woman."

Louise introduced Leigh as they came into the front room, and Leigh shook his hand. After praising her for her courage and for keeping her wits about her under the worst possible circumstances, Tom got to the point of his visit. He apologized for intruding so soon after her tragic experience but emphasized the importance of his task.

"Leigh, you have enabled us to put a would-be serial killer behind bars. We want to ensure that he never sees the light of day again, and that's my job as District Attorney. I'll be prosecuting this case." He went on to explain how crucial her testimony would be, but it would not be easy to testify. "A lot of young women who have been through what you went through last night are reluctant to come forward and testify. They feel that going through it again in court is almost as bad as the actual assault. But for me to prosecute Daniel Lee, your testimony will be crucial. I just need to know how you feel about taking the witness stand in court and telling what he did to you and what he told you about Jeni Gray. Are you going to be willing and able to do that?"

Without hesitating, Leigh replied, "Mr Rusher, I'm very willing, and I'm sure I'll be able to look him in the eye and do my part in putting him away for good. I did nothing wrong, and I'm not ashamed to tell it."

Not only did Tom Rusher breathe a sigh of relief, I did as well. "Maybe she'll be okay," I was thinking.

Tom thanked her, called her a hero, and assured her he would do all he could to make the trial as painless as possible for her.

.   .   .   .   .

Jake's Mountain Road was a very rugged gravel road that led from the outskirts of Boone near the Blue Ridge Parkway down to the little town of Triplett, where Daniel Lee lived. On the best of days it was a bad road, very narrow, with sheer drop-offs. With Hurricane Hugo having just gone through, it was not even negotiable all the way to Triplett. Downed trees and washouts made it impossible to drive. The spot where Daniel Lee took Leigh was only about a half-mile down Jake's Mountain Road. He had found an area just wide enough to turn his vehicle around. The search for Jeni's body began at that site with every available resource from all the law enforcement elements in the area. It became obvious immediately that the search would not be easy. The vegetation was very thick with dense undergrowth, and the terrain was extremely steep. No trace of Jeni was found all day Saturday and Sunday.

On Sunday, a search warrant was obtained to search Daniel Lee's house. Sheriff Red Lyons, Police Chief Zane Tester, Agent Steve Wilson, William Greene, Luther Harrison, and Lieutenant Willie Watson and several other law enforcement officials conducted the search. Several items were confiscated, including a pair of black panties and a white bra. Later that afternoon, warrants for the arrest of Daniel Lee were obtained for one count of robbery with a dangerous weapon, three counts of first-degree sex offense, one count of first-degree kidnapping, and one count of first-degree forcible rape. The magistrate placed Lee under a $3,000,000 secured bond and set an initial court date for Oct 4, 1989. The next day, Monday, October 2nd, Daniel Lee made a statement during an interview with Sheriff Lyons admitting to abducting and raping Leigh but denying any knowledge of Jeni Gray's murder.

The search of the Jake's Mountain Road area continued through Tuesday, October 3rd with bloodhounds and helicopters. Still, no trace of anything. Knowing the spot where he assaulted Leigh was near the Blue Ridge Parkway, officials decided to search other likely areas along the Parkway. On Wednesday, October 4th, an intensive search with bloodhounds was conducted around Price Lake. Some officials began to doubt whether Daniel Lee was actually the killer of Jeni Gray, that perhaps his attack on Leigh was a copycat incident. Knowing their initial suspect was from Tennessee, they searched ponds and lakes in Johnson County, Tennessee.

On Wednesday afternoon, Detective Harrison and Lt. Watson drove the route that Daniel Lee had taken with Leigh in his car. The distance from the spot on Meadowview Drive, where he had abducted her, to the crime scene was 13 miles. From the crime scene to the service station where she escaped was 5.25 miles.

The search for Jeni Gray continued through the weekend. On Friday, October 6th, a team from the Boone Police Department, the Watauga County Sheriff's Department, and Blue Ridge Parkway Rangers again searched the Price Park area. Later that day, Detective Harrison, Detective Greene, and LT Watson went back to Jake's Mountain Road to search. They found a logging road about one-half mile down Jake's Mountain Road from where Leigh was attacked. A couple of smaller logging roads branched off this road. The logging trails were very steep and difficult to negotiate, even on foot. The detectives searched down to about 100 meters from where the trails branched. Again, nothing was found. In spite of the frustration and perhaps doubt creeping into the minds of some of the persons involved in the search for Jeni Gray, Leigh remained adamant.

"They may never find her," Leigh told Louise and me, "but there is no doubt in my mind that she's somewhere along Jake's Mountain Road. I know he killed her."

On Monday, October 9th, Lieutenant Watson, perhaps on a hunch, suggested taking another look at the logging trails they had searched on Friday. He went with Detective Harrison, Lieutenant Farmer, and Sergeant Main. They split up to search the logging trails, Watson and Harrison going one direction and Farmer and Main going another. At 4:00 PM, Sergeant Main contacted Watson and Harrison by radio asking them to meet him at their vehicles. When they arrived, he told them that Lieutenant Farmer had located the body of a white female. The three men walked down the trail to Farmer, who was waiting with the body. Detective Harrison noted that he had walked down this same trail on Friday, but he had turned around about 100 meters too soon. The body was nude and lying face up with a piece of clothing wrapped around her neck. Her neck and shoulders were

130

bruised. The body appeared to be the remains of Jeni Gray.

The DA, Tom Rusher, called us that night. "I want to tell you and Leigh before you hear it on the news at 11 o'clock. We have located Jeni Gray's body, and the manner of death was just as Leigh described it."

Leigh had not returned to her classes yet. She was driving to Charlotte to see Chris when the body was found. When she arrived and got out of the car, Chris hugged her and said, "They found her."

Dr. John Butts, the Chief Medical Examiner for the State of North Carolina, made a positive identification of the body as the body of Jennifer Lea Gray. Cause of death – strangulation. The autopsy also showed a skull fracture on the back of the lower skull with indications of four or five blows to the back of the head, a cracked rib, and internal hemorrhaging on her back. A BB was imbedded in her vagina.

The authorities now had a body, physical evidence and an autopsy showing that the death was exactly as Leigh had described it. DA Tom Rusher charged Daniel Lee with first-degree murder, kidnapping and rape, in addition to the charges already filed for the attack on Leigh. The warrants were served and Daniel Lee was held without bond, with a new court date of October 24.

LEIGH

On Thursday, October 5th, Appalachian State University organized a march through campus and to the downtown parking lot where Jeni Gray's car was found. About 600 people marched in protest to violence against women. Some were cheering, some shouting slogans like "Take back the night." My family and I marched along with them. When the march arrived at a temporary stage set up at the Lois Harrill Center parking lot, a few university officials spoke, and then others in the crowd were invited to speak. The tone of these additional speakers, most of whom were students, began turning to hatred of men in general and criticism of law enforcement officials in Boone and the county. After several critical speakers, I was upset. I turned to Mom.

"Mom, this is not right. Would you go up and say something?"

Mom took the stage and gave a short speech explaining that she was the mother of the girl who had been abducted and raped. She praised the police, the sheriff's department, the counseling center, and the DA's office. She talked of all the support I had received since my escape and said that we shouldn't be blaming men in general for the acts of one person. What had been a raucous and angry crowd suddenly became quiet. She changed the attitude of the entire crowd.

After Mom spoke, the crowd broke up and returned to campus or to their homes. Barbara Daye, Assistant Vice Chancellor for Student Development, who had organized the march, came over and thanked Mom for her comments. She explained that it was her intent to make the march an annual event and assured us that, in the future, it would not be an angry protest. She was true to her word, as all subsequent marches were called the "Walk for Awareness" rather than "Take Back the Night."

.   .   .   .   .

I was relieved when Jeni's body was found. I was sad for her family to learn that she had died such a horrible death, but at the same time, I felt that it must be better for them to know what occurred rather than forever be in doubt. In a way, I was proud that had it not been for me, they may never have known what happened to her.

I credit Jeni Gray for saving my life. I had the advantage of knowing Daniel Lee was a killer. I imagine that Jeni steadfastly resisted him at every point. Perhaps she refused to undress, and he became enraged. I think she may have tried to run from him (she had daylight, which I did not have), and a fallen tree over the logging trail stopped her. It was unclear whether or not he actually raped her, but he was charged with a sex offense related to the BB gun.

I was determined not to let Jeni's death be in vain. Thanks to her, and my knowledge of what had happened to her, I believed I was given a new chance at life. I owed Jeni my life, and I was determined to make the best of what she had given me. When Mom and Dad asked whether I wanted to go back to school, I readily said "Absolutely." I knew I needed counseling, so for several months I made regular visits to the ASU Counseling Center. Dr. Donald Sans and the staff at the Center were a valuable asset as they listened to anything I wanted to talk about and helped me shed, or at least control, the demons that would love to have taken control of my mind. I talked to each of my professors about the class days I had missed. They were all very accommodating in arranging time and tutoring for me to make up missed work and to take my exams. I couldn't have been prouder and more appreciative of being an ASU student. Tom Rusher and his staff checked in on me frequently and kept me informed of the progress of the upcoming court case.

Of course, the media were all over my story, especially the Watauga Democrat, the Winston-Salem Journal, and the Charlotte Observer. A flap arose immediately that bothered my parents more than it did me. Most newspapers had a policy of not revealing the names of rape victims. The Democrat and the Observer ascribed to that policy, but the Journal did not. The Journal immediately released my name. The Democrat, on the other hand, did not publish my name but did publish the lurid details of each sex offense. Readers of both newspapers easily put the two coverages together and knew not only that I was raped, but exactly how I was raped. Several people wrote letters to the editors of both papers in protest of the papers'

133

insensitivity.   My mom even visited the editor of the Democrat in person to explain that my parents and I did not want my grandmothers and my younger sister and brother to know certain details of my trauma.

During the months after my escape and leading up to the trial, I did a lot of thinking. I was keenly aware that I had been sabotaging my potential and that my eating had been out of control.   I now had a second chance at life, and I wanted to take advantage of it. I decided to take control of every aspect of my life.   I also felt an overwhelming obligation to do something positive with whatever life I had left. I owed that much to Jeni, to my parents, and to myself. One aspect of being in control involved a decision which I feared would disappoint my dad, but I knew I had to do it. One evening about a week or two after my ordeal, I approached him as he was reading the newspaper. Mom was in the kitchen, but she could hear our conversation.

"Dad, I need to talk with you about something."

"Sure, Hon, what is it?"

"Dad, is there any way I can get out of my ROTC contract?"

"I don't understand," he replied. "You're doing very well in ROTC, and I'm certain you'll become an outstanding officer."

"Yes, but after what I've been through, I can't bear the thought of anyone being in control over me, or me controlling someone else for that matter. When I was in that car, another man had total control over me, and I'm determined that will never happen again. I know that it's a different kind of control, but someone will be giving me orders, and I will have to obey whether I agree with the orders or not, and I just can't bear the thought of that."

"You can do that, can't you, Dad?" asked Mom.

"Actually, I don't have that authority. She signed a contract with the US Army, so Department of the Army will have to approve it. I'll call General Arnold at Region Headquarters tomorrow. I think he'll support us on this."

"Thank you, Dad. I'm sorry to disappoint you. I love you."

"Oh, Babe, you surely don't disappoint me; I love you too."

"I know I can be a leader, Dad, but I see a different focus for my life now. I think I was put in that car for a reason. Someone else may not have escaped, and Daniel Lee would still be killing young women. I was given a second chance on life, and I am determined to make the most of it. I really want to have an impact in this world; I want to make a difference. I feel like I'm starting my life over. I'm thankful for the chance to start over, and I'm going to make it count."

Mom came over with tears in her eyes and gave me a long hug. "You're going to have a wonderful, productive life," she said. "I'm so proud of you."

Dad stayed in his chair. I know he didn't want me to see him crying, but his eyes were definitely reddening and tearing up.

The Region Commander told Dad to submit the paperwork, and he would recommend approval. I finished that semester in ROTC and was then disenrolled and my contract voided.

A few days after that conversation with Dad, I had another conversation with Mom and Dad. I was taking a nutrition course in my PE major. As a project for that course, I decided to take control of my eating habits. I established target goals for myself: track my food intake, eat three meals a day, always eat sitting down, drink water, eliminate fast food, and, of course, continue to exercise. I explained my project plans to my parents, and for the first time told them how I had been pigging out on junk food for years, and that I did, in fact, have a serious eating disorder. I guess they suspected my eating problem, for they didn't seem totally shocked. They offered to help me take control by setting monetary rewards for meeting my weekly goals. I eagerly accepted their offer, and it certainly helped me to get started, but after a month I knew I had it licked. I told them to stop the monetary rewards, as I was ready to do it on my own. I was finally in control. My weight, as expected, started coming down. I wasn't actually on a diet; I was just very much aware of what went into my body, and I was determined to control my eating habits. My running improved. I started feeling

135

more like a deer and less like a plow horse. The feeling of empowerment was amazing and so self-satisfying.

While I continued to train on my own through that semester, I told Coach Weaver I was looking forward to cross-country in the fall and promised him I would be a different runner.

CHAPTER EIGHT

TAKING CONTROL

The trial in the Jeni Gray murder case began on Monday, April 16, 1990. Since Lee was pleading not guilty to the sex offense charge (firing a BB into Jeni Gray's vagina), the kidnapping and murder charges would be heard first and sentenced, then the sex offense charge would be heard. A motion by the defense for a change of venue had been approved by the Watauga County court, so the trial was held in Newland, in adjacent Avery County. The defense moved on Monday to prevent Leigh from testifying. Judge Charles Lamm denied the motion and ruled that Leigh could testify concerning Jeni Gray's case only but could not talk about specifics concerning Leigh's own case. Since Daniel Lee had pleaded guilty to every offense except the first degree sex offense against Jeni Gray, this would be a sentencing hearing only. District Attorney Tom Rusher made it clear that Daniel Lee's guilty plea to first degree murder and first degree kidnapping was not the result of a plea bargain and that the state was definitely seeking the death penalty. At a pre-trial hearing Daniel Lee had offered to plead guilty to all charges related to Leigh, but the judge refused to accept the pleas because a trial date had not been set for those charges.

Monday and Tuesday of the trial were spent primarily dealing with motions, most of which were filed by the defense. Opening statements were presented on Wednesday. Tom Rusher described the brutal murder as "A crime so heinous it should be punishable only by death." He explained that, "Her skull was fractured, but she lived. He kicked her, but she still lived. He then stood on her back and strangled her with her own sweater."

In opening statements by the defense, Chester Whittle, one of two court-appointed attorneys, argued that Daniel Lee did not deserve to die because he had suffered a brain aneurysm in the spring of 1988 and his character had changed as a result. On Thursday, evidence and testimony were presented by law enforcement officials who had discovered the body and gathered and analyzed evidence such as photographs, clothing and the branch that was found near Jeni's body. Leigh, the star witness for the prosecution, was scheduled to take the stand on Friday.

The *Watauga Democrat* reported Leigh testified "in a calm, composed and even tone." Leigh's testimony was more than calm, composed, and even; it was riveting. Daniel Lee appeared afraid of her, looking down at his hands and fidgeting during most of her testimony. Everyone in the courtroom, and especially the jurors, were on the edge of their seats as Leigh described in detail how he had abducted her at gunpoint, taken her to remote Jake's Mountain Road, and while he was sexually assaulting her, told her of his brutal murder of Jeni Gray. Leigh recounted the defendant's statements to her that he beat Jeni with a big stick, kicked her several times in the throat; and seeing that she was still alive, stood on her back and strangled her with her bra and sweatshirt. Leigh testified that Daniel Lee told her "Jeni had died a slow and painful death and she was hard to kill."

The remainder of the trial was anti-climactic as the defense attorneys attempted to convince the jury that Daniel Lee's brain aneurism had changed his personality and that he could not appreciate his conduct when he committed the crimes. They presented a neurosurgeon and a psychologist to testify in support of their claims. Defense Attorney Chester Whittle argued that they were not excusing Daniel Lee's crimes, but that justice would better be served by putting him in prison rather than sentencing him to death.

On Thursday, April 26, after seven hours of deliberation, the jury of six men and six women returned with a recommendation that Daniel Lee receive the death penalty. Lee merely nodded when Judge Lamm sentenced him to the electric chair. During their deliberations, the jury had made one request of the judge. They had asked whether Lee would ever get out of prison or be eligible for parole should they not decide on the death penalty. Judge Lamm informed them that he was not permitted to answer that question and that they would have to make that call based on the evidence they had heard in court. The jury were not willing to take the chance that Lee would be paroled.

Ironically, and unknown to the jurors, while they were deliberating, Judge Lamm had sentenced Lee on the charges related to Leigh's case. He was sentenced to four consecutive life sentences for the first-degree rape and three first-degree sex offenses against Leigh.

Additionally, he was sentenced to 15 years for the consolidated charges of common law robbery and kidnapping of Leigh. As Tom Rusher put it, Daniel Lee could not "live long enough to ever get out of prison." For each life sentence, he would have to serve a minimum of 20 years before becoming eligible for parole. Thus, Tom estimated that even if he was never executed, he would have to serve an estimated 120 years in prison before becoming eligible for parole. Each sentence was the maximum allowed under state law for the offense.

Leigh was surrounded by the media as she left the courthouse with her family and her team of attorneys. She had said she didn't mind talking to reporters. She wanted everyone to know that she was not ashamed of what happened to her and that she hoped her testimony would encourage other victims of sexual assault to come forward and talk without fear.

Asked for her feelings about the death sentence, she replied, "I guess I was somewhat relieved when the sentence was read. My main satisfaction came during the deliberations when Judge Lamm announced his sentences for the assault on me. After that, I knew that Daniel Lee would never again be a free man, and that he would either die in the electric chair or in prison of old age or sickness or someone beating him to death. I wouldn't have been terribly disappointed with a life sentence for the murder of Jeni, but I certainly had no problem with the death sentence."

She also said that Daniel Lee's description to Leigh of how he murdered Jeni was further motivation to survive, so she could tell about the murder and help find Jeni's body, and maybe ease the pain of Jeni's family and friends.

·   ·   ·   ·   ·

With the kind understanding and generosity of her ASU professors, Leigh finished the semester successfully. Her efforts to control her eating went well; she lost excess weight and ran well. Some of her friends wondered if she would and should run again and cautioned her about running alone, but there was no way she would stop running. She had a couple of male friends who were also runners, and one of them always seemed to be around when she was ready to run. Running with males made her feel more secure, but she would have run whether they were around or not: she was determined to be in top condition when she rejoined the cross-country team in the fall.

She was thankful Chris stood by her. She knew that it is not uncommon for boyfriends, and even husbands in many cases, to abandon a female after a rape. If anything, Leigh and Chris became a stronger couple. They were practically living together, as Chris said he was afraid to let her out of his sight. Not a runner himself, he had no problem with Leigh being accompanied on her runs by other male runners. But her runs were about the only times they were apart. They planned to marry when they graduated from college.

Chris graduated that spring and in the fall he took a job teaching PE at East Burke Junior High in the little town of Icard, NC, just down the mountain from Boone. Leigh continued her studies at App State and visited Chris as often as possible between taking classes and running cross-country. Louise and I enjoyed seeing her compete in cross-country that fall. She finished in the top ten in most meets, and in the Southern Conference Championship race, she finished in 8th place overall in a time of 19:37, earning All-Conference honors. We suspected something was preventing her from finishing higher, and we learned what the next day. Leigh came to our house to hang out and was exhausted the whole day. It was her mom, with mother's intuition, who asked her if she could be pregnant. We think Leigh was relieved that we brought it out in the open first. Of course, it would be a stumbling block to her running, but Louise and I were so happy that Leigh was alive and recovering so well that her announced pregnancy didn't even register on our "Richter Scale." The whole family loved Chris and was excited to be thinking of the two getting married and starting a family.

Louise and I had not seen or talked with Chris after Leigh told us the news until we saw him at our daughter Holley's high school cross-country state championship meet in Charlotte. Chris and Leigh came to support Holley. When we met them, I said to Louise, "Mom, go back to the truck and get my shotgun." Chris's jaw dropped. Then we all had a good laugh. My joke relieved any tension there might have been and made Chris feel better around his future in-laws. He assured us he had no intention of abandoning Leigh or hurting her. After discussing possible plans later that weekend, they decided to get married at the end of December.

We all had to pitch in to plan a wedding in less than two months. My uncle Bill, who was a minister and lived in Morganton, gladly accepted the request to officiate the service. The First Baptist Church of Boone graciously allowed the use of its chapel and fellowship hall for the service and reception. The date was set for December 29, 1990. The proudest moment of my life to that point was walking Leigh down the aisle that day. It was a simple church wedding, well-attended by family and university and community friends. For their honeymoon, Leigh and Chris booked a room for three days at the Grove Park Inn in nearby Blowing Rock. After one night there, though, they decided they would rather be with family and came to our house in University Village. The saying, "You're not losing a daughter; you're gaining a son-in-law," certainly rang true, giving Louise and me great of satisfaction and joy.

Leigh continued running through most of her pregnancy, though of course, she did not compete in track that spring semester. She was determined not to gain too much weight so she could compete in cross-country in the fall. Leigh's penchant for tardiness certainly did not hold true for this pregnancy. Two months prior to her due date, she was standing by her car pumping gas when she felt the first contractions. She knew she was going into labor.

"Oh, my God, no!" she told herself; "It's too early!" All of our family were out of town for various reasons, so Leigh and Chris welcomed Jacob Christopher Wallace into this world by themselves on May 4, 1991. In typical Leigh fashion, she wanted to experience the full effect of childbirth without any pain medication. It was touch and go for a while and very scary; he was so tiny, weighing only 4 pounds, 4 ounces, and lived in an incubator for the first two weeks of his life. He wasn't even strong enough for Leigh to feed him; he had to be fed through a tube. He grew so much later that we could hardly believe he had ever been so small. When Jacob was released from the hospital, Leigh and Chris took their tiny baby home to Icard to begin their life together as a family. She took about a week off from running but then got right back to it. Her final year of college was to begin that fall, and she wanted to be competitive.

Leigh returned to the cross-country team in fall of 1991 and trained with the team three days a week when she was in Boone for classes. She and Coach Weaver planned her workouts together. He wanted to ensure she remained healthy and injury-free. They reduced her running mileage to well below that of most of her teammates, but she continued to do intense water workouts and biking. She was feeling much stronger, and her training times were improving weekly. In her first race, held at ASU, she finished 2nd on the team and 9th overall in a time of 19:12 for the 5K course. She was encouraged by finishing ahead of several runners from the University of North Carolina, an Atlantic Coast Conference school. A couple of weeks later, ASU hosted the ASU Invitational, a race in which most of the Southern Conference schools competed. The race gave runners a good measure of where they stood in the conference. She was the top ASU runner in this race, finishing 4th overall in a time of 18:30. In college, women's cross-country courses are supposed to cover 5 kilometers, although that distance may vary slightly from course to course; but some courses have more hills and the running surface can vary over a given course from loose to compact, smooth to rocky, or grass to dirt. These first two races, though, were both at the same course, Moses Cone Park, so her time improvement was significant and encouraging. Her next meet was at Wake Forest University, a meet which also included Navy. She really looked forward to this meet since the Wake Forest coach was one of the coaches who had told her she would not be competitive in the ACC. Leigh finished 2nd overall, helping ASU defeat both Wake Forest and Navy and proving she was competitive in any league. This trend continued in the next meet, the North Carolina Collegiate Championship meet, which included teams from UNC, Duke, Wake Forest, East Carolina, and other state colleges. Again, Leigh finished 2nd overall on a more difficult course. In the final race of the season, the Southern Conference Championship meet she finished 3rd, earning All-Conference honors. She had established herself as an elite Division I university runner, and she had finally completed a full competitive season of running pain-free.

Leigh had never run indoor track, but she was on a roll physically and mentally and anxious to continue competing. ASU did not have an indoor track facility at that time, so their meets were always held at other schools. Their biggest meet was at Navy on January 18, 1992, a meet in which teams from Wake Forest, Duke, Maryland, George Mason, William and Mary, Delaware, and Mount St. Mary also competed. Leigh ran the 5,000 meters and finished 1st in a time of 17:38. Three weeks later she competed in the 1,000 meters in a meet with Virginia Tech and Wake Forest and won that race in 3:09. The Southern Conference Championship that year was held at East Tennessee State University. Leigh won her first conference championship, finishing first in the 5,000 meters in a time of 17:01. She also placed second in the 3,000 meters in a time of 10:02.

Leigh began the 1992 outdoor track season brimming with confidence, believing she was the best distance runner in the conference and one of the best in the South. She was pain-free, and with her weight down to about 120 pounds, she felt strong. She was 30 pounds lighter than she was in her freshman year, but she was by no means skinny. She had continued her strength training and was powerfully built. Coach Weaver had talked with her about how European distance runners were strong women as opposed to the rail-thin women runners from the US. Leigh was once again confident in her body and regained an appreciation for her physically strong appearance.

ASU's first outdoor track meet was a big one, the Raleigh Relays at NC State's track. Most of the stronger teams from the ACC were there, plus Yale and Dartmouth. It was a very cold and windy day, but being from Boone, the weather didn't bother Leigh too much. She ran the 10K, finishing 6th overall in a time of 35:50. She was a little disappointed that she didn't finish higher but was pleased with her time. She knew she was running against many of the best runners in the Southeast. At the ASU Invitational a couple of weeks later, Leigh ran the 3,000 and won in a time of 10:07.

Her next and last meet was the Southern Conference

Championship meet held at Marshall University in Huntington, West Virginia. Coach Weaver and Leigh discussed which event or events she should run. She knew he was a little concerned about keeping alive the team's streak of five straight conference championships. Leigh had the fastest times of the year in the conference in both the 10K and the 5K, so they were confident she could win either of those races. She had also won the 3K at the ASU Invitational against most of the conference competition. But the unexpected can happen. Leigh was feeling stronger every day and running very fast in her workouts. After some hesitation, Coach Weaver suggested, "Leigh, have you thought about running all three distance races at conference? Do you think you'd like to try it?"

"Absolutely, Coach," she said, "I can do it."

"Well, Leigh, I would never ask any runner to do that, but I think you have a shot at winning all three. If you really want to try, I'm okay with it; but you know, only one other girl in the conference has ever tried it. That was Whitney Ball in 1989, and I think you're dominating this league now as much as she was then."

The first distance race at the conference championship at Marshall University was the 10K. It was run on a Friday morning in late April. As usual, I chose not to sit in the stands. I staked out a position along the fence as close to the track as I could get. I noticed that Coach Weaver was directly across the track from me. When the gun went off, Leigh took the lead. A small pack of girls tried to stay close through the first lap, but they recognized the pace would be difficult to maintain. They gradually fell back. After two laps, Leigh was out front all alone. At about the 10th lap, with 15 laps remaining, she began lapping the trailing runners, without a noticeable letup in her pace. She pulled farther away from every runner with each stride, and I became concerned she might be pushing too hard. After all, she still had to run a 3K that afternoon and a 5K the next day. As she came by on the next lap, I hollered, "Ease up, Leigh, you've got this race. Save a little for the next two." She looked over at me as she blew by and just smiled. I knew I was wasting my breath. She ended up lapping the field in running a time of 36:55, one of the fastest times ever in the conference championship.

146

Leigh's strength was the longer distance races, so I knew the 3K would be her toughest test. No other runner was scheduled to compete in all three races, so after a few hours rest, she was up again that afternoon against fresh runners. Again, she took the lead immediately, daring anyone to go with her. No one took the challenge, as the rest of the field elected to race for second place. Leigh ran by herself for most of the race, winning in a time of 10:07, just five seconds off her fastest 3K ever and again one of the fastest times in conference championship history. Leigh was very excited that evening, knowing she had easily won what everyone figured would be her toughest race. Naturally, she was tired, having raced 13,000 meters that day, but she was in no pain and felt strong. I asked her why she had pushed so hard in both races when she had them easily won and knew she still had the 5K the next day.

"Do you have anything left for tomorrow?" I asked.

"Dad, I didn't really push it that hard. I was a minute off my fastest 10K time and a little off my 3K PR (personal record). I know I can win all three of these races, but I don't just want to win. I want to make a statement that I am an elite runner. Whitney Ball ran all three races with quality times, and I want to do the same thing. If anyone is going to beat me tomorrow, they'd better be prepared for a lot of pain. I'm going to take the lead from the start and control the race."

She was right. On Saturday afternoon, in one of the last races of the meet, she set a blistering pace from the start. After two or three laps, she had a 50-meter lead on the nearest pack of runners. The coach of one of those runners was standing about 30 feet from me near the edge of the track.

As his runner came by on the third lap, he hollered to her, "Keep that pace, she'll come back to you. She's already run two races; she can't hold that pace."

He yelled the same thing for two or three laps as Leigh kept increasing her lead. Finally, he looked over at me, shrugged his shoulders, and said, "Incredible."

Leigh won with a time of 17:12, again one of the fastest times in conference history.

Of course, at the end of the meet we stayed for the awards presentation. ASU's women won their 6th conference championship in a row. The Most Outstanding Performer award could have gone to either of two girls. Melissa Morrison was one of the top sprinters in the country and had won two individual races plus running anchor on a winning relay race. But the award was given to Leigh. She had accomplished something only one other runner in Southern Conference history had ever done: she won all three distance races in outstanding times.

Speaking with reporters afterward, Coach Weaver said, "Seeing her out there leading the pack for so long, it's hard not to vote for her. What she did was very impressive."

I spoke with Coach Weaver later and asked him if he wasn't concerned that she was setting such a fast pace during the 10K after she had the race easily won.

"Colonel Cooper," he said, "when Whitney Ball did the same thing, I worried that she was going too fast in the 10K. I told her to slow down. She just looked at me and said, 'Coach, I can't run slower.' I learned then that there are a few very special runners, and Leigh and Whitney are both in that category; they're going to run the only way they know how. My only guidance to them is to find a pace they are comfortable with and know they can finish with, and I don't worry about how fast it is. So, to answer your question, no, I wasn't worried in the least. After winning the 10K and 3K as easily as she did, I knew that if anyone was going to try to stay with her in the 5K, they were going to have to run the race of their life."

A couple of weeks later, Leigh proudly walked across the stage in Varsity Gym at ASU and received her undergraduate degree.

Leigh	Julie	Holley
Claude	Louise	Graig

CHAPTER NINE
DON'T SETTLE

Chris taught for one year at East Burke Junior High, after which a budget shortfall caused the Burke County School system to reduce expenses. As the newest employee in the system, Chris was terminated. He was very discouraged but decided to take the opportunity to acquire more skills. He, Leigh and Jake came back to Boone, and he began working toward another degree from ASU, this time in accounting. Though sad for Chris, the move suited Leigh fine. She loved living in Boone.

Leigh began running road races to earn money and help with expenses. She felt like she was at her peak as a distance runner, so she looked for big money races in the area. She also ran local races that weren't money races, such as the Big Apple Road Race put on by ASU. These races were good training runs for her and helped to keep her competitive edge. Her first serious money race was the Rhododendron Run in Bakersville, NC, a 10K on an out and back course. She finished second in a time of 36:50 and won $100.

Being back in Boone, she was also able to run occasionally with Holley and Julie, which was great bonding time for the three sisters.

.   .   .   .   .

Leigh was not the only member of the family having success as a runner. As a junior in high school, Holley was the leading runner on the Watauga High cross-country team. She was selected as the outstanding high school runner in the state of North Carolina for the month of September, winning all five races in which Watauga competed that month.

Julie was also running cross-country for ASU in this her senior year. Coach Weaver, at the beginning of the year, was not too optimistic about the girls' chances of a 7th straight conference championship. In an interview with the *Watauga Democrat*, he projected the team to finish anywhere from 2nd to 5th in the conference. In talking about his top runners coming back from the previous year, he didn't mention Julie at all. But I knew she had improved significantly, having worked with Leigh over the summer, and I thought Julie would be a factor on the team. I was right.

In the team's first meet, Julie finished second overall and second on the team to the winner, Carrie Hogg. Julie was only one second behind Carrie in a very respectable time of 18:53 in the 5K race at Bass Lake, running against Davidson, UNC-Charlotte, and UNC-Asheville. She then finished 6th overall and 4th on the team in a 2.2 mile race at VMI. The course guides made a mistake in this race, causing the distance to be almost a mile shorter than it was supposed to be. Another significant thing about this race was that it was on the course where the conference championship would be held at the end of the season. After a weak race at Navy in which she did not place, Julie came back strong with an 18:55 time on a difficult course at Duke in the NC Collegiate Championship meet. She finished 11th overall and 2nd on the team against some of the top runners in the Atlantic Coast Conference.

She then capped a great season at the conference championship meet at VMI. The cross-country course at VMI was the most difficult course I had ever seen, and I've seen many. The course was wet from rains that week, and the first 150 meters were mostly under water. As always, I scouted the course before the race and found a bit of dry, higher ground on the left side of the start area. I told Julie to work her way over to the left immediately at the start. Hilly with slick narrow trails, the course would require strength more than speed, which worked to Julie's advantage. Her ROTC training had made her stronger and improved her endurance. After the straight start, the runners were to complete two loops through the woods and hills before sprinting back over the open start area to the finish line. After the first loop, Julie was in 10th place, but she looked strong.

Louise and I moved to a spot from which we could see the runners break out of the woods just before the sprint to the finish. The first runner emerged wearing the gold and black of ASU, but it was Carrie Hogg. Then the next runner burst out of the woods, also wearing gold and black. It was Julie! I sprinted toward the finish line behind Julie, yelling all the way. She finished five seconds behind Carrie in an outstanding time for that course of 19:10 to take second place in the

Southern Conference. I was as proud of Julie as I had ever been of Leigh. Julie had reached her potential as a competitive collegiate runner. Leigh understood Julie's achievement and shared that pride.

.　　　　　.　　　　　.　　　　　.　　　　　.

Leigh's triumph over the attack by Daniel Lee and her rise as an elite runner in the South began to attract national attention. The December, 1993 issue of *Redbook* magazine featured her in an article entitled "Breaking the Silence," in which she explained that she did not mind being known as a rape victim because she did nothing wrong. Then, early in the summer of 1995, she was contacted by representatives of the Leeza Gibbons television show in Los Angeles. Ms. Gibbons had her own talk show, and her staff were planning a show about near-death survivors. The show's producers wanted to include Leigh's story on this show and offered to fly her and one guest out to LA for the taping of the show, with all expenses paid. Leigh wanted to tell her story; she saw the TV show as a great way to reach other victims and show them they don't have to continue to be victims. Leigh took Julie with her to Los Angeles. Leeza and her staff were wonderful, and Leigh and Julie had a great time being treated like royalty in LA. The show, Episode #512, actually aired on December 6 of that year. While the show did not launch Leigh as a national celebrity, it did give her a degree of recognition outside of North Carolina. Calls for her to speak to women's groups and to high school students increased after the showing.

.　　　　　.　　　　　.　　　　　.　　　　　.

Leigh continued running races whenever she could, especially the money races. She loved to run the local races, such as the Big Apple Road Race put on by ASU, even though most were not money races. At the least, she would get a new pair of running shoes or some other running apparel for winning. She ran in The Springfest Flyer, a big race in Johnson City, Tennessee, in the summer of 1993. She had a growing reputation as an elite runner, so most of the elite races offered her free registration to entice her to race. Free entry was fairly common for the top racers in the area, as each event wanted the best competition possible. The Springfest Flyer, a hilly 8 kilometer race, had a stronger field of elite runners than any race in which Leigh had run to date, with outstanding runners from several states, many of which she knew by reputation. She told me that, at best, she would be running for third place, which would put her in the money. As it turned out, Leigh found herself running almost the entire race stride for stride with another runner. Leigh knew this woman was one of the top runners in the Southeast, although they had never raced each other. Both were really running well, competing for 2nd place. A couple of other women tried to stay with them for about three miles, but they couldn't maintain the pace Leigh and this woman were setting and eventually fell back. Leigh and this competitor were alone and they were flying.

Leigh explained later, "I was hurting, but I knew she must be also. I was a step ahead of her and trying to push the pace and break her. But she kept hanging on; I didn't know if she had anything left or not, or whether she was just waiting for the right moment to blow by me at the finish. We had about 1,000 meters to go and I was really hurting. I didn't think I could maintain the pace much longer. I told myself that I would keep pushing it to an overhead bridge I saw about 300 meters ahead, and if she were still with me when we reached the bridge, she had beaten me. I thought I could not hold the pace past that point. She had to have known I was hurting, but she was breathing hard, right on my shoulder. As we approached the bridge, I was about to give it up when I heard her gasp and she dropped back. I had broken her. Knowing I had broken her gave me energy and determination. I eased off slightly and breezed in well ahead of her to take second place money of $200. After the race and the award of prizes, the woman came up to me."

"How do you do it?" she asked. "I thought I could beat you; I thought I had you beat, but you wouldn't quit. You've got such stamina."

Leigh thanked her but did not say she was within about 20 meters of breaking. She knew they would race again, and she didn't want her to know how close she had come to beating Leigh.

Later, when Leigh became a high school cross-country and track coach, she shared this story and its lesson with her runners. The lesson was, "Don't settle." Leigh could have easily and reasonably settled for her initial race goal of finishing in the money, third place. But her biggest fear in racing was that during a race she might give in to the pain and settle for something less than maximum effort, even knowing that maximum effort might not be enough to win.

Leigh had an uncanny ability to take her mind off physical pain, as she did when she was raped, by focusing on other things. She might sing, or set a goal like reaching the overpass, or otherwise occupy her mind to disassociate herself from the discomfort. She practiced it in her training. She believed that in order to withstand the pain of racing hard, one had to learn to deal with the pain while training: to train the legs to run fast when they're hurting and to train the mind to continue to push the body even when it's hurting. She knew the pain that comes from running was something that could be stopped any time by just quitting or settling to a slower pace. But if she could push through the pain, she felt that she would win the race, or at least finish very high and receive recognition and reward for doing something well. Leigh never settled.

Leigh drew insight from her experience with pain, weighing benefits against the discomfort, so the cost became understandable and tolerable. She went through childbirth twice without the use of drugs, knowing the severe pain would come. She made a choice to endure the pain, and she was prepared for the consequences. She reasoned that if women had given birth prior to our knowledge of drugs, and her mom had delivered her four children without relying on drugs, if any woman anywhere who could deliver without using drugs, then she could.

. . . . .

Leigh ran in the Summer Breeze 5K road race in Charlotte that summer. She won the race with a time of 17:14, but more significant and personally rewarding was the cast of elite runners who finished behind her. The race featured several outstanding former runners from the Atlantic Coast Conference, including Leigh's old high school nemesis, Mary Powell, who had been a star runner for Wake Forest. Leigh enjoyed talking with Mary and catching up on their college careers and lives, but the reward for Leigh was finishing ahead of her former rival.

.   .   .   .   .

In August of 1993, David Ward announced he was stepping down as head track and cross-country coach at Watauga High, and his assistant, Randy McDonough, was named as his successor. Randy immediately asked Leigh if she would be his assistant head coach. Of course, she accepted; she was excited. She would actually get paid, though not much, for what she loved doing. But she told Randy that she had to do more than just run with the team; she wanted to have an impact, to have input into planning workouts and strategy. She wanted a reasonable amount of control.

"No problem," he told her, "you will do that and more. You will be the intense coach; I will continue to be the laid-back coach." Laid-back indeed. Randy was an easy-going, slow-talking, good old boy who taught physical education at Hardin Park Elementary School in Boone. He was an avid runner, though not a particularly fast one. He was one of the few coaches at Watauga High (the county's only high school) who actively promoted his sport at the elementary school level. He organized a running club at Hardin Park Elementary School and promoted county-wide running and racing at the elementary school level.

Randy, or Coach Mac as everyone called him, was true to his word. He and Leigh developed a friendly and efficient relationship that seemed to work to everyone's advantage. He gave Leigh the title of Associate Head Coach for cross-country and Distance Coach for track. Watauga usually had 40 or 50 runners to compete in cross-country on the boys' and the girls' teams. Often, at Leigh's urging, athletes who were cut from football or soccer would come to cross-country. Other athletes who played spring sports tried cross-country to help them get in shape for their primary sport. Leigh worked with the "A" team, usually the top ten or twelve runners, boys and girls. Randy and his volunteer assistants worked with everyone else. Leigh not only ran with the top runners on each team; she also planned their workouts and determined race strategies. She became more than a coach; she became a mentor. She also was allowed considerable input to determine when an improving runner should move up to train with the "A" team. She completed the workouts with the team, sometimes running with the boys, sometimes with the girls. She loved coaching, sharing her knowledge and inspiring her runners, something she was born to do. Her ability to interact with and inspire her runners, plus Coach Mac's efforts to promote running among the youth in the county, led to Watauga High School cross-country becoming one of the most dominant athletic programs in North Carolina high school history.

As a new coach, Leigh inherited a solid girls' cross-country program. The team had been state champions in 1990 and 1992, Holley's sophomore and senior years, and had a second-place finish in 1991, Holley's junior year. The squad began the 1993 season, Leigh's first year as coach, ranked second in the state. Unfortunately, due to injuries, neither of the top two runners on that team, both ranked in the top-five runners in the state, was able to finish the season. With her team leaders ailing, Leigh sought a runner to step up and assume a leadership role. She found that leader in an unlikely person.

Addie Bower had run the previous year as a freshman. She was very shy and lacking in self-confidence to the point she was reluctant to run with the A-Team. Leigh saw something in Addie, though, that told Leigh she could be a very competitive runner. After one of the early workouts in which Addie ran with the slower group, Leigh pulled her aside.

"Addie, from now on I expect you to train with the "A" team. You're too good a runner to be running with the slow group!"

"Wow, I don't know, coach. I'm not sure I'm ready for harder workouts every day."

159

"Addie, you have so much more potential than you realize. Before this season is over, you will be the fastest runner on this team, and I need you to be a leader on this team. And you've got to start doing it now. You have a choice to make: you can be a champion racer, or you can settle for just being a runner." Addie chose to be a champion. She discovered that she could complete the hard workouts and that she loved running fast.

Addie won the conference and the region championships that year and went on to finish third in the state championship, just three seconds behind the winner, to make All-State.

Leigh's biggest accomplishment that first year, though, was with the boys' team. Will Hodges, a young boy on that team, had finished 50th at the state meet as a sophomore the previous year. He was small and, like Addie, rather shy; but Leigh saw in Will a similar work ethic to her own and a willingness to run through the discomfort. Leigh had the ability to see strength and potential in others who might not promote themselves. She and Will developed a special bond over the next two years. Like Addie, Will won conference and region championships and finished third in the state in his junior year. With the boys finishing third in the state as a team, Leigh had accomplished her first goal of making state contenders out of the boys' team, a status they would not lose during Leigh's coaching tenure.

.   .   .   .   .

It was no longer a "Take Back the Night" event; it was now called Walk for Awareness. In September of 1990, Associate Vice Chancellor for Student Development at Appalachian State, Barbara Daye, afraid that she might be asking too much of Leigh, approached Leigh about speaking at the Walk. Leigh told her she would be proud to speak. Not too happy with how the rally had gone the first year, Barbara stressed that the rally this year had two purposes: to serve as a memorial to Jeni Gray and to raise awareness of the need for personal safety. This event was not to be a male-bashing rally; rather,

160

participants would meet in front of the Administration Building on campus where the Chancellor would speak, then walk in silence with candles and flashlights. Every four minutes a bell would chime reminding the participants that every four minutes in this country, a rape is reported. The walk proceeded to the Lois Harrill building downtown where Leigh gave the keynote speech. She spoke of the support she had received from family, friends, the university, and the community, and encouraged others who had been victimized by violence not to remain victims, but to speak out and regain control of their lives.

She told the crowd in 1990, "I know I'm not the same person I was a year ago, but I'm doing fine. I'm glad I played a role in getting Jeni's killer off the streets for good."

For the first ten years of the Walk For Awareness, Leigh was the keynote speaker. Each speech was different, but to the hundreds of university students and townspeople, she stressed three recurring themes:

1) Make good choices.

2) Take control of your life.

3) Don't remain a victim. If you have been victimized, there are resources that can help; you can choose to regain control; you can choose to come out of the closet and live your life.

Leigh knew she had a strong message about regaining control of one's life after victimization or tragedy, and each year she gained confidence in delivering that message. Her speeches and prominence in speaking out strengthened her belief that there was a reason Daniel Lee made the mistake of picking her up that night in 1989; she began to realize her purpose in life.

Leigh's speech at the 1994 Walk for Awareness was typical of the message she delivered in the first few years of the walk:

Five years ago, Jeni Gray was kidnapped from the streets of Boone and murdered. Five days later, the same man who killed Jeni also kidnapped me. He drove me to the same isolated area where he had left Jeni's body and he sexually assaulted me. As I was being raped, Daniel Lee told me that he had killed Jeni and described to me in detail how he had killed her. He let me know that he obviously would have to kill me too, and that I would have to die the same way Jeni had. It is impossible to describe to you how terrifying and emotionally draining this experience was. And although there wasn't a doubt in my mind that I would die that night, I continued to look for the smallest opportunity to escape. My only goal was to survive. I had one advantage over Jeni in that I was aware of the fact that I was with a murderer. There is no way Jeni could have known what this man was capable of. After several hours, I did find a way to escape. I survived and thus began my healing.

Because of the tremendous support I got from my family and this community, I have been able to put this tragedy behind me and regain control of my life. I knew from the start that my family would support me and do all that they could to help in my healing. What amazed me, though, was how people from all aspects of this community reached out to me. The Boone Police Department and the Sheriff's Department were among the first people I came in contact with once I escaped. They were always caring, sympathetic, and patient. In the months and years that followed, they have continued to keep in touch with me and show genuine concern for my welfare. OASIS (Opposing Abuse with Service, Information and Shelter) volunteers were at the hospital that night before I even arrived and offered their support, as did the hospital staff. I spent many hours in the office of Dr Sanz of the ASU Counseling Center. I can't thank him enough for allowing me to talk, cry, and eventually laugh with him. He seemed to always be able to find the most comforting words. Within two days of my ordeal, our District Attorney, Tom Rusher, made a visit to my house to assure me and my family that I would be treated with respect and dignity by those in his office. He always kept me aware of what was going on with the case and he let me know what to expect at the trial.

I was a full-time college student when this happened to me. I felt that going right back to my classes was the best thing to do to help keep my mind off the kidnapping. Concentrating in class was not easy, but I was able to get through the semester and pass all of my classes with the support and encouragement from my professors and fellow students.

And finally, the people of Boone were, and still are, a source of support and encouragement. The point I am trying to make to all of you, and especially to any victims who may be here tonight, is that the support you need to overcome adversity is out there. In my case, because of all the publicity, that support came to me; I didn't have to seek it. But what happened to me is also pretty rare. There are many other types of crime or acts of violence being committed around us, and people are victimized daily. Examples of this are spouse abuse and date rape. If any of you here tonight is one of those victims, please use the resources available in this community to get the help and support you need. There are so many people who are willing to help. And if any of you knows a victim, please reach out to them. Many of the cards I received in the weeks following my kidnapping were from complete strangers. Knowing that people I didn't even know were thinking of me and praying for me was so encouraging. I am absolutely convinced that I would not be leading a happy and fulfilling life today if it weren't for all the help I received.

Two years after my ordeal, I graduated from ASU. I finished out my last two years on the ASU cross-country and track teams with very successful seasons. I eventually married the man I was dating at the time and we have a 3-year old son together. I continue to run and race seriously, as well as coach cross-country and track at Watauga High School. I am a happy person, and I refuse to live my life as a victim. What happened to me is something I'll never forget. It is a part of my history – a part of me. But I don't live with it every day. What Barbara Daye has organized here is a wonderful way for the university and the town of Boone to come together to remember Jeni Gray and to make ourselves and others aware of the potential for violence. It is also a time, I feel, for healing. Whether any of us has been a victim of a crime or has been dealing with hardship or adversity, this walk should help us to realize that we need to rely on each other and our friends in the community and university to see us through. I know that every year that I participate in this Walk for Awareness, I am reminded of how many people care. I am reminded that, although this is a safe community, I still must take precautions and do all that I can to keep from becoming

163

a potential victim, and not to fall into the trap of convincing myself that it could never happen to me again, or to anyone in my family. I'd like to thank Barbara Daye for bringing us all together to remind us of the potential for violence and for giving me the opportunity to share my story and to help make others aware.

The Walk for Awareness grew in attendance every year, and Leigh was particularly pleased to see more and more males in attendance.

Leigh had an impact on the track program at Watauga as well as the cross-country team. For track, she had responsibility for all distance runners, to include the 3200, 1600, 800, and the 4x800 relay events. Watauga's boys that year, '93-'94, won their first conference track championship since 1978. Leigh's distance runners certainly had much to say about that championship. Will Hodges won four events himself: the 3200, the 1600, the 800, and he anchored the winning 4x800 relay. Shane Austin took second in the 3200 and the 1600 meter races. While the competition for the boys was close, the girls dominated, finishing first in 11 of 17 events. Again, the distance runners were strong with Addie Bower, Kathleen Mertes, and Kim Deni winning the 3200, 1600, and 800 respectively.

A few weeks later, Will Hodges finished third in the state in both the 1600 and 3200, qualifying for the scholastic national championships in both events.

.   .   .   .   .

While Leigh's teams were winning, she continued to compete as well, running several road races that summer. The most competitive were the Winthrop Eagle Run in Rock Hill and a return to Summer Breeze in Charlotte. The race in Rock Hill was fun for her because her aunt and uncle, Jane and Jimmy Blackmon, and her uncle Les Dickert, all of whom she loved dearly, came to watch her run. It was an 8K race which she won in a time of 28:50. She finished fourth at Summer Breeze this time, although she ran a very respectable 16:56 over the 5K course, faster than her winning time of the previous year.

164

Being Strong

In the 1994-95 school year, Leigh's second year of coaching, Watauga High produced cross-country and track teams which were among the most dominant teams in North Carolina cross-country and track high school history. Based on the success of her teams in her first full year of coaching, Leigh was confident in her ability to coach and mentor these athletes. All her runners had tremendous respect for her because she was still an active, successful racer. When she planned high intensity workouts for them, and actually ran these workouts with them, talked race strategy and emphasized exercise as a lifestyle, they listened to her and believed in her. Some of the new runners might have been a little intimidated by her until they got to know her. But Leigh always made a point to single out each new runner and run with each for a portion of the workout. Her goal was to convince each runner he or she didn't have to settle for being just a member of the team or even for being just a good runner. Leigh taught every runner that he or she could be competitive to a greater extent than he or she might believe. Any athlete who ever trained with her heard Leigh say on more than one occasion, "Don't settle" or "You're stronger than you think."

When cross-country practice began in '94, Leigh was particularly observant of one new runner, freshman Whitney Woods. Louise had taught Whitney at Green Valley Elementary School and encouraged her to run, as she had done well in the county sixth, seventh, and eighth grade races. After about a week of practice, Leigh moved Whitney up to train with the "A" team, again, giving her the choice of being a racer or settling for just being a runner; and Whitney immediately started showing great potential.

Watauga dominated the Northwest 4A Conference championship race in the fall of 1994 as all seven members of the boys' team and all seven members of the girls' team finished in the top ten to earn All-Conference honors. And both boys' and girls' teams repeated as regional champions. At regionals, Watauga's girls defeated the defending state champions, Providence High of Charlotte, with Addie Bower, Jennifer Phelps, and Whitney Woods finishing 1, 2, and 3 in the race. Leigh was concerned about Addie prior to the race. Addie had confided to Leigh that she didn't think she could beat the Charlotte runners. She had dealt with minor injuries early in the season and didn't feel like she was running her best. Leigh told her that she was in a class by herself in cross-country this year and her toughest competition would probably come from her own teammates, which proved to be the case. The boys were also impressive at the regionals, beating East Mecklenberg of Charlotte, which had won three of the past four state championships.

Both the boys' and girls' teams of Watauga went to McAlpine Park in Charlotte with the notion of winning the state championship. Each team, though, would have to beat one of the strongest fields in North Carolina history; several other teams were also talented enough to win it all. Leigh felt that if all her runners ran close to their best times, both teams could win. She was also convinced that Watauga had the best individual runners in the state in Addie and Will. To capture boys' and girls' team championships and boys' and girls' individual championships in the same year would be a monumental achievement. Addie's performance in the regionals had boosted her confidence; from the regionals' finish line to the starting gun at State, Leigh focused on Addie maintaining that confidence. With Will, Leigh needed a race strategy to give Will an edge on Justin Niedzielak of Providence, who had narrowly beaten Will at regionals. At McAlpine, the course begins with a long straight stretch, after which the course follows a fairly narrow path through the woods. When the runners finally break out of the woods, they have about a half-mile to go around a pond to the finish line. Leigh told Will to put some distance between him and Justin before they broke out of the woods. During every race, Leigh sprinted to points along the race course from which she shouted encouragement and instructions as her runners passed. Will was just off Justin's shoulder going into the woods. As they came by Leigh in the woods at about the midway point, Justin didn't look comfortable. Will was pushing the pace.

Leigh shouted, "DO IT NOW, WILL, DO IT NOW!" He nodded slightly and put on a spurt. Justin could not go with him. When they came out of the woods and approached the pond, which was the next time Leigh and most of the other spectators would see them, Will led by about 30 meters. Leigh was screaming "Go, go, go!" as we all watched Will increase his lead around the pond to win by 7 seconds in a time of 15:38. With teammates Jody Corum, Shane Austin, Dylan Wright, Chris Kitchens and Caleb Thorp also running strong, the boys captured their first state championship. After the race Will told Leigh that he, too, was sensing that Justin was struggling at the point where he put on his spurt.

Leigh was elated after the boys' race. Watauga had accomplished what Leigh thought were her teams' two toughest goals, winning the boys team and the boys individual championships. The girls race turned out to be the closest spread between the first four teams in North Carolina history. The winning team finished just five points ahead of the fourth place team. Unfortunately, it was Watauga who finished five points out of first place. A spread that close means that if two or three of Watauga's girls had picked off one or two runners, the girls also would be state champions. Leigh was very proud of her girls, though. Addie became the first Watauga girl to win the state championship, running a time of 18:44. Whitney Woods made All-State as a freshman by finishing sixth in a time of 19:35, ahead of Jennifer Phelps who finished in eighth place.

Track season in the spring of '95 brought more domination by Leigh's distance runners. On May 20, 1995, Will Hodges gave perhaps the best performance of any individual in state outdoor track championship history. He won the 800, 1600, and the 3200. The 30 points he racked up by winning three events, plus the one point that his cousin, Shane Austin, earned by finishing sixth in the 1600, allowed Watauga to finish fourth in the state in the team competition. Winning those three races on a given day is an outstanding achievement against any competition. Will's performance was made even more remarkable because his wins came against some of the best distance runners in NC high school history. In addition to Niedzielak of Providence High School, Buddy Priest of Roxboro Person High entered the meet with the fastest time in the state in the 3200. Will set a school record in the 800, running a 1:57. He ran a 4:17 in the 1600, beating Priest by two seconds and Niedzielak by five seconds. In the 3200, he blew by Priest with two laps remaining and won by seven seconds in a time of 9:26.9, a personal record for him.

Will and Leigh planned how to win each race. She knew Will might not have the greatest speed of anyone in the state, but she also knew no one could match his endurance and strength, so every race plan stressed his endurance and strength. They both knew that Will couldn't wait until the final lap or the final straight to make his kick. He had to push the pace early and break the competition, take the kick out of them. He never doubted Leigh when she told him to surge, to make his move.

She later told me, "I don't think I ever coached a runner who was more like me as a competitor than Will was. His strengths and weaknesses as a distance runner were so much like mine, and I believe he understood that. He was not the most talented runner I ever coached, but no one worked harder and no one was more competitive."

Watauga's reputation in cross-country grew beyond state boundaries. Watauga was recognized nationally for several years during Leigh's coaching tenure, as either the boys or girls teams or both ranked among the top teams in the nation. Success in prestigious events such as the Wendy's Invitational, where the top programs in the Southeast were invited, justified Watauga's national ranking.

Leigh didn't always have the best athletes at Watauga High for her cross-country teams. On the contrary, she would often visit the football and soccer tryouts in the fall and seek the athletes who were cut from those teams. Her message to them: "You don't have to settle for just being a student who didn't make the team. You can still be an athlete, and if you're willing to work hard, I'll help you become a champion." One such athlete was Joe Lion, who had attempted wrestling without much success. Joe became one of the great stories of Leigh's coaching career. It's actually a story about Joe and his mom. Cathy Lion was battling cancer while Joe and his younger brother, Todd, were in high school. She was an extraordinarily courageous woman, and she challenged Joe and Todd to fight for what they wanted as hard as she was fighting her battle against cancer. As a result, they both had tremendous determination. Neither was a natural runner, but Joe reached levels far beyond what anyone would have believed possible. He had a high pain threshold and was willing to run through pain. Although running through pain was very much in line with Leigh's racing philosophy, it's not something she taught him. He would say, "Considering what my mom's going through, I can take anything." Leigh said she never coached a more focused runner. As a freshman,

169

Joe's 5K times were in the high 19 and low 20 minutes. When Leigh saw his determination, she told him at the beginning of the '95 season, his sophomore year, that he would be running under 17 by the end of the year. At the time, he didn't see that as a possibility. At the ASU Invitational that year, he ran a 16:29. He had reduced his 5K time by three minutes in one year, a monumental achievement. Sadly, Joe and Todd lost their mother that spring.

On Nov 4, 1995, Watauga ran in the Regional Championships at Freedom High School in Morganton and achieved an amazing result in such a highly competitive event. The boys swept all seven of the all-regional spots, and the girls took four of the top five spots. Shane Austin led throughout the boys' race and won in a very fast 15:35, but every Watauga runner stayed close to him and finished well under 17 minutes. In the girls' race, Addie, as usual, led the pack with a time of 19:14. Erinn Struss showed tremendous grit. She fell at the start of the race but got to her feet and fought her way from last place to fourth. She could easily have settled for simply finishing the race, but she didn't. That was not the Watauga way.

Watauga's success in cross-country over those five years was no secret. And although there were several other great teams in the state, Watauga's boys and girls teams were considered the teams to beat. To win a state championship, any team, whether boys or girls, knew they had the daunting task of facing Watauga. Some coaches suggested Watauga's success could possibly be the result of training at an altitude of over 3500 , implying that Boone's altitude gave them an advantage. Leigh never believed that the mountains gave Watauga an advantage, other than perhaps providing beautifully scenic venues; she believed it was a matter of attitude, not altitude. She always stressed to her runners that running is a way of life, or at least a major part of a particular way of life. Running should be enjoyed. Racing, on the other hand, was an attitude: a determination not to settle, not to give in to pain. A race only lasts for a few minutes, and to be competitive, one must be willing to endure more than one's opponent is willing to endure.

.   .   .   .   .

At every practice, Leigh typically ran a mile or two farther than anyone on either the boys' or girls' teams ran. She normally went out with the fastest runners, talking to them about racing and ensuring they were running the pace she had prescribed for that particular day. Then she often circled back and picked out one or two of the slower runners and talked with them about whatever she felt they needed to improve. One of the team's training runs prior to the 1995 state championship was on an out and back course. Leigh ran with the leaders through the turnaround, and on the way back she saw Erinn Struss running alone. Leigh turned back to run with her. Erinn was a sophomore, very unsure of how good she could be and hesitant to go out fast, afraid she might not have the strength to finish the race or workout. Leigh talked with her about nothing in particular. Leigh sensed Erinn was thrilled that Leigh had picked her out for special attention. As the two ran and talked, Leigh gradually increased the pace. Erinn stayed with Leigh, carrying her share of the conversation. They finished the workout, and Erinn was shocked when Leigh told her the pace she had run. That practice session opened Erinn's eyes to just how fast she was capable of running.

McAlpine Park was cold and wet for the state championship race on Nov 11, 1995, with standing water in many places on the course. As the runners lined up for the start of the 4A girls race in a driving rain, I noticed a stark contrast. Girls on the other teams wore their warmup suits until the last second. They were huddling together, shivering. Watauga's girls, on the other hand, discarded their warmups before approaching the line and went through their pre-race routine, oblivious to the inclement conditions. The result was a team that appeared ready, eager and intimidating. The girls' team recaptured the state championship with Addie Bower and Erinn Struss finishing third and fifth respectively to earn All-State. Erinn far exceeded expectations, running a brilliant 19:24 through the mud. The wide smile on her face and the obvious pride she felt were in sharp contrast to how her body looked, covered in mud. Seeing her joy after that race was one of Leigh's proudest moments as a coach.

As the boys finished their race, it appeared that Watauga had won both boys and girls championships, even though the boys had lost four seniors from last year's team, including Will Hodges. When the points were tallied though, Watauga and Leesville Road were tied with 109 points each. Rather than declare co-champions, the officials employed a tie-breaker system and scored the points down to the sixth man for each team. Leesville Road's sixth man had finished in 38th place; Watauga's had finished in 44th place, making Leesville Road the winner. In the post-race critique conducted by Leigh, no one blamed the 6th runner. Rather, each runner talked about what he could have done to make the difference.

Leigh's joy with Watauga's success on this day was short-lived, as Louise met Leigh after the meet to inform her of the unexpected death of her aunt Lil the night before. Lil was only 47 years old and left behind a husband and two beautiful children.

.   .   .   .   .

Junior Whitney Woods had struggled all of the fall, 1996 season. She had nagging injuries, and Leigh could sense she had lost confidence in her ability to be competitive at the highest level. Toward the end of the cross-country season, Whitney usually finished runs in 7th or 8th position on the team. Leigh knew Whitney was a much better runner than that, and she struggled to decide whether to include her on the team that would advance to regional and state, as only seven runners from each team could compete in those championship races. One day in the week prior to regionals, Leigh asked Whitney to run with her. They talked constantly throughout the run, with Leigh of course doing most of the talking. Leigh had more confidence in Whitney than Whitney had in herself, and Leigh was determined to reignite the fire and the confidence in this highly emotional athlete. At the end of the run Leigh told Whitney that she would run at regional and state. She told her "Forget the past and concentrate on the future. It may not happen this year, but I'm absolutely certain that you have state championship potential. You're stronger than you think."

At regionals that year, on a cold, blustery day that probably worked to their advantage, Watauga's boys and girls dominated again. For the boys, Ryan Woods and Jody Corum were 1 and 2 as usual, both breaking the 16-minute barrier. Joe Lion, who had improved by leaps

172

and bounds over the year, barely missed the 16-minute mark with a time of 16:04. Leigh had told an unbelieving Joe that he would break 16 minutes before his high school career was over, and she had no doubt that he would. The boys placed six runners in the top 10. The girls did almost as well, placing three runners in the top five, led by the race winner, Marina Chase. Leigh always admired the natural self-confidence that Marina possessed, a trait that took Leigh years to develop in herself.

Obviously Watauga's training program worked. After finishing behind Leesville Road twice during the season, the boys' team beat them at the state meet to capture another boys' state championship. Ryan finished second individually in a time of 15:40, with Jody less than a second behind him in third. Joe Lion had another great run to finish 11th in 16:05. Greg Horn beat his regional time from two weeks earlier by four seconds to finish 19th. Watauga's top four runners barely edged out Leesville's top four, so the race between each team's fifth runners was crucial. Britt Marlowe and Jesse Lile ran almost the entire race with Leesville's fifth runner. As they came by Leigh with less than a mile to go, Leigh recognized that Leesville's fifth runner was with them, and she hollered at Jesse and Britt, "THIS IS YOUR RACE RIGHT HERE, GUYS! BE STRONG!" The Leesville guy put on a spurt near the end to edge ahead of Jesse, but he was unable to hold it. Jesse edged back ahead just before the finish line to beat him by less than a second. Britt wasn't far behind. Leigh was proud of both Jesse and Britt for the determination they displayed. In a great show of sportsmanship, before the awards ceremony, the entire Leesville boys' team came over to the Watauga tent to offer their congratulations. They knew that the race was between them and Watauga and had been tallying points as each runner finished. The girls' team was unable to defend its state championship, finishing sixth. Marina finished fourth individually and earned All-State honors with an excellent time of 19:04. Having lost two All-State runners from last year, and with such a young team, Leigh was proud of the girls' effort.

Leigh's ability to combine coaching with motherhood was never more evident than at that state meet. On November 5, just before regionals, Leigh and Chris welcomed Haleigh Lynn Wallace to their family. Three weeks early, Haleigh already exhibited the ability to follow in her mom's footsteps and make sure she was the center of loving attention. The cross country teams gathered at the hospital to shower her with attention, and this continued throughout the years when Haleigh was a steady presence at practices and meets. Her first experience accompanying her mom to running events came at the age of ten days, when her grandmother, Louise, stayed in the car with her at the state meet while Leigh coached her runners through their races. Between the boys' and the girls' races, Leigh ran to the car, nursed Haleigh, then resumed her coaching duties. Haleigh seemed perfectly happy with this way of life.

At the end-of-the-season team banquet each year, Leigh always gave a speech about each senior. Her proudest duty as a coach was to stand in front of the team and their parents and say something meaningful about each departing athlete. Whether they were state champions, or All-State, or just runners who tried their best, Leigh felt that it was important for a coach to honor their efforts. She took this responsibility very seriously and knew that the parents especially appreciated hearing Leigh's words.

Leigh was so much more than a coach to her athletes. She was a part of their lives, on and off the course or the track. On the anniversary of the death of Joe and Todd Lion's mother, Leigh invited them both to her house for supper. She wanted them to know that she remembered. Leigh often wrote to her athletes. They all cherished the "focus cards" she wrote each individual prior to the State Championships. But she also wrote letters of encouragement and inspiration. Her letter to Joe Lion when he was a senior would have added meaning and significance 15 years later:

My Thoughts on Joe Lion

When someone is extraordinarily special to you, it's hard to put into words the reasons why without sounding foolish. Often times, it's hard to pinpoint the exact reasons why. And even if you can list several reasons why someone is special to you, you then have to find the words that adequately express just how you feel. I find it almost impossible to do. But I feel I owe it to Joe to try my best.

174

I first began to really notice Joe at the beginning of his sophomore year. Although he ran on the team as a freshman, I did not know him well. He was quiet and never did much to draw attention to himself. And sure, I was preoccupied coaching what I hoped to be Watauga's first boys state-champion cross-country team. I regret now that I missed out on that year of Joe's life. But as a sophomore, I took a strong liking to Joe. As a coach of a large team, you try not to have favorites, but you can't help but favor those athletes who push themselves beyond their presumed abilities. I was happy to see that Joe had decided to become this kind of athlete and team member. I admired his desire, his work ethic, and his tremendous heart. Joe began his sophomore year as a young runner who I hoped would be rewarded for his efforts by making it into our top 7. As his season ended with him being our third best runner at the state meet, my dreams and hopes for him began to change. I saw him from then on as a future individual state champion in the making.

As wonderful and amazing things were happening to Joe athletically, his personal life was taking a tragic turn. His strong and beautiful mother was battling the cancer that was spreading through her body. Throughout her illness, Joe outwardly showed a strength that I would never expect from someone so young who is faced with the possibility of losing his mother. My admiration and adoration of Joe grew immensely during this time. I felt the need to reach out to him and do all that I could to help him through his life-altering tragedy. In spite of my efforts, I never felt like I did enough. I would come away from our heart-to-heart talks feeling that he had helped me so much more than I had helped him. His strength and resilience inspired me. And following the death of his mother during these critical early-teenage years, Joe could have easily decided that fate had dealt him a bad hand. He could have understandably taken a wrong turn in life. Instead, he seemed to get stronger, better and even more determined to succeed in all areas of his life. I truly believe Joe has handled this tragedy so well because of the way his mother raised him. And though her time on earth with her son was way too short,

175

she undoubtedly used that time to its fullest. I can only wish that I am able to instill the values in my son that she so effectively instilled in Joe.

When I think about the fact that Joe only has one more year left to run in high school, I can't help but cry. I can't imagine coaching anyone like Joe again. I'll never enjoy watching someone grow from a boy into a young man as I've enjoyed watching Joe's transformation. Will I ever coach another athlete whose smile and mere presence makes me happy? I can't imagine it. It is easy to think that when Joe walks out of Watauga High School's doors for the last time, I should walk out of them as well.

Leigh Wallace

.   .   .   .   .

The start of cross country season is always an exciting time at Watauga High School, and this was especially true for Leigh. During her coaching career more athletes tried out for cross-country than for any other sport at Watauga. High school cross-country enthusiasts knew the Watauga Pioneers were developing a dynasty and expected both the boys' and girls' teams to be serious competitors for a state championship every year. The boys' team began the '97 season having lost four outstanding runners from the previous year's team: two of the all-time greats, Ryan Woods and Jody Corum, plus steady Greg Horn and Jesse Pipes. But outstanding senior leaders returned in Joe Lion, Britt Marlowe, Jesse Lile, and Joe Kitchens. The team also had Ricky Brookshire, a sophomore who was beginning to show the potential to be the best runner ever at Watauga and perhaps in the state. The girls' team lost Erin Byerly and Ashley Norman to graduation, but the girls had some outstanding young runners returning, including Marina Chase, Whitney Woods, and Leigh Suggs. No doubt Watauga would be in the running for state team and individual championships again.

Leigh always felt privileged to work with many outstanding high school runners in the years she coached. Some were not great natural runners but achieved success through a tremendous work ethic and determination. Surprisingly, not many of Leigh's best distance runners

176

had great speed; they had strength, endurance and a high pain threshold. Ricky Brookshire was certainly an exception. And it's not that he did not have the attributes mentioned above; he had all of them, but he also had the natural gift of speed. When Leigh saw him run as a freshman, even though he didn't break into the top five runners on the team that year, she knew he had more natural running talent than any runner she had ever coached. Not breaking into the top five as a freshman was not unusual, even for someone of Ricky's innate talent; after all, he was on the best team in the state. But part of not being a top-five runner his freshman year was his not realizing how good he could be, so Leigh's efforts in coaching Ricky were mainly directed at building his confidence and constantly challenging him to find his potential. Leigh never considered tampering with or even tweaking his stride or any mechanics; he was a natural.

In the first race of the '97 season, held at the Bunker Hill course, Ricky, now a sophomore, broke the course record set the previous year by Ryan Woods. He ran a 16:35, leading Britt Marlowe and Joe Lion across the line for a one-two-three finish for Watauga. With those three runners plus junior David Stroupe, senior Joe Kitchens, and junior Jason Carter finishing in the top nine, the boys looked better at this point than last year's state championship team. And the girls looked just as good with Whitney and Marina breaking 20 minutes, and Leigh Suggs, Erin Struss, and Megan Keefe finishing in the top eight.

As expected, Watauga breezed through the season, the boys' and the girls' teams dominating almost every meet. At the prestigious Wendy's Classic, featuring many of the top teams in the country, the boys finished fourth and the girls finished third. Three Watauga boys, Ricky, Joe Lion, and Britt Marlowe, ran the course in under 16 minutes, with Ricky and Joe finishing one-two. For the girls, Whitney ran a sub-19, while Marina ran a respectable 19:18. At the conference championship race, the boys won the title for the seventh straight year, while the girls continued a winning streak that began in 1989. With Ricky battling the flu, Joe Lion led the boys with a time of 15:53. Joe had developed from a 19-plus minute runner to a sub-16 in three years. Watauga also had five other boys finish in under 17 minutes. Whitney led the girls, running a 19:06, and the girls' team placed seven girls in the top ten.

After blowing away everyone at regionals, they went to the state meet with confidence. Again, they knew they had a legitimate shot at capturing both team titles and both individual titles. In the boys race Leesville Road edged Watauga for the championship, despite Watauga having three runners under 16 minutes and two making All-State. Ricky Brookshire finished in third place in a time of 15:38, while Joe Lion finished fourth in a time of 15:42. In many years, those times would have been good enough for one-two finishes. Watauga's girls fared no better, finishing second to Cary. Whitney Woods made All-State, finishing sixth in a time of 19:21.

Three weeks later Watauga had the rare distinction of having two runners finish in the top ten at the Footlocker South Regional Championships as Joe Lion finished 7th in a time of 15:27 and Ricky Brookshire finished 9th in 15:31. Joe's top-eight finish qualified him to run in the Footlocker National Championships, an event which recognizes the top individual cross-country runners in the nation, where he placed 30th nationally.

Joe's trust in Leigh as a coach was evident; he asked her to accompany him to the national championship. She was very touched by this honor.

Leigh with Haleigh

Entering her sixth season of coaching cross-country, Leigh was known throughout the state as one of the top distance running coaches in the state. During Leigh's first five years of coaching, either her girls' team or her boys' team, or both, had finished no lower than third in the state. In the past four years, she had placed one or both of those teams in the top two in the state. She had coached numerous all-state runners and several state champions also. Other coaches were watching her. It was not uncommon for a coach of a competitor team to approach her before or after a meet and ask her how she was generating such success. She loved to talk shop with fellow coaches, and she readily shared her workouts with them. Most were amazed her runners were not putting in the mega-miles that other top teams required. Leigh thought quality of training was much more important than quantity, and that timing, peaking at the right time for the critical meets, was very important. She didn't go the high-mileage route because she expected many of her runners to run at the college level, and she did not want them to be burned out when they entered college.

Each summer, Leigh worked as a counselor/trainer at ASU's summer camp for cross-country. She always asked Coach Weaver if she could work with the fastest group of high school runners. Leigh's runners also attended this camp and got to know personally many of the top runners in the state. Watauga and Leesville Road had an especially good rapport, as they had been the top two programs in the state for the past three years. Her presence at the camp helped make ASU one of the premiere running camps in the state.

When some of her runners questioned Leigh about giving her workouts to the competition and training them in the summer, she explained, like a Zen Master, that workouts alone did not make champion runners, saying:

"Anyone can come up with good, solid workouts that will improve a runner's stamina and even his or her speed. But it's what's in your heart and mind that makes a champion. It's your ability to maintain a pace when you're in pain, your determination not to settle for less than your absolute best performance. That's what I strive to instill in you guys, and I'll never try to coach that into a competitor."

180

Leigh meticulously developed workout schedules for her runners. Every workout had a specific purpose and, along with the other workouts, was intended to get the maximum performance out of each runner and to insure that the team peaked at the right time. David Stroupe had learned the sanctity of Leigh's workouts the hard way a couple of years earlier as a naïve freshman, and the rest of the team learned from his example. Leigh empowered her runners by always explaining the purpose of each workout and how the workout would improve their performance.

One day during track season, David wasn't paying much attention as Leigh explained that day's workout and its purpose. After a warmup run they were to do three sets of 400, 300, 200, and 100-meter runs on the track at pace. The sequence was to be 4,3,2,1, then 4,3,2,1, then another 4,3,2,1. The workout was intended to develop and improve speed, particularly closing speed when tired. After the warmup, David suggested to his running partner that they just do all three 400s first, then the 300s, and so on. Of course, Leigh noticed. When she saw them go into another 400 after the first one, she sprinted over to them.

"WHAT ARE YOU GUYS DOING?" she yelled.

"Well, we just thought we'd do the 400s first," explained David meekly.

"Where were you when I explained this workout?" she demanded. "I spend a lot of time developing these workouts, and each one has a specific purpose. You will not change my workouts. If you want to run for me and Watauga, you will do my workouts exactly as I specify. This particular workout is not just about giving you some mileage to run; it's designed to develop closing speed. Now, is that going to be a problem for you?"

"N- n- no, Coach. I'm sorry, Coach."

.   .   .   .   .

In July of every year, the Highland Games are conducted on Grandfather Mountain. One of the highlights of the Games is The Bear, a five-mile road race from Linville at the base of the mountain to the mile-high swinging bridge at the summit of the mountain. It's one of the most grueling road races in the country, climbing 1,568 feet, and it attracts hundreds of runners from all over the US. Leigh decided to take a crack at it in 1998. She also encouraged her runners to continue their training over the summer and run The Bear. The race of 1998 was an excellent example of the quality of Watauga High's distance running program under Leigh's guidance. Leigh finished second overall among females, with Whitney Woods finishing fourth. Among the men in the race, the list of Watauga runners is truly remarkable: Ricky Brookshire won the race with David Stroupe finishing second, Joe Lion fifth, Ryan Woods sixth, Britt Marlowe ninth, Jason Carter tenth, Jason Klutz twelfth, and Jesse Pipes thirteenth. This race marked the moment when Leigh truly realized that the pride she felt in her runners' accomplishments far surpassed pride in her own accomplishments.

Leigh did not run The Bear again until 2002 due to scheduling conflicts. She ran in 2002 and again finished in second place among females. Our family beach reunion prevented her from running The Bear in 2003, but she then had a six-year stretch during which she ran the race every year. In 2004, she was the top female finisher. She finished 5th in 2005, 2nd in 2006, 2007, and 2008, and 4th in 2009. After her 2004 win, she always told me that she was running The Bear just for fun and not concerned about winning. Yet, at some point during the race, her competitive urge took over, and she increased her pace to see how many runners she could catch. When Leigh ran The Bear, I stood on the summit of Grandfather Mountain looking down at the final 300 meters to the finish line, so steep, with the wind howling in the runners' faces at 50 or 60 mph. What a thrill to see Leigh leaning into that hill and wind and driving to the finish line. She was indeed a well-oiled and powerful machine.

.   .   .   .   .

David Stroupe's sister, Kristen, a freshman, joined the team in the 1998 cross-country season. Somewhat shy and lacking confidence, she completed her training run with the slow group of beginners on the first day of practice. This group was composed mostly of girls who had never run before, so they were doing a combination of running and walking to get their mileage. David finished his workout and waited for Kristin. When he saw her walking in with the slow group, he pulled her aside.

"Kristin," he said, "You've got to get out of this beginner group and run with Leigh and her group; you are a runner!"

Leigh knew Kristin had potential but had not noticed she was with the slow group. Leigh was glad David jumped on her because what a runner she became!

At the Wendy's Invitational that year, Watauga again was competing against some of the best high school teams in the South. Leesville won the girls race, with Watauga's girls finishing fifth, led by Marina's fourth place. Kristin, nursing a minor injury, missed this race and the next one. For the Appalachian Invitational Race, Leigh listed Kristen to compete. Kristen approached Leigh before the race and said she wasn't sure she was ready to run.

"You are ready, Kristin," Leigh replied, "and I expect you to finish in the top three. Just get out there and relax and let it flow. You're stronger than you think."

About two-thirds of the way through the race, Kristin caught Marina, who was leading the race at the time. She told Leigh after the race that she wasn't sure what to do; she was hesitant to embarrass Marina by passing her. She remembered Leigh's mantra never to settle for anything less than your best effort. She passed Marina and won the race. After the race Leigh gave her a big hug. Kristin later said Leigh's hug after that race was a very big moment for her; it was the first time she knew she had Leigh's approval.

Watauga's boys and girls dominated all the races preceding the conference championship meet. Of course, they dominated the championship race also. Ricky shattered the boys record by 11 seconds as he ran an amazing time of 15:12, and the boys' team placed seven runners in the top 10. In the girls race, Marina finished second to Alisha Little of East Burke, but the girls' team easily won, as the team placed 11 runners in the top 20. Watauga then cruised to wins at regionals, with the boys having an incredible day. With Ricky taking first in 15:34, the boys' team placed six runners in the top eight, winning regionals for the eighth consecutive year. The girls' team won for the ninth consecutive time. Kristin Stroupe was the top girl, finishing fourth, just ahead of Marina.

At the state meet, everyone knew that both the boys' and the girls' races would be between Watauga and Leesville. It turned out to be just that; unfortunately, in two very close races, Watauga was slightly behind in each. Leesville beat Watauga's boys by four points and the girls by eleven points. Ricky finished second to Brad Wilshire of Orange County, and David Stroupe finished fifth overall. Interestingly, if the scoring had included each team's top seven runners instead of just the top five, Watauga would have easily won both races. Leigh was mildly disappointed that again her teams had come so close to sweeping both the boys and girls races at state, but as always she was very proud of both teams.

.   .   .   .   .

With Ricky Brookshire and Brian Greer a solid one-two punch and Jason Klutz a strong number three, Watauga's boys were ranked 13th in the US in cross country early in the '99 season. On September 25, a race would reveal the accuracy or inaccuracy of that ranking. A running enthusiast, Rick Hill, helped sponsor and direct one of the greatest high school cross-country showdowns in the history of the sport, the Great American Cross-Country Festival at McAlpine Park in Charlotte. Among the teams he attracted were five of the top eight boys teams in the United States and three of the top five girls teams. The race showcased a level of competition previously unseen in high school team cross-country. This was not a mere regional race; he had most of the best teams from all over the United States at this event.

The race received enormous pre-race chatter on the internet; interest in the race was extraordinarily high. Much of the talk was about Ricky Brookshire, clearly one of the top high school runners in the nation. Rick Hill, the meet director, posted his thoughts on how the boys' race would develop and projected Ricky Brookshire to finish third individually. Leigh knew that Ricky was reading all the chatter and promotions and was concerned it might go to his head. She stressed to him that he had to run his own race and not what someone who didn't even know him projected. Ricky had the best combination of strength and speed of any high school runner Watauga had ever seen. He and Leigh talked about his strategy for the race, the most important of his career to date. She wanted him to go out with the leaders early, hoping someone would pull the runners along to a fast pace. Then, at the two-mile mark, he was to put the hammer down and use that awesome combination of strength and speed over the course of the last mile. Leigh knew that if he ran that kind of race, anyone who beat him would have to be one hell of a runner.

The race was one of the greatest high school races ever in North Carolina terms of the quality of competition, the times run and the sheer excitement of the final 600 meters. Ricky ran a brilliant race. He was with the lead pack of about ten runners when he made his move at the two-mile mark. Alan Webb, from Weston, Virginia, went with him. Webb was a great runner, who later, while still in high school, ran a sub-four minute mile. As they came out of the woods, Ricky had about a 20 meter lead on Webb. Approaching the pond, Alan came even with Ricky, then the lead changed hands several times as they went into a full sprint for about the final 200 meters. At the finish line, Webb pushed ahead ever so slightly, winning by the blink of an eye, as both were timed in 15:03 and change. Their nearest competitor was 18 seconds behind. Of course, Ricky's 15:03 shattered his previous best time at McAlpine of 15:11 and set a new state record. Brian Greer, battling a nasty blister, finished in 13th place, and the team finished eighth overall. Watauga's girls, led by Kristin Stroupe and Lindley Swartz, finished 14th overall in their race. Not bad for a team whose top five included two sophomores and two freshmen.

Later that year at the conference championship, the boys' team swept the top five spots, and the girls took four of the top five spots to continue their domination of the Northwestern 4A Conference. Ricky broke the course record at Freedom High and the conference record with a time of 15:05. Brian Greer also ran a sub-16, finishing second in 15:59. Kristin took second in the girls race in 19:01, followed by Lindley Swartz in 19:13. After dominating performances throughout the year, Watauga expected to walk away with two regional championships again. It was a little surprising but not exactly deflating when both of Watauga's teams took second. North Mecklenberg beat the boys by 11 points, and Freedom broke the girls' nine-year run on the regional championship. Leigh again reminded both teams that their goal was to win state, not regional. Also, they ran regional without two of their top five boys, as Jason Klutz had nagging back and hip problems, and Elliot Austin had a lower leg injury. Brian Greer ran, but he too suffered from lower leg pain and was nowhere near his peak. Ricky easily won the boys' race in an excellent time of 15:08, while Kristin and Lindley finished fifth and sixth in the girls race. Leigh hoped Jason and Elliot could run at the state meet, which would put Watauga in contention for the championship.

At the state meet, both the Watauga boys and girls proved that their performance at regionals was just a bump in the road and reinforced Leigh's philosophy: "We aim to peak at state, not regional." Ricky broke the state championship meet record, running a 15:05 to beat North Mecklenberg's Stephen Hass by 14 seconds, and the boys recaptured the state championship. Jason and Elliot ran, with Jason finishing seventh to earn All-State and Elliot finishing 21st running with a probable stress fracture. Brian Greer, also running in pain from a lower leg injury, pushed himself to a 14th place finish. As he did at the Great American Cross Country Festival earlier in the season, Ricky made his move to break away from Hass at about the two-mile mark. He spoke with grace and class after the finish, giving all the credit for the team win to his teammates, especially Brian, Jason, and Elliot for running through pain. Watauga's girls came back strong from the week before to take second place. They beat their nemesis, Leesville Road, but were nosed out of first by Southeast Raleigh. Kristin earned her second All-State honor by finishing fourth in a time of 18:48, twenty-nine seconds faster than her regional time. Lindley ran a strong race but just missed All-State, placing eighth in 19:04.

Two weeks after the state meet, Ricky ran in the Footlocker South Regional Cross Country Championships, hoping to qualify for the Footlocker Nationals, to be held in Orlando in December. Scheduled at McAlpine Park, the Footlocker South Regional was another thrilling showdown between Ricky and Alan Webb of Virginia. Both runners broke the 15-minute barrier with Webb running a 14:52 to Ricky's 14:57, making this race the fastest South Regional ever run to date. The top eight runners from each region were invited to compete in the Footlocker National Championship in Orlando, and they were allowed to bring a coach. It was a testament to another runner's trust in Leigh as his coach that he asked her to accompany him to Orlando. Although he did not run his best, as the Central Florida heat really affected him, his time of 15:15 broke the previous race record. Unfortunately, 13 other runners also broke the record in the fastest national race ever run at that time. His 14th place finish was enough to earn him All-American recognition.

.   .   .   .   .

In the track state championship meet in spring, 2000, Ricky easily won both the 1600 and 3200, while Kristin took second in the girls' 3200. Ricky was determined to break the state record in both the 1600 and the 3200 at the State Meet. An extremely fast pace set by Stephen Hass of North Mecklenberg helped him accomplish his goal in the 1600. Ricky pulled away in the final two laps to run a 4:07:99 to break the state record by .02 seconds. Although he won the 3200, the brutal heat was a major factor preventing Ricky from getting the state record in his final high school race. He did share in one more state record, though, as he teamed with Brian Greer, Nathan Giles, and Patrick Murphy to shatter the 4x800 record, running the seventh fastest time in the nation for the year in 7:49. As a team, the Watauga boys scored more points than ever before in a state meet, finishing second to Vance.

The Great American Cross Country Festival was again held in Charlotte on September 23, 2000. The best teams in the nation competed, including two from North Carolina: Watauga, and last year's state champion girls team, Southeast Raleigh. The Watauga girls, led by Kristin Stroupe, finished a respectable 13th of the 22 teams in the premier race, the Race of Champions, well ahead of Southeast Raleigh, in 19th place. Finishing first and second in the girls' race were teams from Wyoming and Colorado respectively. Watauga's boys didn't fare as well, as the team's top runner, Elliott Austin, had to drop out due to a knee injury. Two weeks later Watauga ran in the Wendy's Invitational, again in Charlotte. This race, becoming more prestigious every year, featured over 80 schools from six states as well as Canada. Watauga's girls won this race, beating their top opponents in the state, Raleigh Leesville Road, Southeast Raleigh, and Winston-Salem's Mount Tabor. Kristin, just a junior, broke the Watauga school record with a time of 18:41 to finish fifth overall. Watauga's boys, still struggling to find a clear frontrunner to replace Ricky Brookshire and Brian Greer, finished sixth.

After dominating wins for the boys and girls in the Appalachian State University Invitational, Watauga won the conference championships, the 16th straight conference title for the girls, and the 19th straight for the boys. Both teams qualified for the State meet, as the girls won the Regional Championship and the boys finished fourth. Kristin was the individual Regional Champion, running an 18:48. The boys understandably found it difficult to focus, as senior team member, Ethan Dobson, lost his father in an automobile accident earlier in the week.

Kristin was running exceptionally well, and Leigh felt good about Kristin's chances to win a state championship. Two of her top competitors, Casey McGraw from Freedom and Julia Lassiter-Lucas from Myers Park, would miss the state meet with injuries. Leigh considered Kristin the girl to beat even if Casey and Julia were in the race. It was primarily a matter of keeping her confidence up and demonstrating that confidence on the starting line. Leigh knew that no one in the state had worked harder than Kristin to make herself an elite runner. Leigh had experienced the pain and disappointment of breaking down physically in a big race. But that disappointment was nothing compared to her feelings for Kristin when Kristin broke down at this state meet. Leigh was not disappointed in Kristin; she was disappointed and heartbroken for her. Kristin was battling Ginger Wheeler from Mount Tabor, well out in front of everyone else, as they were about to leave the woods for the final half-mile. Leigh was positioned there to give her a final bit of encouragement. As they came into view, Leigh saw Kristin gasp and begin to stumble. Leigh knew from her own racing experience that Kristin's race was over. Leigh didn't know if she had an illness or an injury, but she knew that Kristin was suffering from over-exertion; she had run herself into the ground. As she struggled up to Leigh, Leigh held out her arms and Kristin collapsed against her.

"It's okay, Kristin," Leigh said, as she held her.

"I'm sorry, Leigh, I've let you down and I've let the team down."

"Kristin, you gave it all you had. It's just a race; you don't owe anyone an apology."

Another Watauga runner, freshman Sarah Bastarache, also went down in the final mile. Losing those two, the Watauga girls finished fifth in the state. The boys finished in eighth place, which was about where Leigh expected them to finish.

.   .   .   .   .

With the exception of Kristin Stroupe, neither Watauga's boys' nor girls' teams were as strong as they usually were in track in spring of 2001. Although both won the conference championships, each finished in 7th place in team standings at regional, and neither team placed in the top ten at state. Kristin, though, ran brilliantly, and made Leigh very proud. She beat some tough competition at conference and regionals, including a former state champion from Freedom High, Casey McGraw, in the 1600. At regional she won the 3200 easily and anchored the winning 4 x 800 relay team. Then at state, she barely missed first place in the 3200 to repeat last year's runner-up status. Her time of 11:19 equaled last year's winning time.

.   .   .   .   .

Leigh always felt that she was meant to coach. But her family was her first priority, and Leigh worried that coaching duties took her away from her own children's athletic events and development. She considered giving up coaching. After discussing it with Chris, she decided to coach through 2001-2002, and then re-evaluate. She really wanted to work with Kristin during her last year of high school, and she also felt she owed it to several other girls and boys to whom she had become very attached.

Leigh often said that her favorite part of coaching was watching her runners receive recognition for their hard work. She was very proud again this year to see three of her runners sign scholarships to run at the college level. She was especially gratified that, although the boys distance runners were not as strong as some teams in the past, two of her runners, Elliott Austin and John Tumbleston, showed the work ethic and potential to be recognized and rewarded by moving to the college level. Elliott signed with East Carolina, and John signed with Elon. Of course, Kristin was courted by several colleges. She signed to take her talents to the University of North Carolina.

At the end of each school year, Watauga High holds its Senior Awards Ceremony. The most prestigious athletic awards are the Hall of Fame Award, given to the top female athlete in the school, and the Trailblazer Award, given to the top male athlete. Cross-country and track did not normally receive the spotlight that football, basketball, and baseball enjoyed, so it was unusual for a runner to be recognized as the top athlete in the school. In what was probably her proudest moment as a coach, Leigh had the privilege of introducing the winners of this year's top awards. Kristin won the Hall of Fame Award, and John Tumbleston won the Trailblazer Award. Of course, Leigh was grateful to Coach Mac for giving her the honor of delivering the speeches to introduce each of them.

The satisfaction and pride she felt at the awards ceremony convinced Leigh to coach for one more year. She was sad to lose Kristin, but she had quality runners coming back and was excited about the girls' team's chances. And she felt good about the returning boys as well; no great front runners, but a hard-working, very coachable group.

Leigh knew the girls had potential, but she didn't expect them to win the Wendy's Invitational. They surprised her by placing five runners in the top 26 to beat a strong Mount Tabor team. The boys finished in eighth place. Both teams went on to win the conference championship. The girls won Regional and the boys finished second. At Leigh's last state championship meet, her girls finished a strong third and the boys finished in seventh place with Michael Sutton losing a shoe in the first 100 meters to finish the race with one shoe.

.   .   .   .   .

Leigh didn't want to make a big deal of her decision not to coach; no press release or media event was held; but at the conclusion of track season in 2003, with a twinge of sadness, she informed head coach, Randy McDonough, that she would not be coaching cross-country in the fall. Of course, the news spread quickly, and Leigh experienced several emotional moments with runners expressing their shock and regrets and thanking her for the lessons they had learned. Leigh wanted to spend more time with family, especially with Jake and Haleigh now becoming very active in youth sports. Haleigh, at six years old, was just beginning to play youth sports, but Jake was showing outstanding ability in Little League Baseball as well as youth football and basketball.

A brief review of Leigh's coaching record in cross-country alone is an indication of her success. Neither her boys' nor her girls' teams ever lost a NW4A Conference Championship. Her boys' and girls' teams both were regional champions for six straight years, and she coached a total of 16 regional champion teams in her ten years of coaching. She also coached four state championship teams and six state runner-up teams. A look at the individual accomplishments of her runners is just as impressive: 15 individual conference champions, 12 regional champions, 3 state champions, and 18 All-State runners. But these numbers are merely the tip of an iceberg if one also included the conference, regional, and state champions in indoor and outdoor track who were coached by Leigh in the 800, 1600, 3200, and 4 x 800 events.

Throughout her coaching career Leigh was proud that most of her runners became runners for life, and many competed at the university level. She did everything she could to encourage those athletes she believed could be competitive at the college level, trying to help them realize which college might be a good fit for them, and also talking to coaches at the colleges they were targeting.

Leigh considered it an honor and a responsibility to help her athletes with college scholarship applications. She also helped those runners who were not good enough to earn a scholarship select a college where they could compete and have a rewarding experience, academically and athletically. Leigh loved to talk to the coaches of colleges where she thought one of her runners might be successful. She was very proud to see many of her runners continue competitive running at the college level, many of them on scholarship. Leigh's runners had outstanding careers at programs like Brevard, Appalachian State, UNC, NC State, East Carolina, Elon, West Point, and other top schools. Most of her runners who did not compete in college continued running as a life style. She always said that seeing her former runners in later years running for the sheer joy of running was her greatest reward as a coach.

Her greatest legacy as a coach and a teacher, however, proved to be the life lessons she imparted to young people by her teachings, her example, and her inspiration.

David Stroupe

Leigh was always recruiting. She would grab guys who were cut from soccer or other sports and encourage them to try cross-country. I didn't run cross-country my freshman year but I did go out for track. I was really impressed with her enthusiasm. It was contagious. She immediately started recruiting me and other newcomers to join the cross country team the following year. Even after my first track season, I was naive about the commitment and dedication required to be a great runner. I didn't fully comprehend the summer training that made her top runners great. When I started my first cross-country season running JV races, I knew I wanted to be better. Leigh pushed me to run with the top guys whenever I could handle it. They were so dedicated and fast. She convinced me that if I trained with the top guys, I would improve. I ended up improving my 5k time by over two and half minutes over the course of the season, and I was close to making the top eight, the group which traveled to the state meet. At the final conference meet before the team was set, I ran my best race of the season and set a personal record. Unfortunately, I was still the ninth runner and I didn't make the travel team for the regional or state meets. That year the boy's team won the state title. I was disappointed that I didn't get to travel with the team, or get a ring, but after frequently training with the top guys, I had an appreciation of what it took to be part of the best team in the state. After that season Leigh let me know I would be an important part of the team's success the following year. That next summer Leigh mapped out a customized training plan for me, and I trained all summer getting ready for cross-country my junior year.

At our first track practice as freshman, she got all the distance runners together and talked to us. She said that she wanted running to be fun. "I don't want anyone to ever look at running as punishment, like some other sports do," she said. "I hope most of you will become runners for life."

Leigh made a point of developing and supporting the senior leaders on the team. She used them as role models, and because so many of her runners were successful and improved every season, it was clear to younger runners that if you follow their lead and listened to the coaches, you could be a good runner.

She also really did a nice job of promoting the Watauga running family. Whenever a former runner would visit, as they often did when they were home from college, she would invite them to practice, introduce them to the team, and brag about their accomplishments. It was really inspiring because Leigh would tell us about their successes and relate old running stories. She was very proud of her former runners. I remember former greats like Will Hodges, Shane Austin, and Addie Bower stopping by practice or training in the area with their college team. I looked up to them; I wanted to be fast just like them. They were legends of the program, and their success before me helped me understand what was possible for Watauga runners.

If you were not yet established in the "top" group, the top seven or eight, it was hard to hang on with that group and with Leigh on training runs. I remember one day, during my freshman season in track, we were training out at Bass Lake. It was a slower training day for the top guys and Leigh invited me to start with this group. It was the first time I was able to stick with Leigh and the top guys for more than a quarter mile. As the run progressed, I was even more determined to stick with them for as long as I could. We ran the maze, which has a couple of really long, steep hills, and Leigh and the regulars in that group were just talking away like this run was a piece of cake. I was sucking wind, using every ounce of energy I had, but I was fighting to stay with them. I hung on for 4 miles until we finally got back down to the lake where one lap around the lake usually ended the run. I was really hurting but so excited I had run with the group. Then as we were almost to the point where I was sure we were going to stop, Leigh said, "Okay, let's go one more lap around the lake." I looked at Leigh in total distress and pleaded for permission to stop. She realized I had put everything I had into completing that run with them, and she probably didn't want me to pass out, so she congratulated me on my run and gave me permission to end my run as she and the rest of the guys cruised another mile around Bass Lake.

I was excited that I was able to run that far with the top group, but I was humbled at how easy they made it look and how they kept going after I stopped. By Leigh encouraging me to start that run with them, she had set me up for a breakthrough. I ended up doing more than I thought I could, but I still was a long way from where I wanted to be. Days like that were both satisfying and humbling. I came into the program hoping I could make a more immediate impact because I was a good runner, but I was constantly reminded that my female coach had a significantly faster 5k PR than me and could run me into the ground on an easy training run. There was the constant reminder and motivation that you weren't really one of the top guys until you beat Leigh's 5K time, which I didn't do until the end of my junior year of cross country, when I finally cracked the 17 minute barrier.

I got chewed out my freshman year in track for not doing a workout exactly in the order she wanted. I naively figured that if I ran the amount she prescribed the order of the sets and rest didn't matter. I was wrong. There was a logic and a plan with everything she had us do, and it gave us confidence that what we were doing would always make us better. By believing in our training and understanding the reasons for everything we did, we always felt like we were more prepared and had an advantage over our competition.

Leigh usually specified our training runs by time rather than by distance. For example, she would say, "I want a 30 minute run, out and back," rather than run 2 miles out and 2 miles back. That way, each person was getting a workout suitable for his/her ability and we all finished together. We almost always did strengthening exercises such as pushups and crunches after our run.

In training, Leigh was all about building your confidence, both physically and mentally; she would say that when you start hurting in a race, you need that confidence in yourself and your preparation to help you push through the pain and discomfort. During my freshman year of track, she paced each of us freshman through a mile time trial, just to give us the confidence that we were ready to race. I set my first mile PR in that time trial with Leigh. She would always look for ways to get a baseline of your fitness. She would use time trials, specific races, and workouts to assess each runner and project their individual time goals throughout the season.

Everyone close to the program knew what an impact she had on our success. Coach Mac was often the face of the program since he was the head coach. To his credit, he and Leigh took on different roles and split responsibilities. While he managed much of the administrative details and non-distance events in track, he gave Leigh the reins to really focus on coaching the distance runners. Although they worked together, Leigh was the mastermind who constructed most of our workouts, and she was the inspirational and strategic leader behind the distance teams' success. Coach Mac deserves credit for empowering Leigh, especially when it came to coaching the boys' team. In the 90's, none of the other top boys' cross country teams in the state of North Carolina had female coaches. I remember at races runners from other teams approached us and asked us about our coach. They were often shocked when we explained that we had a female coach. From my perspective it just seemed normal, but in reality she was a trailblazer.

195

Leigh often told us that other coaches would ask her about our training. She explained to me that she never worried about sharing her workouts or her training program with competitors. She believed that the training plan alone wouldn't make other teams and runners succeed. She knew there are intangible aspects of our program's success, such as dedication, mental preparedness, strategy, and community, that were much more difficult to emulate.

Anyone who was an athlete or followed our program closely knew Leigh; they knew of her history and of her impact.

She never said "You have to do this." She would give each of us a suggested schedule geared to our fitness level. Once you had been in the program, she didn't have to reiterate that in order to be competitive for a state championship, which was always our goal, we needed to work hard throughout the summer. We knew that because it was ingrained in the culture of the program. We wanted to do it, and we organized our summer training ourselves. She didn't believe in high mileage. She wanted her runners to have the opportunity to increase their mileage in college, when our bodies were more mature. She planned our peak mileage for August, before we started workouts. Her summer training plan would normally have us build up mileage for three weeks, then back off for a week to recover to ensure we adjusted to the increased volume. After the recovery week, we would increase mileage again for three more weeks then reduce our mileage for a week.

Leigh really believed in the mental aspect of racing, and she knew the importance of mental preparation. One of the things she stressed was to always make the runners next to you or around you think that you were stronger than they were – to make them believe that you still had something left in your tank. She always said to focus on keeping your breathing under control and to even say a few words like "good job" to competitors to show them that you aren't distressed.

Leigh paid close attention to details. She ensured that we all warmed up properly and together before each race, that we had appropriate attire for the weather, that our uniforms always matched, and that we had the right shoes and spikes for the surface we were racing on. She insisted that we didn't walk around in our uniform, and that we all wait to take off our warmups until it was time to race. Once we were in our uniforms that meant it was time to do our final strides and race. We looked like a team that had its act together. We knew the weather could be cold or wet at McAlpine for the state meet, so Leigh made sure that we were mentally prepared for anything. On colder days, she would tell us to warm up closer to the start-time of the race, to make sure we didn't cool off too much. When we went to the start line, we were ready to execute our race plan no matter the weather conditions. Leigh believed that on cold or wet days when we showed up to the line warm and oblivious to the weather, that alone psyched out a lot of teams that would be standing around shivering.

She always scouted the course before the race, and she knew where she wanted to be during the race to ensure that she could be seen and heard. She would typically position herself away from the crowds and other coaches. She would sprint to those spots. It was always positive comments from her; calm, composed and encouraging. We always knew where she would be, especially at McAlpine, and I really believe that we all got a lift each time we saw her.

Of course we had the tradition that every year after the conference championship, we would tape the fastest freshman boy finisher to the flag pole.

Kristin Stroupe

When I joined the team as a 9th grader, it was clear that Leigh ran the show. I could tell that the team was in awe of her and had the highest respect for her, as did I. I wasn't intimidated; but I didn't want to let her down. I still remember the first time Leigh "noticed me" and gave me a hug, I was a 9th grader and it was after the ASU Invitational and I finished first on our team – I remember feeling pride in that I must have impressed her to earn that hug . That was our first photo together, I still have that photograph.

For high school practices, she would hand out the workout sheet for the entire week and go over it in detail with us, talking about the specific goals and paces for each workout, the mental aspect of the workout, and how it would prepare us for competition. She was very deliberate in explaining the purpose of each workout. If we were approaching a race, she would talk very specifically about how to

197

prepare for the race, not only physically, but mentally as well. Leigh knew the value of the often-overlooked aspect of the mental training piece of distance running. She believed and showed us that mental strength can outperform physical strength. She was tough as nails. On our cross-country and track teams, she helped build our mental strength and pushed us beyond our physical limitations to reach our goals.

My senior year, Leigh and I ran all of my workouts together. This was a reflection that she would never give us a workout that she couldn't do herself and that she was willing and able to put in the work, which, I think, really helped her empathize and understand her runners both as athletes and as people. Having Leigh as my training partner, I got to experience her mental and physical strength. We shared an unspoken bond, appreciation, and understanding of what each other was going through. These workouts, these runs, they meant the world to me, they still mean the world to me. I can still remember what it feels like to run with Leigh, the swing of her arms, her stride, her breathing. I treasure that I will always have that and can carry it with me.

Before big meets and races, Leigh would give every runner a focus card – a specific goal for the race that included a message or quote for each runner. I still have my focus cards. For the cross-country state championship race my senior year, she knew how important this meet was to me, and that I was disappointed by what had happened to me in my junior year, so she wrote me a long note: "KRISTIN – Your strength is your EXPERIENCE. You have been through just about every conceivable race situation in your four years of competing at the state's highest level. You have had disappointment and you have had the kind of success that many runners only dream of. Every race in your past, good or bad, has prepared you to be successful tomorrow. In my mind, there are no limits to what you can do, Kristin. If you truly believe this yourself, then you will surely look forward to this race instead of dreading it. Let your excitement about what can happen be your motivator and not the fear of what might or might not happen. Don't doubt your ability...don't doubt your instincts. If something in you tells you to make a move, then make that move and don't look back. You have trained and prepared like no one else I have ever coached. Be confident and enjoy the thrill of the competition. You make me proud to be your coach. Good Luck.'

My junior year, I was one of the favorites going into the state championship cross-country meet. I was physically prepared; I was confident in our training, and I was mentally prepared. After two miles, I was positioned right where I needed to be with the leaders going into the woods, when the strangest thing happened. Something in my body failed me, which had never happened to me before. I was always so consistent, and I had never had a "bad" race. Out of nowhere, I felt like I was going to pass out and I struggled to keep running. I remember thinking, "This is okay, I'll still get all-state" which I had gotten my first two years and hoped to join the select few girls to get all-state all four years of high school. Then I watched girls blow by me as my dreams and body slipped away from me. Barely moving, I finally came out of the woods and I saw Leigh. She had her arms open to hug me and I fell into her arms until a teammate carried me to the medical tent. I was examined at the hospital, released the same day, then tried to pick up the pieces of this missed opportunity and restore my faith in my dreams and myself after I unexpectedly failed to reach my goal. As I was regrouping from this setback, I met with Leigh for several runs together. She shared the story about how her brother, Graig, was the favorite to win the state wrestling championship but made a mistake in the final match and lost. She told me I would come back from this setback. It was such a heartbreaking race, and I wondered how I would recover and relearn my love for running when I had invested everything and failed for no explicable reason. I ran with Leigh all through that winter and we had many discussions about how to get the fire back.

We had a tradition of taking Leigh to Makodo's, a Japanese restaurant in Boone, on her birthday. Another tradition we had on the bus trip to the state meet was to write personalized songs for each member of the boys' team to be performed at the hotel. The boys' team wrote personalized poetry for the girls' team. All of this was performed at the hotel the night before the state meet and was a reflection of the many ways we bonded as a team.

My freshman year the girls 4x800m team won the state meet; it was one of the most incredible and memorable moments of my running career and I felt so honored as a 9th grader to share in this experience with three seniors. The following year, I was the returning sophomore veteran on the team. I remember being incredibly nervous because in my rookie mind I was no Donna Bealer. Donna was a state champion in the 800 who anchored us to the state championship the year before. I remember my sophomore year of track I was on the 4 x 800 team. We were getting ready to run in the state championship, going for our third state championship in a row in that event. Before the race, one of the girls mentioned praying for us. I distinctly remember Leigh's response, that she didn't have an issue with praying, but that we control our own destiny, that praying wouldn't determine the outcome of the race. We would finish second in that race, but Southeast Raleigh had to break the state record to beat us.

After every race, the first person I sought out was always Leigh. I could always hear her voice during races. Assuring and steady (until the end when she was thrilled and jumping with excitement!), I could feel her pride and shared excitement from her investment in us as people and athletes as she shared in our successes with us.

To say that she made a difference in my life would definitely be an understatement.

I remember Leigh defining courage as not the absence of fear but rather being brave in the face of your fears. I readily admitted my fears to Leigh, the pressures of racing and living up to the high expectations I had for myself and that others had for me. She valued courage and helped me summon my own during a defining moment in high school. This has nothing to do with running, but it says a lot about Leigh as a mentor and what she meant to me. My senior year, I was on Student Council. I saw another council member cheating during an election. I told the advisor, who didn't take me seriously and just tried to sweep the incident under the rug. The student's parents rushed to their daughter's defense and went to the principal. The story was spun that I had made this story up because I was jealous. The advisor did nothing, the principal did nothing, and the student spread rumors that I was a liar. I lost faith in teachers and adults in authority at our school, but Leigh stuck by me. She was the only teacher and adult who believed me. She praised me for standing up for what I believed was right. And when I won the Hall of Fame award that year, Leigh, in her speech at the assembly, openly talked about my integrity and doing the right thing over the easy thing. Leigh stood by me and I'll never forget that.

Leigh later became the Student Council Advisor and would use that experience to emphasize integrity to her members and to ensure

200

that would never happen again. Many years later the student who cheated contacted me and apologized for the incident. Of course, I shared this with Leigh, thanking her for standing behind me at the time and for never doubting me. She deserved the apology and truth as much as I did. Leigh felt strongly that everyone who had been impacted by this incident deserved the truth and the apology as much as I did. Her strong feelings about the incident showed how invested she was in making the situation right and supporting me many years later.

I carried Leigh's lessons with me as a runner in college and beyond. We continued to stay in touch after high school and developed a true friendship; whenever I was back in town, I would call her and we would run together, meet for a meal, scrapbook together. We'd talk about life, goals, and laugh until our abs ached, and be excited about the burn, and laugh some more. I treasured our friendship and could go to Leigh for advice or call her with news; she was such an important mentor and friend.

After graduating from college and facing the real world, as I was soul searching, figuring out what I wanted to do with my life, grappling with what I thought success was "supposed" to look like and how that didn't quite fit with what I love doing, I reflected upon my happiest times and the most important people in my life. Leigh loved what she did; I felt that every day we shared. Leigh made my life better. She helped me fall in love with running - with competing. She introduced me to some of the most important aspects of my current life. Though it took me a while to find my own path and how I wanted to spend my days, my time, my life, I realized that I returned again and again to Leigh's love for coaching and the impact she had in my life.

I'm a high school coach now and I have reflected so much on Leigh's coaching in developing my own coaching style. I still talk to my runners about her. At my job interview for my first high school coaching position, I talked about Leigh, the positive influence she had on me and on others. It's just an incredible feeling to know the influence she has made on my life, and I hope I can make that same kind of impact on my runners. The last time we talked on the phone, I called Leigh to tell her I had gotten the high school co-ed head coaching job and was going to be a PE & Fitness teacher.

Leigh was also open and honest about her struggles with eating *disorders and body image. Her honesty and openness were refreshing and valuable. As a high school athlete, in the running world where disordered eating can be prevalent, her openness and honesty on the subject made it less scary and secret. She shared her struggles so that others could know that they weren't alone. She modeled that it was okay to be vulnerable in talking about struggles and that admitting and facing your fears takes courage, which she valued. She modeled that it was okay for women to be competitive and strong. I loved that Leigh was all of these things, not realizing until much later that this helped me as a female entering the "real" world, particularly the coaching world.*

I thought it was normal to have a female coach; I didn't notice that all of the other teams were coached by men. I didn't know anything else. I just knew I had a good coach. So what? The strongest person I know is a female. My guy friends and teammates felt the same way. I later learned from my brother, who was on the boys' team, that at big meets, other guys in the state came up to them wanting to know all about their training and program...how they were so successful... and was it true that their coach was a female? I now realize how special it was that I had a female role model and coach; because of this, I had no self-imposed limits on what being a "coach" looked like. She helped pave the way for me to be a strong female.

CHAPTER TEN

YOU'RE STRONGER THAN YOU THINK

"I don't know . . . I guess I just love to inspire people. I love to see the light go on when someone realizes that being strong is one of the greatest feelings in the world ... and to know that running makes you just as strong mentally as it does physically! To know that no matter what life's circumstances are and no matter how hard the world may seem to be trying to hold you back, our own personal strength and belief in ourselves is something that no one can take away without our permission. I believe this more than I believe anything and am committed to helping others believe it, too."

Leigh Cooper Wallace

Endurance Magazine, **May, 2009**

Leigh and Chris were struggling financially, and she knew she needed to work outside the home in addition to her coaching. She had obtained her teacher certification but had put off applying for a job in order to stay with her daughter Haleigh. At the end of the 1999 school year, Leigh applied for a position that opened up in the Health and PE Department at Watauga High School.

She accompanied Louise and me on a trip to visit her brother Graig at West Point Military Academy when, on the return trip home, she got a message to call Mr Gary Childers, the principal at Watauga High. Leigh dreaded returning the call because it meant that he would offer her the job. The thought of not being with Haleigh all day was very disconcerting to her, but she also saw an excellent opportunity to make a real difference in young peoples' lives, not just runners, but every high school student in the county. She finally made the call and learned that Mr Childers was in fact recommending her for the job, and he was confident she would be approved by the school board. She began teaching Healthful Living in the fall of 1999.

Leigh already had a well-established reputation at the high school as an outstanding coach and mentor. The students were in awe of her, and the faculty had the highest respect for her. She quickly became a popular teacher in the school, and her class was always in high demand. Of course, she had the benefit of having as her tutor and mentor the finest teacher in the county, her mother, Louise. Every evening, Leigh would either call or come to the house to discuss issues she had encountered or anticipated.

Leigh loved teaching and her students loved her. She was becoming very concerned, though, about the fitness level of the students, especially the non-varsity athletes, many of whom had never been involved in any type of athletics or physical activity. She knew some students were inactive simply because they were lazy. Many, though, she realized were not involved in an exercise program because they did not have an athletic background and did not have the knowledge to start an exercise program on their own. Leigh thought most students wanted to be fit and wanted to feel good about their bodies; they were at a time in their lives when they definitely had an increased awareness of their bodies and body image. She wanted to find a way to reach those students.

When each department in the school was asked to suggest courses to offer as electives, Leigh proposed a fitness-based course. She presented her idea to the school board, along with a proposed curriculum, for a course geared primarily toward students who were not varsity athletes. The Fitness Training course was approved and was first offered in the fall of 2001, when 33 students enrolled. Word spread quickly among the student body that if you wanted to get into shape but didn't know how or were having a hard time finding the motivation, then sign up for Leigh's class and she would make it happen. The demand for the class was so great that in 2002 a second section was added, giving her 68 students for the course. In addition to teaching her Fitness Training course, she also taught Healthful Living each semester. By teaching both Healthful Living to freshmen and two sections of her Fitness Training class, Leigh directly influenced virtually every high school student in Watauga County and in many cases changed existing life styles for better ones. She not only accepted, but encouraged, special needs students to take the fitness course. When one such student in her class competed in a Special Olympics Swim Meet, Leigh took the entire class on a field trip to cheer this student on. A special needs student in another class dreamed of being a beauty queen and loved to watch and talk about beauty contests. This girl's classmates, with Leigh's supervision, organized a fitness contest and crowned her as the Class Fitness Queen.

Leigh quickly developed great self-confidence in the classroom. She took on any topic and convinced even the shy students to participate in discussions of the most sensitive subjects. This confidence and openness allowed Leigh to maintain absolute control in the classroom without ever showing anger or frustration. She loved what she was doing and she showed it. Very rarely did a student test Leigh's composure. One such incident occurred during the first week of class in Leigh's second or third year of teaching. In her Healthful Living class for freshnen, Leigh had her students do a "get acquainted"

206

exercise. For homework they were to write something about themselves that they were willing to share with the class, preferably something that others did not know about them. The next day, they all turned in their papers, and for the next two class periods, Leigh selected papers to read to the class and have the class guess who the writer was. As she was scanning the papers, she discovered a paper from a freshman male student which disclosed that he "had Elephantitis (sp) of the nuts." Obviously, the author was one of the few new students coming to the high school who did not know Leigh's reputation. Leigh put this paper aside, determined to deal with it the next day. As she went through several papers that first day, she noticed one student had a constant smirk on his face, so she suspected he was the one testing her. She also did not read his paper on the second day. Instead, as the other students filed out at the end of the class period, she told the boy with the smirk to stop by her desk.

When just the two of them remained in the room, she told him, "I didn't want to embarrass you in front of the class, but I want you to know how sorry I am for your condition. I've given it a lot of thought, and I've read about it, and I met with the school nurse yesterday afternoon. She confirmed what I had read about the disease, and there is now a simple treatment for Elephantiasis in which they just insert a needle into your testicles and draw out all the excess fluids in there. So, I've arranged with the school nurse to perform the procedure. She's waiting for us right now, and we can visit her now and have you back in class in no time at all."

"Oh no, Mrs. Wallace, I don't really need to do that; I'm fine."

"Oh, I insist. I feel that since you opened up to me about this delicate situation, you were screaming for help. I cannot let this go unresolved. Let's go." And she took his arm and practically dragged him down the hall to the nurse's office.

All the way to the nurse's office, he was pleading with Leigh, "I'm sorry, Mrs. Wallace, it was just a joke; there's nothing wrong with me."

As they walked into the nurse's office, the nurse, who had been previously briefed by Leigh, said, "Ah, so this is the young man with the problem. Wait just a moment while I get my needle."

The poor kid was practically in tears now, insisting that it was just a joke.

Leigh grabbed him firmly by the shoulders and looked into his face, "OK, now listen to me. Everything I do has a purpose. You tried to make a mockery of my class and I won't allow that."

"Yes, Mrs. Wallace; I'm so sorry. It'll never happen again, I swear!"

The kid was a model student from then on.

No subject was taboo in Leigh's class. She used her abduction and rape as an opportunity to talk about control, violence, victimization, and getting your life back together after being victimized.

In her second year, when several teachers asked if she could help them get into a fitness routine, she started early morning workout sessions for teachers. She also provided guidance for teachers on nutrition and weight loss. It wasn't long before word about her work at the high school reached Appalachian State University. Leigh received a phone call from Donna Breitenstein of the Department of Curriculum and Instruction at ASU. Donna was a professor and also the Health Education Coordinator for the University and the Director of the North Carolina School Health Center. She asked if Leigh would be interested in teaching a course at the University. Eager for any opportunity to bring in a little more money and expand her influence on young people, Leigh became an Adjunct Professor at ASU teaching an introductory health education class once a week.

As if Leigh weren't already spending enough time on fitness (with her daily runs and her high school fitness class where she did the workouts with her students and her teacher workouts), she was also spending considerable time at the Wellness Center in Boone. She would usually get in at least one workout a day at the Wellness Center, a workout that might include running on a treadmill or on the indoor track, spinning on a stationary bike, and weight lifting. She became such a fixture at the Center that Jody Cash, the Director, hired her to lead stationary bicycle spin classes. The mountain trails and roads around Boone are often filled with bicyclists, and Leigh's spin sessions became a very popular workout for serious bikers in the county.

Leigh always taught one of the freshman PE classes at the high school. Pete Hardee, the varsity baseball coach, usually taught another PE class, and they shared the gym, at least for a portion of the period. One year, Leigh's class was convening in the bleachers on one side of the gym, Pete's class on the other. Pete is not a big man, but he can be an intimidating presence. He has a gruff voice, does not hesitate to raise his voice when he sees something going wrong, and has little tolerance for mistakes. On one opening day, a young freshman boy was assigned to Leigh's class, but he, unfortunately, was probably the only student in the school who did not know who "Coach Wallace" was. He made the terrible mistake of going to the wrong side of the gym and parking himself in the bleachers in front of Coach Hardee. After Coach Hardee called the role, he asked if anyone present had not had his name called. This poor soul raised his hand.

"Well, what's your name son?" asked Pete, obviously annoyed at this potential discrepancy. The boy told him his name.

"Well, you're not on my roster," said Pete, his irritation growing. "Let me see your schedule." He looked at the schedule, which read PE 101, Coach Wallace." Pete's face reddened and the hairs on the back of his neck bristled.

"MY GOD, BOY!" yelled Pete, shouting loud enough now that he had the attention of not only his class, but Leigh's class as well, across the gym floor. "YOU'RE SUPPOSED TO BE IN COACH WALLACE'S CLASS! DON'T YOU HAVE ANY IDEA WHO COACH WALLACE IS? YOU SEE THAT PHYSICAL SPECIMEN OVER THERE?" He was pointing across the floor to where Leigh stood with her hands on her hips looking back at Pete, obviously amused. " THAT, MY BOY, IS COACH WALLACE! DO I LOOK ANYTHING AT ALL LIKE THAT? DO I HAVE POWERFUL ARMS LIKE THAT? DO I HAVE LEGS THAT CAN RUN FOREVER LIKE THAT? IS MY BODY CUT LIKE THAT FINE-TUNED MACHINE YOU SEE OVER THERE? DO YOU THINK I COULD DO ONE-TENTH AS MANY PUSHUPS OR PULLUPS OR SITUPS AS SHE COULD? NOW GET OUT OF MY CLASS AND GET OVER THERE

WHERE YOU BELONG AND QUIT WASTING MY TIME!"

Most of the kids in both classes stared in shock, but those who knew Coach Hardee began laughing, knowing he was really a nice guy and fun to be around. Leigh was laughing inside but trying to maintain her composure, as the young boy hurried across the gym floor, glad to get away from Pete's wrath.

Leigh was not just a coach and teacher at Watauga High School. She immersed herself in the life of Watauga High School. She never missed a home basketball game and rarely missed an away game. She didn't just attend the games; she was a cheerleader. She always sat next to the student section, even though the students had a tradition of standing the entire game. Whenever the spirit waned, Leigh jumped up and got the students going by starting a cheer or encouraging them to make some noise.

.   .   .   .   .

In the year 2000, beloved teacher, swim coach, and Leigh's colleague, Lan O'Laughlin, was battling cancer, a battle he eventually lost. To help with his treatment expenses, the Watauga High Student Council sponsored an event known as "Mr. WHS," a male "beauty pageant" in which male student contestants raised money to enter the contest, performed talent or comedy acts on stage, participated in a themed "fashion" show, and answered questions from a panel of judges. In its first year, Mr. WHS raised over $4,000. Two or three years later, Leigh became the Student Council advisor, a role which included responsibility for the pageant. As was her custom in every phase of her life since the rape, Leigh threw her heart and soul into the pageant which effected quite remarkable results. In 2008, the pageant brought in enough money to include multiple families as benefactors. By 2010, ten years after its origination, the money raised had increased ten-fold to over $41,000 per year. Leigh provided the guidance, advice and encouragement, but the students ran the show: emcee'ing, decorating, directing, managing the funds, and selecting the families to support. Struggling families benefited from the financial aid, and, of course, the students learned one of life's valuable lessons: give back to the community.

In 2002 a group of prominent business men and sports enthusiasts in Boone began an initiative to recognize the greatest all-time athletes in Watauga County. The first five people, all men, were inducted into the Watauga County Sports Hall of Fame class in 2003. After the first induction, a Hall of Fame Committee member informed me that Leigh was high on the committee's list for eventual induction. He gave me the nomination forms and suggested I work on her nomination. I did so, and when the third class was announced in 2005, both Leigh and head track coach, Randy McDonough, were among the five inductees. At the ceremony on September 8, 2005, in what was certainly one of the proudest moments of my life, I was given the honor of introducing Leigh as a member of the Watauga County Sports Hall of Fame.

The next year, a local magazine, *All About Women*, featured an article on Leigh written by Marie Freeman. The article, accompanied by a half-page photo of Leigh leading a spin class at the Wellness Center, described Leigh as a "fitness diva." Interestingly, the article made no mention of her abduction in 1989 or her role in putting away a serial killer for good. Instead, it focused on what she had done since 1989 to influence healthy living in Watauga County.

"Powerful is not a strong enough word to describe the physical and mental prowess of Leigh Wallace," wrote Freeman. "Still, the Watauga High School Healthful Living teacher, mother of two, and local fitness diva intends to make more of an indelible mark upon the health of the High Country."

Freeman quoted Leigh: "Fitness should be a way of life. Many people don't work out because they don't know how to get started or don't know how to motivate themselves. The motivation to work out and the discipline to continue to do so are lessons that transcend into

211

other areas of our lives. These kids have to get up and move more."

When asked what was the motivation for her rigorous exercise schedule, Leigh said, "I like to train hard for no particular reason other than it is a feeling of empowerment which I continuously feed off. Each day I try to push myself harder than the day and week before and that in turn makes me feel good about myself. My workout is a form of meditation. When everything else is hectic in my life, I know my workout is a peaceful place to retreat."

Leigh heard about an organization called "Girls on the Run." Molly Barker, social worker and four-time Hawaii Ironman triathlete, was the founder of the organization, and its function was to establish local clubs where women would coach and mentor young girls toward a life of fitness and a love for running. Molly began this program in Charlotte, NC, but it became a nationwide program serving over 200,000 girls and women each year. As this program emphasized empowering young girls, Leigh wanted to get involved in the program and start a group in Watauga County. She signed up for a clinic conducted in Charlotte by Molly to train women as coaches and mentors. After attending the clinic, Leigh became the first Director of Girls on the Run in Watauga County. When these two powerful women met (Leigh and Molly), the impression each made on the other was obvious. Molly wrote a beautiful article for the May, 2009 edition of *Endurance Magazine* (a running/fitness magazine published in Durham, NC) describing Leigh's early battles with eating disorders, her abduction, rape and escape, and how she took control of her life. "I've got to be honest with you," Molly wrote, "when I met Leigh I was intimidated by her. Her physical strength is obvious. She is one of the strongest looking females I have ever met. Her energy, though, was a little reserved. She was probably intimidated by my extroversion and wide-open persona. We had a kind of mutual intimidation society, if you will; me of her physical presence and she of my emotional one." A full-page picture of Leigh was featured on the cover of *Endurance Magazine*

Leigh summed up her personal philosophy and her message by these words written on the wall in her classroom:

"YOU'RE STRONGER THAN YOU THINK!"

These words became the motto of her fitness class as well as every activity in which she was involved.

.   .   .   .   .

Leigh made believers out of the people with whom she came in contact. Almost all of the young people Leigh coached in cross-country and track are still runners. Many of the people who took her fitness class are now runners for life. Her spin sessions at the Wellness Center were always full, as were her strength and aerobic exercise classes there.

In the spring of 2008, a TV producer from the Oxygen Channel contacted Leigh and asked if she would consent to doing a show about her abduction. Seeing another opportunity to get her message out to a broader audience, she readily agreed. Interviewers, camera crews, and producers converged on Boone and produced a show as part of their "Captured" series, a true crime series featuring women who have been victimized. Extensive interviews were conducted with Leigh, with Steve Wilson of the State Bureau of Investigation, and with detectives; Chris, Louise and I were also interviewed. Professional actors played the roles of Leigh and other key figures. The show aired later in 2008 and focused primarily on the abduction, Leigh's escape, and her actions to bring Daniel Lee to justice.

.   .   .   .   .

In September, 2009, Leigh was asked to give the keynote speech at the 20th Walk for Awareness. It had been ten years since she had last spoken at that event, although she still attended regularly. She accepted the invitation and delivered her longest and probably most powerful speech:

Some people can pinpoint a defining moment in their lives - a moment when everything changed for them. I am one of those people who has experienced such a moment. Twenty years ago, September 29, 1989, I was pulled away from a life that I knew and forced into a terrifying nightmare. With a gun pressed to my forehead, I faced my own death and the reality that my life would be much shorter than I had thought it would be. My thoughts were dark, consumed with the inevitability of my death. 'Why must I die now? At 20 years old, my life had really only just begun. What kind of wife would I have been? Would I have been a good mother? Will it hurt? My family - they will carry this sadness for the rest of their lives.' I was kidnapped and raped 20 years ago, but the images, the thoughts in my head, and the terror are still very clear to me today. The moment defined my life - not as a victim, but as a survivor. Many never heal from tragedy such as this. In that car, I could think of no life for me beyond that moment; recovery wasn't even a consideration. Without question, one of the happiest moments of my life was when I hugged my parents and my future husband, Chris, after I escaped. My healing, my recovery, had begun. From then on, I defined myself as a survivor, a fighter. As a lifelong competitor, I viewed my triumph over my captor's will to end my life as a victory. I had won and I had given myself another chance at life. Surviving this crime has since been a great source of pride for me. When I talk about being a victim, I speak in the past tense. I was a victim. But from the moment I escaped, I became a stronger, tougher, and more confident person. People often ask me where this strength comes from and how I found the strength to move forward. But the way I saw it and continue to see it, I had no other choice. This is what survivors do; I was a victim only in that car, but no longer. It didn't make sense for me to have survived, only to give up on life in the days and years that followed. I made a choice to continue to live my life; but now, I was living with a renewed sense of life's importance and my power to control my own fate.

When people tell me that they could have never survived what I did or that they could have never recovered, I do my best to convince them that they would have the strength and that recovery is a choice. There were many choices I made on my road to recovery. I could have chosen to pity myself. I could have allowed shame and self-doubt to overwhelm me. But I have never allowed my thinking to go in that direction. It would have been self-destructive. I could have chosen to hide in my house and live in fear. Instead, I made the choice to bravely face the world again. I could have chosen bitterness and isolation. But I found comfort in the counseling and support I received from my family, my friends, and this community. I could have asked myself over and over again, "Why me?" But I would have never found the answer to that question and it would have kept me trapped in the past. Instead, I chose to ask myself another question, "How do I get back up and move forward? How do I persist in being a survivor?" I have never denied that this event happened. I have never tried to forget it. This crime is a part of my history. It helped shape the person I am today and I like that person. My recovery has always been about how to move forward into my future; it has never been about staying stuck in the past. So as long as you have the freedom to make your own choices, you, too, have the ability to choose renewed strength and recovery. If you choose to live your life, no matter what you have gone through, you will find the strength you need. I challenge you not to doubt your own strength. Be courageous when you face life's challenges and choose to overcome them. Be a survivor.

When I prepared to speak here tonight at this 20th Walk for Awareness, I spent a great deal of time reflecting on the past 20 years. I wondered if things are any better now than they were 20 years ago. I believe, in some respects, they are. I believe there is a greater understanding of victimization today. Through social events like the Walk for Awareness, people better understand the many scars that sexual assault leaves on its victims, and society is more sympathetic. I think that instead of pointing fingers at rape victims, we are more likely to open our arms in embrace. We may not be able to stop sexual crimes, but we do have the power to help victims heal and return to life. I know that, as a former victim, I feel a renewed sense of strength and comfort when I come to this walk and see the hundreds of people here to show their support. The silence of the walk fills me with a powerful calm. I walk away with a tremendous feeling of peace and hope. I want to thank you all for that. You are a reason for my continued well-being.

I also want to share my personal reflections of the last 20 years. In gathering my thoughts for tonight, I thought about the path that my life had taken and I wondered if I had served my purpose. I suppose that most people who survive a life-threatening situation come to believe that they must have survived for a reason, that there was something they were meant to accomplish or do. I have often wondered that. And the answer that I come up with is that my greater belief in myself as a result of my survival allowed me to accomplish my running goals when I returned to competitive college running. It helped me to be a better high school coach and inspire my runners to believe in themselves. It has helped me as a teacher as I encourage my students to be passionate about their lives and their futures. The knowledge I have gained from this experience has allowed me to trust again and believe that most men are compassionate and wonderful people. Believing this allowed me to discover the amazing love I share with my husband. And because I never gave up on my life and I always believed in the goodness of life, I wanted more than anything to bring children into this world. My husband and I are the proud parents of two incredible people: an 18-year-old son and a 12-year-old daughter. My life is full and my life is rewarding. So I have come to believe that my purpose in surviving is to show others that being a victim does not have to mean the end of one's hopes, dreams and happiness. Maybe my story can show others that, though the memories still remain, I have not let them cripple me and prevent me from enjoying the great life that I know I deserve.

So how can hearing about my experience and my recovery help you? What do I want you to take away from here tonight?

1) Being a victim of a crime, especially one of a sexual nature, is a terrible crime that leaves many emotional scars. If you know a victim of a crime, please reach out to them. Be patient and understanding as they heal. If you have been a victim of a crime, please seek help. Do not deal with this alone. Reach out to family, friends, teachers, and community resources. I attribute a major part of my healing to my family who embraced me with love; my friends who listened to me when I needed to talk, then showed me that fun and laughter were still a part of my life; my professors who showed compassion when I had difficulty concentrating in the weeks after the assault; the police who believed in me and treated me with dignity and respect; my coach who gave me the confidence to return to the sport of running, and especiallly to the people of this community, many total

216

strangers, who reached out to my family and me with words of comfort. Let the support and love you receive from those who care about you lift you up and restore your faith in humankind. This walk is a reminder that we cannot, and should not, walk alone in our battle to overcome.

2) Be a survivor for a better today and tomorrow and do not remain a victim of yesterday. Acknowledge your victimization and accept it, but then make the decision to move on and grow from the trauma. Find renewed strength and courage as you take the steps to regain control of your life. You do have the strength to do this. Commit to believing that no one can take away your belief in yourself and your strength unless you let them. Empower yourself with the belief that life can be good. And then pick up the pieces and live the life that you deserve. You are stronger than you think.

.   .   .   .   .

Three years after Oxygen Channel aired Leigh's story, the Investigative Discovery (ID) television channel did another take on the same story, only with a slightly different slant. This show was a part of their "Sins and Secrets" series in which they reveal past crimes in small towns. There was a double focus; one being on the town of Boone, the other on Leigh's heroic story. As with the Oxygen Channel series, Leigh was interviewed extensively for this show, but they used professional actors to play the key roles. We received a lot of positive feedback from this show, comments such as, "Every college freshman should watch this show."

Leigh was well-known in Watauga County prior to these two television productions. But the local interest generated by two television programs greatly increased her visibility. It seemed that there was no one in Boone or in the county who hadn't heard of Leigh Wallace, even if they didn't know her personally. One afternoon in late 2011 or early 2012, Louise and I were riding down the mountain with Leigh and Chris to attend one of Haleigh's varsity basketball games. Chris was driving, and as we were going through Blowing Rock on Highway 321, a highway patrolman pulled behind us and turned on his blue lights. Chris immediately pulled into a business parking lot.

"I wasn't paying attention to my speed," he said, obviously embarrassed.

Chris lowered his window as the patrolman approached. "Sir, may I see your license and registration, please?" The patrolman had his note pad out, ready to write Chris a speeding ticket.

As he looked at Chris's license and registration, the patrolman said, "Mr. Wallace, the reason I stopped you is because I clocked you at 47 miles per hour in a 35 mile per hour zone." As he was speaking, the patrolman glanced into the back seat where Louise and Leigh were sitting.

He did a double take, then he said to Leigh, "Ma'am, you're Leigh Cooper Wallace, aren't you?"

"Yes, I am," replied Leigh.

He then told us his name and said, " Ma'am, it's my honor to meet you. We appreciate what you have done for this community." He then handed the license and registration back to Chris and said, "Please drive carefully, Mr. Wallace, and you folks have a nice day."

It wouldn't have been surprising or unusual for a Boone policeman or a sheriff's deputy to recognize Leigh. They all knew her. But for a state patrolman, whom we did not know, to recognize her immediately was a surprise, and a pleasant one at that. And Leigh had one-name recognition. Most of her students and current athletes called her "Coach Leigh." Former students and athletes, and persons in and out of the Wellness Center and ASU knew her as "Leigh." Almost anywhere in Boone or Watauga County, the mention of the name "Leigh" would bring instant recognition. The speaker need not clarify to whom he or she was referring.

CHAPTER ELEVEN

FAMILY

As much as Leigh loved running and coaching, her first love was and always had been her family. When she was so close to death, her thoughts were primarily on her family and how her death would affect them. She had a beautiful marriage with Chris; they weren't making a lot of money, merely living month to month, but they loved each other and were very happy together. With son, Jacob, and daughter, Haleigh, they had what anyone would call the perfect family.

In 1995, Louise's sister Lillian died unexpectedly of a heart attack at the age of 47. Louise was upset that she had never told her sister how she really felt about her, that she loved her. In a discussion at the dinner table a month or two later, Leigh expressed the idea that each member of our family should share our feelings with each other. Having been so close to an unexpected death herself a few years earlier, she especially wanted each of us to know how she felt about us. She asked each of us to write a note to each other immediate family member. The notes that Leigh wrote about her mom and me and each of her siblings speaks volumes of her love for her family.

About Dad - from Leigh:

I discovered early on that an easy way to get through to my dad was through sports. I decided then to put all my energy into being an athlete. Winning races was fun, but the true prize was the smile on my dad's face and the pat on the back and hearing the words, "Proud of ya, Bud." My high school years were not very successful. But like any great coach who sees an athlete with potential, my dad never gave up on me. He wrote me letters in college encouraging me, telling me to believe in myself. He ended most of his letters with, "You can do it!" I finally did do it in my last year of college - I ran at, or near, my potential. I hope it meant as much to him as it did to me because he's the one who got me there. I still race today. Why? Somewhat for the money, somewhat for the fun of winning, but mostly for that pat on the back.

Although he may not even realize it, I have followed in Dad's footsteps. I am not an Army officer, I am not calm and methodical; I don't plan ahead very well; I'm late everywhere I go, and I'm not very sensible and practical. But, I have molded myself into the role that I feel best describes him . . . I'm a coach.

221

About Mom - from Leigh:

I think it's happening. I've been warned about it for years. They say there is nothing you can do to stop it. I'm turning into my mom.

Well, maybe I shouldn't pat myself on the back just yet. As I sit here and reflect on all the things she has done and all that she means to so many people, I realize I have a long way to go. I still have to raise all my children with nothing but love and understanding - with each child believing that he or she is my favorite. All of my children must grow up to become my best friend and always come to me in times of need. To become my mom, I'll have to be the first person my children want to call when they have great news. I'll always have to be fair and honest. I'll have to be willing to help anyone, anytime - even if it means taking time away from myself. I'll need to know all the right things to say to someone who is troubled or hurting. And I can't always expect these people to come to me. I must reach out to them. The list of requirements could go on and on. But already, it overwhelms me. I don't know if I can do it. It's not coming as naturally as everyone said it would. I am finding that becoming my mom is going to be the hardest thing I have ever done. But I look at my mom and I know that all the rewards are worth it. I won't stop trying.

About Julie - from Leigh:

Take one carefree, laid back girl who doesn't mind breaking the rules a bit and who doesn't care when she gets to where she's going. Blend in a slightly younger girl who is the complete opposite - a girl who must play by the rules because that's the only fair way to do it; a girl who is fiercely independent with a quick mind and a tongue to match. Throw these two girls into many situations together as they grow. Move them to a far away land, helping them to see that a great friend can be found in the other. Stir them around a bit to make sure that their taste in boys differs dramatically (this will help to keep the batter from becoming too lumpy). Whisk them off to college together, once again forcing them to turn to each other. Set the temperature at exactly 350 degrees. If either girl gets too hot, there could be trouble and the cake may fall.

Many are tempted to give up on this recipe when this happens.

It's a confusing recipe - calling for ingredients that may not always mix well. But even if the cake falls, don't throw it out. With love and patience and understanding, the cake will rise again. It may not be the prettiest cake, but once you savor its rich flavor, you'll want to try it again and again and again.

About Holley - from Leigh:

"It was a beautiful day. The sun beat down. They had the radio on. She was flyin'! Runnin' down a dream."

This song lyric, by Tom Petty, perfectly describes Holley's conference meet during her junior year at Furman. Leading up to that race, Holley had had a somewhat frustrating season. Her times were a minute slower than they had been the year before, and girls whom she had beaten in previous years were now beating her. As far as finishing in the top-10 to be named All-Conference, Holley was definitely an underdog. Of course, the whole family was there to support her. Each of us must have privately thought, "If I'm there, Holley can do it!" I'm sure we all had our own little pep-talks to give her, too. But, as usual, my dad was the only one who actually tracked her down to give her all the last-minute advice she could ever need. What did he tell her? Were they magic words?

I'll never forget the last 800 meters of that race. It was racing in its purest form. Although she has run faster times before, I have never seen her run as HARD as she did that day. Her arms were pumping, her legs were strong and striding so far. I tried to keep up with her the last 200 meters, screaming the whole way. At that moment, her 9th place finish felt like Olympic gold. We all shared in her glory and we all walked away inspired by what she had willed herself to do. What a great day!

About Graig - from Leigh:

Graig is very special to me. He is the brother I had always wanted and finally got. I'll never forget Dad coming to my school the day Graig was born and calling Julie and me to the office to tell us . . . "It's a BOY!" Great moment. Everyone wondered if Graig would be a sissy since he had three older sisters. That kind of thinking ceased once

Graig began eating three-inch-long crickets and daddy-longlegged spiders. He seemed to enjoy grossing us out by crawling up to us with half an insect hanging out of his mouth. Over the years, Graig continued to prove that he was 100% boy - he was loud, obnoxious, and hyper. But all of this was fine with me because I had always wanted a brother. And he was my brother.

Strangely, Graig calmed down - way down. I guess all those years of being hyper wore him out. He is now a mellow, even-tempered young man. He is everything I had always wanted in a brother - smart, good-looking, athletic. He is also mature beyone his years. Uncharacteristic of teenage boys, he is sympathetic to the feelings of others, he enjoys being around his family, and I have seldom ever seen him angry. I am always proud of him and I truly adore him. He's my brother.

Leigh   **Claude**   **Louise**

As with all my children, I always considered myself Leigh's coach. It's not that any of them needed coaching by me, but I felt so much pride whenever they were competing and I could say, "Yes, that's my kid out there." In Leigh's case, I think the most significant impact I had on her was the fact that I never doubted her ability. Even when she was struggling with her weight and injuries, I knew she was an elite athlete and eventually she would realize her potential. I always tried to drum that message into her and never let her doubt her ability.

Leigh and her mom, Louise, had a special relationship that seemed to grow stronger every year. They were so much alike, neither ever letting a thought go unsaid. Neither did anything or made a decision without consulting with the other. There was no doubt in Leigh's mind that her mom had the answer to any possible teaching situation that might arise. They would have lengthy conversations almost every night about teaching and mentoring. And Louise would not think of buying a blouse or selecting a paint color for a room in the house without consulting Leigh.

Although they had ups and downs as any sisters close in age would, Leigh and Julie were best friends. Relocating as often as we did because of my military career may have had something to do with their close friendship. They always had each other to rely on while trying to develop new friendships. It was uncanny how each of them always seemed to know exactly what the other was thinking. For example, in the year 2010, we had a typical family dinner at our house to celebrate Mother's Day. After we finished eating, we stayed at the table and each presented Louise with her Mother's Day gift. I was the last; I handed Louise three presents, each the same size and shape but individually wrapped by me, each with different color wrapping paper. Leigh and Julie looked at each other with slightly raised eyebrows, each thinking exactly the same thing, that this probably was not going to go well. Louise opened my first gift; it was a blouse. Everyone ooh'ed and aah'ed in unison. She then opened the second gift by me, another blouse, same design but different color. Leigh and Julie immediately looked at each other. Holley also picked up on it, sharing the wide-eyed, mouth slightly open look that her sisters demonstrated. Louise then opened the third gift from me – another blouse, same style, different color. When Louise held this blouse up, the three sisters could hold it in no longer; they all burst out laughing, as did Louise.

"Dad's been to WalMart," said Leigh, as they all laughed.

Of course I had been to WalMart; I do all my shopping there. I was in and out in 10 minutes When Louise took them back to WalMart to exchange them for something else, the clerk asked if there was anything wrong with the blouses.

"No," replied Louise, "my husband picked them out."

"Say no more," said the clerk.

After Leigh's phenomenal success in her senior year of college, Julie decided she wanted to run again the next year, which would be her senior year. She had not run competitively since she was a freshman, and had gained a little weight. Naturally she asked Leigh to get her in shape, that she wanted to run for ASU. Leigh ran with her and coached her throughout that summer. The mental toughness Julie gained from Leigh enabled Julie to finish second in the Southern Conference cross-country championship race to earn All-Conference honors.

Being six years apart in age, Leigh and Holley weren't close until Holley reached her teenage years. As Holley became heavily involved in competitive swimming and running, the activities that Leigh excelled in, they began to develop a strong bond. Although Leigh didn't begin coaching at Watauga High until the year after Holley graduated from high school, she certainly had an influence on Holley's success as a runner. Like Leigh, Holley continued running and competing after college, as she and Leigh ran many road and trail races together. They also did many training runs together, talking non-stop the entire way. When Leigh became the first lacrosse coach at Watauga High, she asked Holley to be her assistant, a natural fit for two coaches who loved working together to inspire their young team.

Leigh was Graig's biggest fan, and she was a true hero to Graig. Like Leigh, Graig was an elite athlete, one of the best high school wrestlers in the state of North Carolina in his junior and senior years. In both years he was the state runner-up at 171 pounds in scholastic wrestling, and he won state championships in freestyle and greco-roman wrestling. As she did with her runners, Leigh gave Graig focus cards before his regional and state championship matches. She actually played a significant role in his success as a wrestler and as a soccer player. To ensure that no one trained harder than Graig, she took him on long runs after wrestling practice, not only improving his stamina, but also building a strong bond between the two of them. In the final match of the state wrestling championships his senior year, a title he was heavily favored to win, Graig made a crucial mistake that caused him to lose the match. The next day, Leigh took a depressed Graig on a long run and told him his life would not be defined by a few minutes on a wrestling mat. "This experience will help you deal with much more important issues and difficulties to come," she said. Those words definitely proved prophetic later in Graig's life. Leigh knew Graig better than anyone in the family. This bond enabled her to counsel and mentor him in later years when he was struggling as a single parent in San Francisco.

Julie, Graig, Leigh, Holley

I retired from the Army in January, 1993, after serving as Professor of Military Science at Appalachian State University and was very fortunate to begin a second career with ASU as the Director of Administrative Support Services. Louise and I loved the Boone area and decided that we would seek the perfect location outside of town to spend the remaining years of our lives. After three months of searching, we found a beautiful 23-acre tract of land near the small community of Todd. Our purchase offer was accepted, and I began a labor of love that would consume me and my family for years. I first began building a road to the highest point on the land where we would eventually build our dream house. I then built a barn, thinking we might eventually put horses on the property.

Leigh and Chris helped clear brush and stack logs from the trees I cut down to create a lane for a road to our likely house site. They also began to talk about building a house for their family. We found a spot in a lower section of the property suitable for a driveway from the county road, and Chris and I became general contractors for the construction of a house for Chris and Leigh and their children. Chris was listed as the contractor since we were building his house, but I did all the coordinating with sub-contractors and inspectors. I was also the bank, as I negotiated a construction loan to fund the project. We built the house in less than a year, and they occupied it in 1995, taking over the mortgage. Then, during Graig's senior year in high school, 1998, we began construction of our house near the top of what we would later call Cooper Ridge, almost directly above Leigh and Chris's house.

It was great being neighbors, but after a couple of years, Leigh and Chris realized that their mortgage payment was eating too much of their monthly income. Chris had not returned to teaching after his one-year stint at East Burke Junior High and was working as office manager for a company called Belzona of Boone. While his boss at Belzona was very good to Chris and became good friends to all our family, the job did not command a high salary, nor did it offer much in the way of advancement. The real estate market was booming in the High Country at that time, though, so Leigh and Chris decided to test their house on the market. When they received an offer that would net them a considerable profit, they sold their house with the idea of eventually building another house closer to our house. After they sold their house, they rented in Valle Crucis while they began planning and building their dream house.

Leigh was not very happy living on the other side of the county and a 45-minute drive from our house on Cooper Ridge. Also, they weren't accomplishing their goal of saving money. They didn't hesitate when we suggested that they move in with us while working on their new house. Leigh, meanwhile, had been studying every magazine she could find on house plans and designs until eventually she had a firm picture in her mind of the house that she wanted. A local designer friend drew up the plans, and we launched this major construction project. I again did most of the coordinating with subcontractors, and Julie's husband, Steve, who was an excellent finish carpenter, did the trim and much of the carpentry work. Chris and I pitched in wherever we could.

The house was not easy to build, particularly with a roof that had many angles and several different slopes. Also, Leigh insisted on a first-class kitchen with tailor-made cabinets and countertops. The house became considerably more costly than any of us anticipated, but they moved into their new home in 2006. Leigh was proud of everything about that house. And she kept it spotless. She loved to host dinners for family and/or friends. Anyone who entered the house found Leigh wiping down countertops or the table or the floor. No speck of dust lasted more than a few seconds anywhere in Leigh's house.

.   .   .   .   .

Chris was an outstanding athlete. He played baseball and football in high school, and was the star running back on ASU's club football team. Chris had great speed but was not a distance runner. As Jake and Haleigh grew and became involved in sports, it was clear they had inherited the best of each parent's genes. Jake began playing Little League Baseball in May, 2000, at the age of nine. Prior to Little League he had played T-Ball and coach-pitch and he was showing outstanding athletic ability. Chris signed up to coach Little League and became Jake's coach. Jake pitched, played shortstop, and sometimes catcher, and was always an excellent hitter. Jake made the All-Star team each year, and Louise, Leigh, Chris and I rode together to all away games. We never missed a game, home or away. Leigh was never happier than when watching Jake or Haleigh play sports. As they grew older they continued to excel in every sport they attempted, Jake in baseball, football, and basketball, and Haleigh in basketball, soccer, and volleyball. Jake made the high school varsity baseball team as a freshman. In football, he played quarterback in youth league through the Junior Varsity team in the 9th grade. He was moved to tight end on the varsity team for his last three years of high school. He also played varsity basketball as a senior in high school. Jake was hampered by injuries throughout his high school sports career, topped off by a severely broken leg prior to his senior year which prevented him from playing football that year. In the final scrimmage before the start of the season in his senior year, on the last play of the scrimmage, Jake was playing quarterback when he was tackled from behind with a horse-collar tackle. His leg was caught under him when he fell and snapped just above the ankle. Leigh called us in tears to tell us Jake's high school football career was probably over. Several colleges had recruited Jake before the injury, but interest waned due to his injuries and his inability to play football his senior year.

Through grammar school and middle school, Haleigh was a superstar in volleyball and basketball. She was also the strongest middle school distance runner in the county. I thought Haleigh was a better runner in the 7th and 8th grade than Leigh had been at that age. But Haleigh wasn't interested in running - perhaps because she didn't want to be compared to her mom - so she chose not to run in high school. She decided to concentrate on basketball in high school, and it was a good decision, as she became the starting point guard on the varsity squad, the only freshman to make the varsity team. At any game we attended, Leigh was the biggest cheerleader; she loved to watch her kids play sports and she was extremely proud of them.

When Jake was a junior in high school, Watauga High participated in a student exchange program, initially with Germany.

Leigh was asked if she would be willing to host a student. She and Chris had plenty of room in their new house at Todd, so they volunteered to host a German exchange student, Hendrik Jodl, who lived with them and attended Watauga High for a school year. He and Jake became great friends, and Hendrik's family reciprocated by having Jake visit them the next year.

A few years later, Leigh and Chris hosted another exchange student, this time a young girl from China, Wendy Xiao. Wendy lived with them for an entire year, which included a trip to the beach reunion with the family.

Haleigh, Jake, Leigh, Chris

Leigh's love wasn't restricted to her immediate family. From childhood, Leigh's favorite time every year was the Cooper family reunion at the beach, where she spent a week with the extended family: cousins, aunts and uncles, and her grandparents. Even when we lived in Puerto Rico in the early-to-mid 80's, we never missed the beach reunion.

A house called "Ruby Red" at Garden City Beach served as our reunion headquarters until 1989, when Hurricane Hugo picked it up and dumped it into the marsh about a fourth of a mile away. We then moved a few miles up the South Carolina coast to Surfside Beach and have been meeting there ever since. Eventually, as the Cooper families grew, we rented separate houses for each family, all within a block of each other.

To ensure quality time together, we began the tradition of the entire Cooper family gathering at the same house once a day for the main meal. Of course, with Leigh around, there was never any doubt that we would have quality time together. She always organized activities and encouraged maximum participation. Quite often, Leigh was the glue that held things together; she was the sparkplug who lit a fire under everyone whenever things slowed down or when the collective energy faded. Leigh planned games and organized activities to bring everyone together, either on the beach during the day, or at one of the houses at night. These daily activities included beach volleyball, softball, or just getting together at a beach site to sun and watch the kids in the ocean. At night, we played Charades, or board games, or marathon Spades tournaments. For Spades, partners remained partners for life. Having the same partners year after year enabled cheating to become sophisticated, with hand signals, cue words, and various grunts and coughs occurring constantly. Everyone, in good humor, accused everyone else of cheating, and everyone was correct.

Leigh was not only the sparkplug; she was also the mediator when things did not go smoothly. Rarely did family members have a serious disagreement at the beach, but on the few occasions it did occur, Leigh took responsibility for ensuring that the disagreement was immediately resolved.

To say that Leigh was everyone's favorite person in the extended family would be unfair. But I think it safe to say that everyone, old and young, looked up to Leigh, sought her approval, and cherished the moments they spent with her. She took it upon herself every year to give individual attention to everyone at the beach and to let them know they were special in her eyes. She never publicly acknowledged any particular cousin or aunt or uncle as her favorite, but she wanted each family member to believe that he or she was indeed her favorite. I think Leigh's desire to make everyone feel special started when she was a child visiting my parents, her grandparents. My mom had many pictures of all the grandchildren scattered throughout her house. On every table in every room, pictures were displayed. Leigh and her cousins, particularly Larry Carl, argued over which of them was Grandmommy's favorite grandchild. And to reinforce one's argument, the first to arrive at Grandmommy's house rearranged the pictures, ensuring that his or her picture was in the most prominent spot on the table or on the wall. These arguments were serious when they were young kids but later became a running joke. But the notion of being special stuck with Leigh, and she wanted everyone to feel special.

While there was not a set venue and time for Dickert reunions (Louise's side of the family), we had frequent gatherings and special occasions with the cousins, aunts and uncles and grandparents as well. Leigh loved when all the Dickert family got together at Granny's house.

Leigh was two years old when I went to Vietnam for my second tour. Louise, Leigh, and Julie went to Rock Hill to live with Louise's parents for the year I was away. Louise's sister, Jane and Jane's husband, Jimmy, and son, Shaw, also lived there. Shaw was Leigh's age, so he became very close to Leigh and Julie; as a matter of fact, he became one of Leigh's favorite people for life. In later years, Shaw would often accompany us on summer vacations, and Leigh and Julie looked for any opportunity to spend time with Jane, Jimmy, Shaw, and Shaw's young brother, Kurt.

When Holley was born, Leigh and Julie spent two weeks with Jane and Jimmy. Leigh's independent streak was evident even at this young age. As much as she loved her time with them, when Jane brought her home, Leigh boldly announced, "Aunt Jane, I'm home now. You aren't the boss of me anymore!"

Leigh's Final Beach Reunion, 2012

**L-R: Claude, Louise, Findley, Regan, Julie, Riley, David, Cade,
Holley, Coen, Haleigh, Jacob, Leigh, Chris**

CHAPTER TWELVE

"THIS CAN'T BE HAPPENING"

CLAUDE

I don't know anyone who was happier than Leigh in the year 2012. She was doing everything she wanted to do. The year before, 2011, Watauga High started a new varsity sport for boys and girls. Lacrosse had been a club sport for a couple of years, but with the new high school came a state-of-the-art lacrosse field. Athletic Director Tom Wright asked Leigh and Chris if they would coach the girls' and boys' teams, respectively. Neither of them had ever even seen a lacrosse game and knew absolutely nothing about the sport, but they agreed to coach. They wanted to continue to impact young peoples' lives. Leigh and Chris fell in love with lacrosse, and their teams were thrilled to have them as coaches. By 2012, their second seasons, both teams were having some success and winning games. During her first year the coach of the club team became Leigh's assistant, and he taught her some of the finer points of the game. Then, for 2012, she hired her sister, Holley, as her assistant.

In addition to coaching lacrosse, Leigh taught her fitness and healthful living classes at the high school; she taught future health education teachers at ASU; she taught spin classes at the Wellness Center; she was heavily involved in Crossfit at the Wellness Center, where she set the standard for drive and determination; and she still ran 5 to 10 miles almost every day. Leigh was widely known and respected in the county. She was the brightest star in any room she entered, sharing her love of life with others.

During fall semester of 2012, a group of Pakistani students and teachers came to the Watauga County school system as part of an exchange program, and Leigh volunteered to be a host family. Two of the teachers who were leaders in the group were assigned to live with Leigh and Chris for two weeks. Samina and Muzzana were beautiful ladies who seemed very comfortable with our western lifestyle.

The first night that Samina and Muzzana stayed at Leigh's house, Leigh invited Louise and me to eat with them. She wanted her guests to meet her parents and see the closeness we shared. As usual, the house was spotless, and Leigh prepared a wonderful meal. The conversation was mostly about family, as Leigh shared many of our family stories. At one point toward the end of the evening Leigh asked Samina, obviously the more outgoing of the two, what was the most surprising thing she had learned about the US since she arrived. Samina answered that she had always heard that Americans don't treat the elderly well: that as soon as parents showed a little age or the least bit of senility, the family shipped them to an old folks' home, a managed care facility. She was surprised to learn our family had a different approach. At this revelation, Leigh was even more determined to show her love for us. She boasted that one reason she wanted to live so close to Louise and me was so she could take care of us in our old age. And Leigh assured them that any of her siblings would gladly do the same.

A few nights later, we had Samina and Muzzana to our house for dinner with the entire family, including Holley's and Julie's families. As usual, after the meal, we all sat around the table for two more hours telling family stories and laughing non-stop. I can't imagine a happier family. Leigh had been feeling the effects of flu-like symptoms for a few days, but you wouldn't know it by her laughter and spirit at the dinner table.

At the Pakistani farewell dinner
Friday, Dec 14, 2012

LOUISE

Her Final Days

The nightmare began the next night after a farewell dinner for the visiting Pakistani teachers and students and their host families. Leigh finally faced a battle that even her strength could not overcome.

Leigh was at her finest at the farewell dinner, wearing a beautiful Pakistani dress to show her complete embrace of the culture of her guests. Americans and Pakistanis alike shared stories of their time together, and it was a time of true understanding and peace among people of very different cultures. As many recalled, Leigh was the last one to regale the group with the story of a young boy named Balal and his antics at the high school, her natural storytelling ability leaving the crowd laughing as they prepared to say good-bye to their new friends.

After returning home, Chris realized that Leigh was very ill. She had complained of flu-like symptoms all week but in her typical way had ignored her illness in order to make it through the evening's event. They decided at midnight to go to the emergency room at the hospital in Boone. For several hours, Leigh was evaluated with routine tests: a flu test, chest x-ray, but no blood work. With no apparent red flags, she was diagnosed with acute bronchitis, given several prescriptions, and sent home. She had weakened to the point that she could not walk unassisted, and the hospital even offered a wheelchair to enable her to get to the car. With the various drugs she was given and the night without sleep, it didn't seem unusual to us that she slept soundly throughout the next day. I checked on her a few times and tried to talk with her, but she remained in a deep sleep. She did manage to text Julie that she felt "like death."

With family always at the forefront of her thoughts, Leigh had planned a family "Christmas" celebration for her two Pakistani guests that night, asking our entire family and other friends to come for dinner and a traditional gift exchange. These plans, of course, had to be changed, and Chris left to take their guests to town for dinner elsewhere. With the same mother's intuition that I had when Leigh was missing, I sensed I needed to stay with her while Chris was gone. Leigh slept on, stirring only to reach for her meds by her bedside. I wondered if perhaps she had taken an overdose and even counted the pills to check. She managed to stumble out of bed for the first time that day to go to the bathroom. When I helped her back in bed, I realized how very weak she was - no muscle tone and a gray pall to her face. At that moment I realized her illness was not simply acute bronchitis. Something serious was wrong. When Chris returned, Claude came down and we all agreed she must return to the hospital. I volunteered to take her, as Chris was exhausted from his previous night without sleep. We had to carry her to the car and at that point, she was unable even to say good-bye to Chris; she just waved a slight farewell.

I parked at the emergency entrance and ran in to get help. They took her into the hospital in a wheelchair while I parked the car; and by the time I got inside, she had been rushed to a treatment room, and six or eight people were frantically working on her. This was my first moment of true fear; the attending doctor was a fellow Crossfit partner of Leigh's and her first words to me were, "She is very, very sick; you need to call her husband." A few minutes later, maybe half an hour, they took me out for a consultation. One of the doctors showed me the x-ray of her lungs, a total whiteout of one lung and the other lung approaching a whiteout. Dr. Newell, a friend of ours who was there for another patient, came with me, and when they asked me for permission to intubate her, I was at a loss. What did this mean? How was I supposed to answer this question? I turned to Dr. Newell and he nodded. They sent me to the waiting room while they performed the procedure, which required sedating her heavily. Our Leigh, as we knew her, was gone from us forever.

The hospital staff prepared Leigh for medical evacuation to Johnson City Medical Center in Tennessee. The weather on the east side of the mountains that night prevented travel to the medical centers in Charlotte or Winston-Salem. Chris and Jake had arrived at the hospital by then, and we were ushered into a small room to speak with a doctor. After explaining that she had severe pneumonia, he repeated over and over, "I'm sorry; I'm so sorry." We were puzzled by his words; weren't

240

they sending her to another hospital to get treatment for her recovery? How could she be so sick that she would not recover?

As she flew by helicopter, Chris, Jake, and I flew in our car through blinding rain to Johnson City. I remember that trip as one of almost complete silence, each of us absorbed in our own thoughts: "Please, God, don't let them tell us that she has died."

Our last glimmer of hope came when we arrived. She was resting peacefully in a bed in ICU, still in an induced sleep, tubes already in place, machines beeping. The doctor spoke to us briefly, saying that pneumonia this severe was usually fatal but that Leigh was young and strong, so he felt confident she would recover. The race was on to discover the bacteria causing her infection to enable them to treat her with the right antibiotic. We sat with her and waited, watching her numbers on the ever-beeping machines, looking for signs that her body was fighting this monster.

I had called Claude from the hospital in Boone before we left and asked him to wake Haleigh and bring her to Johnson City, not knowing what to expect. Word was quickly getting out to others that Leigh - Mrs. Wallace - Coach Wallace - was very ill and hospitalized. By morning, Julie and Holley had arrived, and my sister Jane and brother Les were there. Throughout the day, other friends came to offer support, staying in the waiting room to speak with us as we took turns "visiting" with Leigh in her ICU room. Our phones were lit up with texts, and one text in particular stood out; it was my friend Todd, a critical care nurse at Baptist Hospital in Winston-Salem. He gave me questions to ask, numbers to look at, options to consider. He was a medical resource - and a true comfort - in this time of fear and uncertainty.

The doctors had few answers, but one thing stayed with me. On Sunday morning, the doctor on duty spoke to Chris and me about her prognosis; I will never forget her words: "Leigh is on a high level of oxygen, which in and of itself can be toxic. She is in septic shock, and if she recovers, she may be an invalid the rest of her life." Was it at this point that I began losing all hope? Perhaps it was later that day when the doctor told us her white blood count was so low that Chris and I would be the only ones allowed to be with her, and we would need to wear masks. I became fixated on the machines, willing her blood pressure to rise, her oxygen level to rise - anything to give us hope.

By midnight, everyone except Chris, Jane, Les and me had left to rest at a nearby hotel. Around 2:00 am, another doctor gave us the news that her organs were beginning to fail - warning us, I'm sure, of what was to come. A vision replays in my head to this day: the nurse coming in to check on her, looking up, then opening the two wide doors of her room. Chris had stepped out for a few minutes and they told me to get him. As I raced down the hall, I could hear the words that every patient's loved ones fear: CODE BLUE! CODE BLUE! Efforts to resuscitate her were in vain.

Our precious Leigh died at 4:45 that cold Monday morning. Despite her strength and determination, she could not beat the MRSA pneumonia that took her life at the age of 43.

.   .   .   .
.

The next few hours were a blur. Claude, Julie, and Holley had rushed to the hospital to find Chris and me huddled on the floor outside Leigh's room. We were ushered into a small room. A family gathering - our best times for many years, now a time of disbelief and mourning. A call to Graig, so far away in San Francisco and so alone in his grief. We each said our good-byes to Leigh, then made the long trip back to Boone, heading back to a home that would never be the same.

The news of Leigh's death spread quickly. Before the day was over, there were several posts on Facebook showing a picture of the huge rock at the high school. It was painted blue and black with white letters saying, "You're STRONGER than you think," lacrosse sticks and hearts painted on either side of the lettering, and "LW" at the bottom – a beautiful and heartfelt display of love and respect from the Watauga High students.

HOLLEY

The Visitation and Memorial Service

December 19, 2012

Thursday night, I think. No wait, Wednesday. I've lost track.

We're at Watauga High School thanks to the generosity of Marshall Gasperson and Tom Wright, Principal and Athletic Director respectively. They had come by the house on Monday evening and offered the use of the high school for the visitation and memorial service.

I've been standing for three hours. I still can't see the end of the line.

Someone is holding up the line, speaking to my mother. I have a chance to grab some water. I turn around and look on the floor where I left it. Not there. My cousin Kelly sees my look of despair. "What is it? What do you need?"

"I left my water right there."

"I got it. Don't worry." She runs off to get me another one. By the time she returns, the line is moving again. Water will have to wait.

Next person. "I'm so sorry for your loss. She was such a wonderful person." I've heard this phrase at least a hundred times tonight. It means something every single time. I'm not sure who is the current speaker of the phrase, and she doesn't feel compelled to tell me. I thank her, and she moves on to my brother.

I look to where the line disappears around the corner, to the people waiting to cry with us. I immediately recognize Colleen, Leigh's best friend from high school. Does she still live in Kansas? Did she come all this way?

When I think I'm too exhausted, dehydrated, and empty to cry anymore, someone comes along and helps the tears flow again. My friends, my co-workers, my boss. I'm so moved by the people who are here for me.

I've been talking to a young man who wants our family and me to know how much Leigh, his health teacher, influenced him in high school. She encouraged him to exercise, eat healthy food, make smart choices. We've heard this story many times tonight. As he walks away, I turn to see a familiar face from work coming through the line with the parents of my sweet Elli, a young child in my special needs class at Hardin Park Elementary School. My eyes immediately drop to their hips, and there she is, dutifully walking along with her parents, holding her dad's hand. Is she wondering why they've brought her out past her bedtime to greet all these somber strangers? Or are her thoughts not that complex? We don't know. She can't tell us.

More people...

"Thank you."

"Thank you so much."

"Yes I know. She was. Thank you for coming."

Elli produces smiles throughout the line. Her father has picked her up to give her tiny legs a break and to be at eye level with my parents. She tilts her head and focuses her right eye on my mother's broken face.

More people, more "thank you's."

Elli's father sets her down and holds her hand again before they get to me. I squat down to her eye level, and Elli's serious face breaks into a smile. Her father lets go of her hand, and she takes a few unbalanced steps into my arms. "Hi, Elli. I'm so happy to see you!" This time there are no tears, just a genuine smile brought on by this precious nine-year-old girl.

I hug her mother, her father, and Cindy, the physical therapist from school, who was walking through the line with them. We talk for a couple minutes, but I know that Elli needs to get to bed, so I thank them for bringing her and let them go.

I can finally see the end of the line. I don't know how we made it through this night. I'm exhausted physically and mentally, but *exhausted* doesn't even begin to describe how I feel emotionally. I think about the number of people tonight I've had to speak to, touch, hug. Close friends and family, co-workers, acquaintances, and complete strangers. It suddenly occurs to me that my usual social anxiety, my extreme fear of talking to people and having attention focused on me, has been strangely absent tonight.

After the final visitors have moved on, Tom lets us know they are ready for us in the auditorium if we still want to watch the video. It's about 9:30 now, but as tired as we are, we all want to see it. This video has played on repeat throughout the night. Visitors were directed first into the auditorium as they arrived to watch the video, and then they took their place in the receiving line after it was over. This process repeated itself for about four hours, with an estimated 3000+ people, according to Marshall. Not everyone came through the line. Some simply watched the video and left, perhaps not realizing the time commitment involved in this particular visitation.

Tom and Marshall lead us into the auditorium. We sit together in the center aisle, near the front, and the video begins. The video is a collection of photos Graig, Julie, and I had picked out and set to music. We sorted the photos by time period and other categories (friends, family, running, etc.). We even pulled some out of their frames from around the house if we thought they needed to be included. And then there were all the more recent ones we had on our phones. This was not an easy task, but I have a feeling it will always be significant to me. Graig, even in his grief, couldn't help but make fun of our 80's styles. We laughed together, and I immediately wondered if we should be laughing right now. *Is it OK to laugh without her? Is it OK to laugh when I am so torn apart inside?* But laughter was so important to her.

245

It's what this family does so well. Maybe it's even more important now than ever. I allowed the laughter to come, and maybe just a hint of healing began.

.   .   .   .   .

December 20, 2012

Thursday. I sleep in as long as my restless mind will allow. David took the boys to school this morning. They stayed home on Monday as they absorbed the shock of what has happened, but I didn't see any reason for them to continue to stay home all week, surrounded by overwhelming sorrow. Their teachers would let me know if I needed to come get them.

Last night wore me out, but it was a welcome change after two days of sitting around thinking about how everything is different now. Plenty of friends and family have been visiting at my parents' house and helping out. Jane Graham and Pegge Laine seemed to show up right away, and I'm not sure they ever left. They've been greeting visitors at the door, answering the phone, and making sure my mother eats and sleeps enough that she doesn't completely fall apart. The amount of food that has been delivered amazes me. Of course, none of us wants to eat, but at least we have something to offer all the visitors.

I walk into my closet and find my black skirt and a grey turtleneck sweater. It's raining, but at least it's not freezing cold for December. I cry in the shower. It's become a thing. I don't know why the shower brings my tears out.

After I'm ready, I find nice pants and sweaters for both boys and put them in a bag. David and I exchange very few words, but I appreciate his presence. He's going back to work tomorrow.

"Ready?"

"Yeah. Let's go."

We drive to Green Valley School and have the receptionist call the boys from their classes. They take their clothes into the closest bathroom and change. Then we all walk together to the cafeteria, where four different schools have set up a meal for all of our family and some close family friends, an opportunity to gather, coordinated by my mom's friends, Sandra, Brooke, Erin, and Erika. There are over 100 people here.

As I'm going through the line, I can't figure out what to eat. I pick out the things I would normally get - almost anything without meat - and find a table where there's enough room for the four of us. One of my cousins is talking to me. I hear him, I answer him, and I pick at my food. I imitate normal conversation, normal eating.

After lunch, we get in the car with the boys and take our place in the procession, heading towards the cemetery. Driving past the high school, we can see the parking lot is already filling up for the memorial service. We pass policemen directing traffic, some with tears in their eyes. We turn into the cemetery and head up the hill. Everyone who was at the lunch was also invited to the burial. Not open to the public, but still a large gathering of people, more than will fit under the canopy provided by the funeral home. Umbrellas pop up as the cars empty.

From the hilltop gravesite, we can look to the south and see the high school and the lacrosse field. When Chris came here with my parents on Monday to pick out a plot, he was discouraged by the lack of options. Most of the available plots were either too close to the highway or were on the back side of the hill. My parents, who had picked out their choice plots at this same cemetery years ago, looked at each other with the same thought. They gave Chris their plots.

Rain steadily falls as my cousin Shaw says a beautiful prayer to open the ceremony. My father then introduces my sister's "favorite uncle" Les, who tells some of his favorite memories of her. When he's finished, my father gets up again and introduces my sister's "favorite uncle" Mike. A sweet, quiet chuckle travels through the crowd. Leigh had convinced everyone they were her favorite. Both of my uncles' speeches are filled with more smiles and laughs than I thought were possible right now.

My father concludes the ceremony, and we all file back into our cars for the short trip to the high school. We are escorted into the side entrance, where there is a large classroom set up for family to gather before the service. I greet and hug a few family members who have just arrived in town. Someone gives me a handful of tissues to take in with me. I don't have pockets, so I stuff them in the waist of my skirt.

Marshall appears in the doorway. "We're ready." I grab another water bottle before taking my place in line, with David beside me, and our boys, Cade and Coen, right in front of us.

The line pauses in the hallway beside the gym. I take a deep breath before heading through the back door into the crowded high school gymnasium. The bleachers are filled, and rows of chairs cover the entire floor. Four empty rows in front await us.

I reach for David's hand as we walk down the aisle toward our seats. I feel so many eyes on me. Rather than sending my anxiety soaring, however, I am strangely comforted by the attention. Being the center of attention is welcome, necessary even. How long will this last? Has sudden extreme grief relieved me of my greatest flaw?

A stage is set up at the front of the gym. There are flowers, of course, and a podium and microphones. In front of the stage is an enlarged picture of my sister. After I sit, I look at the front of the program in my hand.

My head is spinning. This is real. No matter how much this feels like somebody else's story, I cannot deny that my own sister's name is on the front of the program:

Celebrating the Life of
Leigh Cooper Wallace
1969 - 2012

My sister, my best friend, next-door neighbor, running partner, coaching mentor. She's gone.

My father walks to the stage, and I pull my mind up from the swirling puddle it has become on the floor. I hear him thanking the school administrators on behalf of our family, and I hear him saying how difficult speaking at his daughter's memorial service is for him, this man who has been in combat twice and has been wounded and received numerous medals for valor and service.

I'm able to focus more on what he's saying as I hear him quoting Leigh:

"While I love to win races, I've never been the kind of person who says 'I hate to lose.' When I race, it's not just to win. I want to prove something. That is my prime motivator. And I don't know if I'm trying to prove something to myself, or to my competitors, but I feel like I have something to prove and I'm not going to give up easily. If I'm in a race and someone is faster than me, and they're beating me because they're just a faster runner, I can live with that. I can handle losing a race, but what I can't handle and won't stand for is not competing with every ounce of energy and strength that I have. For then, I let myself down, and I let my teammates down. I want to make people proud of me and prove to them that I can be good."

My dad talks about Leigh winning the three distance races at the conference outdoor track championship in her senior year.

He continues, *"Leigh's race is over now, but I know her legacy will live on. Those of you of faith can be comforted and perhaps inspired by the belief that Leigh is looking down on you with pride. We can all be inspired by the memory of the way she competed and coached and lived her life. If you're going to pick up your stick and go onto the lacrosse field, you know that she's going to expect you to give it everything you've got for the entire time you're in the game. Don't settle for anything less than your best."*

Despite his grief, he manages to give words of comfort to Chris, Jake, and Haleigh. He walks off the stage and takes his place next to my mother. This man doesn't look like my dad anymore. He looks ragged, older, fragile, yet I can't imagine him being stronger than he is right now. My dad spent 28 years in the Army and served two tours in

249

Vietnam. He helped his oldest daughter through a horrific nightmare no father should have to deal with. And now, 23 years later, he just stood in front of 3,000 people and said goodbye to her.

Louise and I decided that rather than have a minister preside at the memorial service, we would have selected speakers and some of Leigh's favorite music. I struggled through my short talk, thanking so many for coming to show their love and respect for Leigh. Watauga High Athletic Director (and Leigh's closest friend at school) Tom Wright spoke of the impact Leigh had on the high school and how she was loved and respected by students and faculty. Close family friend Jane Graham reminded all that God was in charge and that he had a plan, though we may not always understand. Shaw Blackmon, representing the Dickert cousins, praised Leigh's love of her family, particularly her cousins, all 27 of them. Larry Carl Nohrenberg spoke on behalf of the Cooper cousins. Knowing that any celebration of Leigh's life wouldn't be complete without some laughter, he recounted some of the youthful antics of Leigh and her cousins, including his constant debates with Leigh about who was Grandmommy's favorite. Joe Lion, speaking on behalf of Leigh's runners, made a beautiful and impassioned speech illustrating the impact Leigh had on others. He first read quotes sent by some of Leigh's former runners. He expressed admiration for the myriad activities in which Leigh was involved, the intensity with which she attacked every endeavor, and the dominating and powerful force she was in so many lives. Leigh's son, Jake, spoke of Leigh's love of family and how Leigh had inspired him to overcome the many obstacles and injuries he had suffered in his athletic career.

While listening to the speeches, each one wonderfully thought out and perfectly appropriate, Chris indicated he wanted to say something after the speeches ended. I wasn't sure he would be able to complete whatever he wanted to say, so I told Jake to remain on stage after his talk to help his dad if needed. Chris's final words captured the essence of Leigh's life when he encouraged everyone to "Look at the person next to you and tell them that you love them. Don't let that go unsaid."

The musical performances by Cam Haas and Abbie Foster, two

of Leigh's former students and Student Council leaders, were brilliant and added a wonderful touch to the ceremony. Julie and Chris had agreed on two of Leigh's favorite songs, "A Thousand Years" and "You Are So Beautiful," and Cam also sang a song he wrote, "Walking Dream Come True."

Each speaker had something different to say about Leigh, but the bottom-line message was the same for all: Leigh made an impact on people's lives. A line from Shaw's remarks still rings true: "Don't cry because it's over; smile because it happened."

After the memorial service, I am eager to change into jeans and a long-sleeve T-shirt. We all go up the hill to my parents' house. There is food everywhere - both refrigerators, the kitchen counters, the dining room, a couple of trays in the living room, and even in the laundry room.

Food everywhere, but not a whole lot of eating happening. The boys are hungry, so I help them fix their plates. I fix myself a plate and pick at it. I realize I'm going to have to force myself to eat at some point.

"Have you eaten anything since you got home?" I ask my mother.

"No."

"You should try to eat something. Want me to get you anything?"

"No, thanks. I'll try a little later."

Family members who are staying in town for the night arrive at the house. Many of my most treasured memories from my childhood include extended family on both my mother's side and my father's. My dad has three sisters and a brother. He and each of his siblings have at least three children. I have spent one week every summer at the beach with this family for as long as I can remember. We have also had countless Thanksgiving dinners, Christmas reunions, and Easter gatherings, mostly in the charming, historical towns of Sumter, SC, and Rock Hill, SC, where my grandparents lived.

Our greatest family legacy is love, despite any differences we have. This family spans the spectrum of political ideologies. We believe in a variety of philosophies on how to live our lives. Debates over current events are common, even when we vow to avoid them.

Sometimes debates lead to arguments, and sometimes feelings are hurt. Behind it all, however, is an immense love.

My mother grew up with one brother and four sisters. Her sister Nina didn't have children, but she and I share similar values and interests, so I have always felt a connection with her. My mother's other siblings gave me numerous cousins, some of whom I have spent entire summers with as a child. I also saw them regularly for holidays and other celebrations. I even went to college one year with my cousin Kelly, both of us on the cross-country and track teams. During the fall of my junior year, two years after Kelly graduated, her mother (my mom's sister Lil) was rushed to the hospital with a mystery illness that turned out to be a heart attack. The next day, still in the hospital, her heart gave out for good. The circumstances of our current situation with Leigh are eerily similar to Lil's sudden and shocking death seventeen years ago, a fact I heard mentioned more than once earlier today.

Having both my mother's and father's families together at the same time is unusual. Despite the tragedy that brought them all here, we can't help but smile and laugh as we catch up with each other's lives and reminisce about adventures from long ago. A nagging thought that keeps popping into my head is, *"Leigh is going to be so upset that she's missing this."* It's as if she's off traveling the globe, and when she gets back, I'll tell her everyone was together at our house having a good time.The reality returns quickly, however, and I am sad at the thought that there won't be an opportunity for her to be upset about missing anything anymore.

My dad gathers everyone together and thanks them for coming: "Leigh would love this gathering of both sides of our family, and if she were here, I'm sure she'd be the center of attention. Leigh loved her family more than anything, and you all know that she loved telling stories. So I think it would be good for us to tell some of her favorite stories. Now, most of the stories she told around here were at my expense, so I'll start with one of those. For a few years in a row, Leigh went down to the Myrtle Beach Marathon with some of her runners. One year, she talked our family into putting together our own team. Originally, it was supposed to be the men against the women, but the women in the family must have known they were gonna get beat because they kept mysteriously backing out."

Laughter erupts throughout the room. Julie chimes in, "Um, I was pregnant and Mom tore up her knee!" More laughter.

My dad continues, "So the team was me, Steve, Holley, Leigh, and Chris. The first four legs were to run 5 miles each, and then Chris would finish it up with the final 6.2. They decided I would be the lead runner to get us out to a good fast start."

I smile and roll my eyes. Leigh and I had come up with the order. We decided Dad should be first because we didn't want one of our faster runners getting slowed down by the crowds at the start. My dad was an incredible athlete and was certainly a great runner in his day, but he was in his early 60's when we ran this race in 2001, and he hadn't exactly kept up his running lately. Steve, Julie's husband at the time and our least experienced runner, would go second, I was third (about six weeks pregnant at the time), Leigh was fourth, and Chris was last. Leigh was by far our fastest runner and in the best shape, but Chris really wanted the challenge of doing the longer distance of the final runner. We decided Leigh could continue running after handing off to him to encourage him the rest of the way.

Dad continued, "Since Julie and Louise weren't running, they were in charge of driving the van around and dropping everybody off at their prospective exchange zones. They dropped me off at the start while it was still dark, and I headed over to scope out the starting area. There were thousands of people in this race, and I knew from experience that things could get pretty jammed up at the start of these big races. I didn't want to get caught up behind a bunch of slow people, so I made my way toward the front of the crowd. As I was investigating, I noticed there were grassy areas on either side of the road that would give me some extra space to avoid the crowd. There was a tree line along the left. I stationed myself on the far left near the tree line. I figured I'd try to get out as fast as I could but stay along the tree line until I settled into my pace."

"Now, most of you know that I don't hear so well. So as I was standing at the starting line, a guy got up on an overhead walkway and started making announcements over the speakers. All I hear is, 'Wah wah, wah wah, wah wah wah.'"

Everybody is cracking up at this point. I notice even my mom is chuckling.

"After a pause, I saw the starter raise the gun and evidently stated, 'Take your marks...' and then POW! The starter fired the gun! I took off running at a good sprint down the road. I knew there were several elite runners in this race, and I was sure they would quickly pass me, but somehow I was still alone at the front of the race. I could hear the huffing and puffing behind me, but it was taking them much longer than I expected to reach me. Then, sure enough, here they came. I looked to my side ... and saw several wheelchair athletes zoom past, some of them glancing over at me with glares on their faces."

My dad gets so animated when he tells stories. He is practically running in place when he describes starting out at a sprint, and now he is pumping his arms like a wheelchair racer and mimicking the dirty looks some of them gave him. The room is roaring with laughter as everyone pictures my dad starting the marathon with the wheelchair racers.

When the laughter dies down, he continues, "I figured the only way I could get out of this with any dignity was to act like I was just doing a stride to warm up for the race, so I just peeled off to the side into the trees and turned around to jog back to the starting line."

When the next round of laughter settles, Julie continues the next part of the story. "That afternoon as we ate at a restaurant, everyone told stories from their part of the race. My dad told us that story, and none of us believed him. We knew he'd done some embarrassing things in the past, but we thought this was too ridiculous even for him."

My dad motions for me to tell the hot tub part of the story now. I look at Julie, "No it's OK. You go ahead."

"So later that night as Leigh sat in the hot tub with some of her runners, they all told stories from the day. One of the guys said, 'I was the first runner on my team, and you guys won't believe what happened at the start! The gun went off for the wheelchair race, and some *old man* took off running with all the wheelchairs!'

As the others all laughed hysterically, Leigh said, 'Oh my God, that was my dad!'"

This revelation at my dad's expense produces another roar of laughter, of course. My dad loves laughing at himself and all his mishaps. It has never bothered him when people laugh at his expense. In fact, he often invites it. I inherited many qualities from my dad, but this is definitely not one of them. I also clearly did not inherit his storytelling ability. I can write it down, but speaking it out loud is a completely different ballgame. All three of my siblings are good storytellers, but nobody could entertain a room like Leigh. She had confidence and enthusiasm that captivated her audience. And she had such interesting stories.

December 22, 2012

Today is Coen's 9th birthday. We had his party with friends last Saturday. There is no way I could do it now anyway. I'm up early putting on layers of warm running clothes and waiting for my dad to pick me up. When I get in the car, he tells me that Graig is driving separately, and then we are quiet for much of the 40-minute drive out to Bass Lake.

Randy McDonough (Coach Mac) has been the head cross-country and track coach at Watauga since 1993. He was an assistant coach when I ran there in 1990, 1991, and 1992. His wife called me on Tuesday to say that several of Leigh's former runners were getting together at Bass Lake on Saturday to run together as a memorial for her. She invited me and any family members who wanted to come. I thought it was a great idea, and I knew I wanted to be there, but I didn't think I'd be able to run. I've had a bad upper respiratory infection for about a week, and I was only running about once or twice a week any way, so I'm in pretty bad shape. When my brother and my dad both said they wanted to go, I decided I would go and just walk around the lake.

When we arrive, I recognize several of the runners I got to know when I moved back to Boone after college. I also see a few of the friends I ran with in high school who are a couple years younger than I am. It is sunny, about 20°, and a light layer of new snow covers the ground. After battling traffic because of the bad road conditions, Graig finally arrives.

There are lots of hugs and "How are you's." We pose for a few quick pictures, and then we all walk down to the lake trail. When everyone starts jogging, I can't resist. I start running with them. Eventually the group separates into smaller groups, and I settle in with some who are running an easy pace. The runners talk about what they have been up to; it's nice to just listen to people having a normal conversation for the first time this week. Halfway through the run, the conversation turns to Leigh, and I make an amazing discovery. Running may just be my key to helping me through my grief. All this week, every time I've talked about Leigh, I either cry or I feel empty and lost. While I'm running, however, I am able to talk about her without crying. This discovery doesn't mean I'm done with crying, but it gives me another method of working through my feelings.

Toward the end of the run, Graig, who was pushing the pace with the front pack, comes back and runs the rest of the way in with me. As our feet crunch through the snow, my thoughts turn to a snowy winter two years ago, when Leigh and I ran an 8-mile hilly loop through about 10 inches of snow, with big, fat flakes falling on us the whole way. A run that should have been extremely difficult was made easy by our conversation and camaraderie. Now, here at the lake, it suddenly hits me that I will never run with Leigh again. I stop my watch when we reach the congregating runners, and then turn around and walk away from them. I sit down on the snow, facing the lake, and for the first time that week, truly think about how sad and lonely my life will be without Leigh.

CHAPTER THIRTEEN

FINDING STRONG

CLAUDE

On December 28 Leigh's death certificate was signed; a week later we received a copy and learned what ended her life. The death certificate indicated that Leigh went into multi-system organ failure approximately 12 hours prior to her death and went into severe septic shock approximately 24 hours prior to her death. The underlying cause of this catastrophe was listed as methicillin resistant staphylococcus aureus (MRSA) pneumonia, with an estimated onset of 36 hours prior to her death. We learned later that MRSA is a very powerful staph infection that has become resistant to most antibiotics commonly used to treat ordinary bacterial infections. It was hard to imagine that any kind of infection could kill someone as strong as Leigh in 36 hours, particularly by attacking the lungs as it did.

It's my belief that Leigh never knew she was dying. I'm convinced she felt as I did that this illness, as painful and uncomfortable as it was, was not a serious threat to her life. This was one time when her high pain threshold betrayed her.

.   .   .   .   .

Louise and I have received hundreds of cards and letters since Leigh died. Many remark on Leigh's strength. Some express the thought that Leigh got her strength from Louise and me. That's nice to read, but none of us had or have the strength that Leigh had. We all knew beforehand, but her passing has made it more evident she was the sparkplug of our family. Her motto for the last 23 years of her life was "You're stronger than you think," and it was her purpose in life to help others find their strength, their "strong." And now, we, her immediate family, are struggling to find our strong. It isn't easy, and it is not getting any easier four years after her death.

Each of Leigh's immediate family members has made life-altering decisions since her death. At every decision, we have asked ourselves "What would Leigh want me to do?" The answer, of course, is obvious: Leigh would want us to live our lives, to be happy, to be strong. And that thought is what is driving our decisions. With the possible exception of Holley, whose teaching opportunities might take her elsewhere, leaving Cooper Ridge or the Boone area would have been inconceivable for any family member if Leigh were still alive. But we all left. Each had his or her reason, but at the core, leaving all came down to Leigh's absence in our lives. Without her, Cooper Ridge could never be the same.

.   .   .   .   .

For the 2013 Walk for Awareness, which was the first one since Leigh's death, Appalachian State University wanted to do something special to honor and remember Leigh. They asked that someone from our family present Leigh's speech from the 20th anniversary event, the 2009 Walk. Jake volunteered to do so. He stood on the steps outside the Student Union and delivered Leigh's speech to the largest crowd ever at the Walk. It was a beautiful moment honoring Leigh's legacy.

Chris and Leigh

June 2012

CHRIS

No End in Sight

The first time I saw you there was no end in sight.
Selecting your hockey stick, I knew you were Ms Right.
You fought for your life and inspired us all;
You taught us how to get up no matter the fall.
Teacher, coach, role model, wife and mother,
All the things you have accomplished could be done by no other.
At night I hold your pillow, opening and shutting my eyes,
Hoping that this has just been one big pack of lies.
Often at night I can't remember your voice or your smell;
There is just no way to be released from this hell.
My days are long and the rooms are dark;
When you walked in the door, there was always a spark.
I wish that I had one more chance to hold you tight;
I had no idea the end was in sight.

I've told people often that the first time I laid eyes on Leigh, I knew I was going to marry her. We were in an equipment room in Broome-Kirk Gym at ASU picking out field hockey sticks for a PE class that we had together. When she walked by me, she glowed. That light illuminated her whole life and all who were fortunate to see it were blessed by it. Leigh was bigger than life and that has never been more evident than after her death.

Leigh had "it." Not sure how to define "it" other than to say she was a dynamic person, the strongest woman I have ever known. Unknowingly and fortunately some of that strength was passed on to me and our children. When I lost Leigh, I felt like I had lost everything. My future was gone. Everything we had planned for, dreamed about, worked toward was suddenly meaningless. Everything I did for 22 years was for her, because of her or with her. Now I had nothing.

The first year without Leigh was a blur. I can't recall much, but

I made a tremendous number of mistakes until I finally realized I wasn't doing what Leigh would have done. Leigh was a fighter. She loved life and wouldn't let anything get in the way of her making the most of it.

I knew that I needed to follow her example, but the challenge to me of living without Leigh seemed far greater than anyone should have to face.

There are numerous ways to measure how truly accomplished Leigh was in life: her many awards, her speeches, the countless student athletes whose lives she inspired. But none is more telling than the huge void that has been left in her death.

Before Leigh's death, I was living the perfect life with the perfect family. My son was in college, my daughter was in high school starting on the varsity basketball team at point guard – a true partnership and marriage of two souls. We were similar in so many ways, yet different enough to keep it exciting. It wasn't a perfect marriage, but it was perfect for me. At no point in our 22 years of marriage did I ever think I would be without her. I never thought to prepare for life without Leigh.

On January 20, 2014, I posted on Facebook:

Here I am sitting alone in Leigh's dream house that we built in 2005. The silence is deafening. Leigh used to sit in bed watching Dancing with the Stars while I sat in the living room watching Dirty Harry for the 12th time. Neither one of us could understand why the other was watching what we were watching. Suddenly I'd hear Leigh scream at the top of her lungs. "Chris, come watch this" I'd yell back that I didn't wanna. "Emmitt Smith is about to dance."...I don't care...."CHRIS!!!". I would mope on back and make sure she knew I wasn't happy. She didn't care because she wanted me to see Emmitt dance. I'd give both arms and my left foot to have that chance again. She'd yell for me and I'd get back there as fast as I could with no arms and one foot. Shoot if I had it to do over again, I would have already been in the bed watching with her. No arms, no foot, no regrets.

I would love to say that everything is good now and that I am stronger than I think, but that would be a lie. At this point I just can't see things getting better. Each day is like the movie *Groundhog Day*. I wake up in the same horrible situation and my wife is gone. I miss you so much, Leigh!!!!

Jake and Leigh

JAKE

My History is Not My Destiny

Her voice is slowly starting to leave me. Her smell is no longer around, and it is hard to recall how her arms felt when she wrapped them around me. I realize these are the physical things that I have a hard time remembering and that loss is sad. But it is the things that I remember well, the things I will never forget, that I want to highlight. The life lessons, such as love of family, honesty, and responsibility, that she instilled in me from a young age that I rarely thought about until she passed away are the things I remember about my mother and the things I will never forget. Just recently I came across a quote that really made me evaluate my life. The quote is my mother in a nutshell, and when I heard it, I immediately decided to change how I looked at my past and what I wanted for my future. "Yes, my history happened, but it doesn't have to be my destiny."

I was sheltered as a kid, although I grew up in what I thought was the perfect family. We were all extremely close: every holiday spent together, every sporting event attended together and every Sunday spent at my grandparents' house at the top of the hill that we called "Cooper Ridge." I saw a family that was perfect, and I felt that our family was looked up to and admired. After my mom passed away, I felt that my family was broken. Everything changed. Sunday dinners stopped. Everyone moved away from "Cooper Ridge," and we lost the desire to get together. We all needed time to grieve and figure out how to manage the hand we were dealt.

This is where the quote comes into play. I am going to change "my" to "our" for this situation. "Yes, our family lost Leigh, my mother, but it doesn't have to be our destiny." In the time since my mom's passing, our family has reconnected and learned to move forward and accept each other for the new people we have become. We don't live within 500 yards of each other anymore. We don't see each other every day, week, or even month anymore, but when we do see each other, we make the very best of it. We all acknowledge the changes in

269

our family since my mother has passed on, but we are determined not to allow that sad event to shape our future as a family. I owe this determination to my mom. She would not allow a tragic experience to define who she was. We do not want to be the family that fell apart during a tough time. We have decided to adapt to our new situation and find a way to turn a very negative event into a positive future. Our relationships have all changed, that is undeniable; but the unconditional love is still there and to me, that makes our family perfect once again.

I'm proud to say my mother was my best friend. Towards the end of her life, I had really started to open up to her and let her know who I was. She was smart enough and tuned in enough to know to an extent who I was and the little battles that I was fighting at the time. I reached out to my mom for advice that I wouldn't have felt comfortable seeking from anyone else. She had an intense way of listening and then responding that encouraged me to open up to her. She walked me through the troubles I was having, but I hadn't fully moved past those troubles before she passed away.

Not having her to talk to put me in a really dark place for a long period of time. On the surface I felt like I was handling myself well, but deep down I had a million different voices pulling me in different directions. I was deeply troubled and at a point in my life where I was going to go one of two ways. I was going to continue in the downward spiral, or I was going to face the pain and beat it. I wouldn't have my mom around to guide me on this journey to change my life, but I did have her past to learn from and inspire my actions. When she was my age, she had been through what I would assume Hell would be like and she did not let it define her as a person. My mom was not a victim. She was a survivor. I could not let losing her define me.

"Yes, my history happened, but it doesn't have to be my destiny." My goal was to overcome this tragedy and turn it into inspiration for others during tough moments of their lives. I decided to do what my mom valued more than anything other than her family: helping others realize that they were stronger than they ever thought they could be. "You're stronger than you think" is a saying that I use in my job. My mom used that line as a teacher, on the field as a coach, and when someone was having a tough time as a friend.

I decided to become a personal trainer in hopes that I could help others realize just how strong they really were. In an interview my mom did for *Endurance* magazine, she said, "Our own personal strength and belief in ourselves is something that nobody can take away without our permission." That quote summarizes my mother's life to perfection. No matter the challenges she faced and the adversity she encountered, she faced them head-on. Now I am doing my best to live life that same way. I have accepted the fact that life can be very cruel sometimes, but I have also accepted that it is up to me to not allow these moments to define me and break me but rather lift me up and allow myself to learn how strong I am.

Mental strength is very hard to teach others. You can't pour it into a person, but one's example in life can help others learn it. Moreover, strength to me is something that you have to learn on your own through times of adversity. My mom found her strength when she needed it the most, and her life turned out to be extremely rewarding. If I could talk to my mom just one more time, I would let her know that she was my hero. I would let her know that her strength was second to none and that I admired and loved her for it. I would tell her that I was doing my best to follow in her footsteps and exhibit the kind of strength that she did throughout her life so that I can inspire someone in a time of weakness and allow him or her to find their strength. I am carrying on my mother's legacy. I tell her story every chance I get. I would not be the person I am today without my mom's guidance, love, courage, resiliency, and determination... all of these qualities made up her strength. My goal is to one day feel confident enough to say that I possess the type of strength that encompassed who she was her entire life.

Haleigh and Leigh

HALEIGH

My Mommy, My Angel

Teacher, coach, mentor, friend, mother; these are the words that would be used to describe Leigh Cooper Wallace by anyone who knew her. Yet she was so much more than that to me. She was my late nights staying up to watch House Hunters, my early morning car rides to school filled with tired laughter, my phone calls when I needed advice on anything, my loud cheers in the crowd during basketball games; and now, she is my angel.

I was only sixteen years old when my mom passed away, such a crucial age in a young girl's life when she's in the midst of high school, dating, and finding out who she really is. And just like every other teenage girl, I was embarrassed by my mom when I was around friends. She was a health and PE teacher at my high school, so most of my friends were in at least one of her classes. I would be embarrassed to learn from my friends that my mom had started dancing in class, or especially when she gave the sex education lesson. On my birthday, she came into my math class and started singing "Happy Birthday" and dancing around. Everyone got a huge kick out of it, but I sank down in my seat and covered my face. I should have cherished these moments. I wish I had gotten up and danced with her. Now I crack a smile every time I find myself starting to dance in the car because I realize happily, "I'm turning into my mother!" Three years ago, that thought would have terrified me; but now, it makes me happier than anything.

As I sit here thinking about my mom, I realize I cannot put our memories or my unconditional love for her into words. We had such a close bond that my memories of her are very personal and may not make sense to anyone else. The things we talked and laughed about were personal and tailored to our own unconventional sense of humor. In my head, I can entertain myself for hours thinking about my mom, but it is so hard to put it on paper. All I can really say is that the love my mom had for me and my brother could never be matched in this lifetime. I am forever grateful for the values she instilled in me and the lessons she continues to teach me even after her passing. Her courage, strength, wisdom, and love will live on forever in my heart, and the hearts of the hundreds of other people she touched in her short life.

I often say to myself the beautiful words from Robert Munsch's book, *Love You Forever*, but I substitute the words, "As long as I'm living, my mommy you'll be."

Posted on Facebook, December 16, 2015:

On this day three years ago, my whole family and I were sitting in Johnson City hospital, waiting for my mom to get better. The turn my life took the next day was so unexpected, so dramatic, and so heartbreaking that I am still struggling to wrap my head around it. She had only gotten to the hospital the day before, only showed signs of illness three days before, and had spoken her last words to me three SHORT days before.

I was a very sheltered child from a middle class family, with a picture-perfect family of four. The worst thing that had happened to me up to this point was as minute as a middle-school breakup or a bad grade. I was so oblivious to the heartbreak that this world has, and would have to offer; I never fathomed the immense depression that the next days would bring me.

But here we are, three years later, and that naivete' is a distant, distant memory. Our family is no longer whole, our hearts are broken, and our days are not as bright as they used to be. BUT, if there is anything positive I have taken from losing my mother at the age of 16, it is that LIFE WILL ALWAYS GO ON. It certainly didn't feel like it a few years ago, but now I am living with Grandma and Grandpa Cooper, I have an incredible relationship with my dad and Jake, and I'm finally smiling a genuine smile. As much as I wish my beautiful mother was here to experience this life with me, I am comforted in knowing I have 16 years of wonderful memories of my mom, and I will lock them away in my heart FOREVER.

I love you, Mom, and I always will. I will never stop chatting with you before I go to bed, and I will never stop missing you.

GRAIG

My Hero

Struggling with the overwhelming task and emotions of writing about my sister, I went for a run to clear my head and find my strength. Leigh has that effect on me.

"Put the phone on speaker and do 50 push-ups, then 50 sit-ups, then 40 and 40, then 30 and 30, 20-20, 10-10."

This Leigh commanded of me and I obeyed, drunkenly. I had been calling her almost every night - almost always drunk - for the last several weeks to cry and vent about an emotional break-up I was going through. Living on my own with my son Findley seemed to be a constant struggle. Leigh would remind me to focus on three things: my health, Findley's health, and my job.

Leigh had always been my go-to person for advice or talk therapy. This began around high school when we'd often run together. After I'd finish a two-hour wrestling practice, Leigh would somehow convince me to go on a run with her. She would do most of the talking, as I struggled to stay with her.

Our first runs together actually started when I was eight years old. That's when she left for college. Each time she returned home, one of the first things she'd do is chase me down to give me kisses.

She doted on me as a child. So much so that when she went to a summer camp when I was two, I was bothered by her absence and started calling my other sister Julie by Leigh's name. When the "real" Leigh returned home, I was confused but solved this problem by giving Julie a name that made sense to me: Leigh-di-Leigh. Of course, I don't remember any of this. It's family lore.

When I think back, running away from my sister's kisses is one of the only vivid memories I have of her from before her abduction. Had she not escaped, I would have grown up to barely even know the kind of person my sister was.

She was my hero. A young boy growing up could have no better example of a strong, beautiful, intelligent woman than my sister. She helped me navigate major life challenges, and I've had some big ones. She gave me inspiration as I trudged through West Point. She helped calm me down when I found out I was going to be a father, and later, when my son's mother took our child to Alaska and refused to return home, she kept me focused and hopeful during the arduous court process to get my son back. And as single fatherhood in San Francisco threatened to swallow me, she helped me resurface and find strength to stay afloat.

I could never do wrong in her eyes. Well, nearly never. The one time I ever made her angry is now a vivid memory because of its uniqueness. In high school I trained with her track distance runners to maintain my stamina during the off season for wrestling and soccer. At the start of practice one day, I was joking around with people by putting them in various wrestling moves. I then grabbed Leigh and put her in a move that pretty much made her constricted and immobile. She started screaming at me to let her go, so I jumped up in shock and felt sick with remorse. It was the only time I can remember that my sister had been mad at me like that.

As I apologized, she explained to me that after her abduction, she never wanted to be in a situation where she wasn't in control, both mentally and physically. When I held her down, she felt that feeling of vulnerability, helplessness, and lack of control that she had worked so hard to escape – both literally in the form of her escape from Daniel Lee and figuratively in her escape from the imprisonment that her eating disorder held her in as a teen.

Another reason this incident stood out to me was that it was the first indication I'd ever seen of the emotional scars she carried from her abduction. Leigh's strength wasn't that she could completely block out or forget about what happened to her. In fact, I feel that approach isn't an emotionally healthy way to deal with tragedy. Her strength was her ability to learn and grow. She learned something about herself during and after her attack, and she resolved to grow into a person who was in control of her life.

We talked about this quite a bit as she was thinking about how to tell her story – what message she wanted to convey to others – and this topic of control came up often. What she went through mentally during her abduction was like a microcosm for her struggles in life and the struggles countless other people go through who struggle with addictions or eating disorders.

At first she felt helpless, that she had made a poor decision to get into the vehicle and now she was doomed to pay for that decision. Her thoughts were dominated by the inevitable pain and death she would face. When Daniel Lee placed the gun to her head, she was certain it was the end. But then she was given another chance by outsmarting her abductor.

Many people sadly never get another chance, and part of me feels that Leigh's determination to escape, after having resigned herself to certain death, was fueled by the determination to control her own destiny. This determination carried over into her struggles with her eating disorders.

With such addictions or eating disorders, people often must hit the bottom before they realize just how much they've lost control. At this point, at the bottom, it becomes infinitely harder to fight back out. It often takes a very strong support network and medical/professional intervention. After her abduction, Leigh's resolve was to never see the bottom again, and to do that, she had to find her strength to gain back control in her fight with food.

This was, I feel, her message of "find your strength." You have to know what it is you are struggling with, you have to understand it and know how it is negatively impacting you, and you have to find your strength to overcome it.

HOLLEY

Learning from Leigh

Leigh was a teacher and a coach to so many people, including me. I learned many valuable lessons from her, mostly in the last 23 years of her life. Some of these lessons she taught me directly, as we ran together, drove to lacrosse games together, or just sat around talking. Many of these lessons, however, she taught by example. I am grateful to have grown up with such a stunning example of qualities that get to the core of what a human was meant to be. While there are many qualities to choose from, I will address the three qualities that drive almost everything I do now. As I think about the challenging, exciting, heroic, too-short life that my sister lived, I am grateful that I learned from her:

1.   Strength – Leigh was strong. She was physically strong. Like the beat-all-the-boys-in-arm-wrestling kind of strong. The power-through-three-conference-championship-distance-race-wins-in-one-weekend kind of strong when she was in college. And of course, the pedal-hard-nonstop-while-teaching-a-100-minute-spin-class   kind   of strong as an adult. Just to look at her with that golden tan, the powerful but beautiful body, and the long hair, and the eyes that exuded confidence was intimidating for some people. But even more impressive than her physical strength was her mental strength. She ran most of her remarkable high school and college races with terribly painful injuries. Her strength of mind was what allowed her to make family, teaching, and exercise true priorities in her life. There were several times when her mental strength outdid her physical strength. For instance, the time she woke up in an emergency room after a road race and asked, "What place did I get? Did I catch that girl?" In fact, she had collapsed before crossing the finish line.

I don't try to compare my own physical strength or mental strength to Leigh's. I have a different body type, a different personality, and different life experiences than she had. What I learned from her,

278

however, is how to strive for strength. As I continue to face challenges in my life, I don't think I will ever stop trying to develop my strength.

2. Courage – What gets an overweight teenage girl to step onto a track, in front of the father she wants so badly to impress, and race her heart out, beating most of the injury-free girls with typically lean runners' bodies? Courage. How does a 20-year old female escape from a killer when her physical strength is no longer an asset? Courage. How is a young woman, after experiencing such a horrendous ordeal, able to go on to tell her story in the courtroom, in front of large crowds, to classes of high school students, and to countless strangers through television interviews? She had courage.

I thought running my first marathon took courage, and then I thought running a 50K took courage. Leigh's motivation certainly helped me through those events, but my real test of courage came after she was gone. First, of course, it took courage to face life after such a tragic loss. Within months, though, I decided that just "getting by" in life wasn't enough. While Leigh was not there to witness my quest for happiness, the courage she taught me played the leading role in making it happen.

3. Pride – Leigh didn't talk openly about pride the way she did about strength and courage, but it was important to her just the same. Her struggles with body image as a teenager led to emotional difficulties many couldn't imagine her having. She eventually realized her physical strength was something she could be proud of. Not only did she learn to take pride in her own body, but she also felt tremendous pride in her family, her children, and her role as a coach and teacher.

These lessons I am still working on, but I am learning to appreciate what I am making of my life. I feel it when I see my 10-year old take the snap as quarterback of his football team. I feel it when I watch my 12-year old run out ahead of me on the trail because I can't keep up with him. I feel it when I get a text from a parent saying her son has never been happier at school and that I must be doing something right as a teacher (in my third week of teaching). And I feel it when I walk hand-in-hand with another woman, sure that everyone who sees us must be jealous because I am with the most beautiful person in the room. This is pride. I know it is what Leigh wanted for me, even if she didn't know what it would take to get me here.

The year after Leigh died, I volunteered to be a host family for the Pakistani exchange program. For two weeks, I had a bright, funny, polite, respectful young man living in my home. At only 16 years old, Baqir left his home and his family to travel halfway around the world, live with strangers, and experience something so different from the world he knew. Aside from never-ending jetlag that had him exhausted and wanting to nap every afternoon, he adjusted beautifully. He was fascinated with American culture and accepted that we do things differently than he had experienced in Pakistan. Surprisingly, he tried every type of food I put on the table, as long as I provided a bottle of hot sauce for him. He even cooked a delicious traditional Pakistani meal for us one night, which my sons not only agreed to try but actually ate full servings of. We discovered that humor is a universal language, as Baqir and I had each other laughing at our shared experiences and sometimes at his perceptions of our culture.

I had several reasons for wanting to host as part of this program. I wanted to do something helpful and interesting. I wanted my sons to get to know someone from another culture and learn from that person. Most of all, however, I did it because the year before, just before she died, Leigh participated in this program. She hosted two incredible women, sharing not only her home, but also friendship, food, customs and ideas. She loved getting to know these women and was so happy to have new friends from the other side of the world. She discovered that for as many differences as they had, they had just as many similarities. Their differences made it an intriguing friendship, and their similarities would have made it a lasting friendship.

When Leigh hosted, the Pakistanis visited in December. At the beginning of their second week here, my parents had the family over for dinner one night so that we could all meet Leigh's new friends. It was important to Leigh to show these women that there are Americans who value their families and who stay close to their parents and siblings even as they grow up. There was a great deal of sharing of cultural ideas and, as was typical at our family dinners, a great deal of laughter as well.

That Friday evening, there was a farewell dinner for all of the participants of the program. Leigh went to this dinner and spoke on behalf of the host families about her experience. That farewell dinner was the last time she saw anyone outside her family. Later that night, she was in the hospital emergency room, and 24 hours after that, she was in intensive care. Leigh's new friends spent their last two night in Boone alone at Leigh's house before traveling to D. C. on Sunday. Monday morning, as all of Boone was in shock and devastated over Leigh's death, there was a small group of travelers in our nation's capital also mourning.

As I sat at the farewell dinner at the end of my hosting experience, I thought about what that evening must have been like for Leigh. I'm sure she was trying to enjoy the good food and good company as I did. She may have been just a little nervous about speaking in front of the group, because although she had given many excellent speeches in her life and was often in the spotlight, what many people didn't know about Leigh was that speaking to a group was actually not easy for her. I imagine she was feeling sad to see her friends leave but optimistic that she would see them again. Through all of this, though, she was very, very sick and probably trying hard not to let anyone see just how bad she felt. Leigh didn't get sick often, and when she did, she usually didn't let it slow her down. I'm sure she thought this was just another one of those times when she had to push through it. *Get through tonight, and I can rest tomorrow.*

It's always easy for me to talk about Leigh. It's usually the unspoken thoughts that bring me to tears, and even then it takes some unknown trigger to get me going. So while I sat at dinner, I talked openly with the group at my table, several of whom had been at last year's dinner and remembered Leigh speaking about how moving this experience had been. When they saw that I was willing to talk openly about it, they asked questions about what happened the rest of that weekend, questions they had kept to themselves for almost a year, questions of understandable curiosity. I answered with the information I knew, what the weekend had been like from my perspective, and what I learned in the weeks following. I appreciated the compassionate ears of my friends, allowing me to talk about something so serious and sad at an event meant to celebrate hope and change for the better.

The speeches began, and I listened as different people got up and spoke about the program and their experiences. When a woman stood in front of the group and spoke on behalf of the teachers from Pakistan, something about her reminded me of one of the women who stayed with Leigh last year. That was my trigger. I used my napkin from dinner to wipe the tears, and while I had thoughts of leaving the room to curl up in a ball in the hallway and sob into my knees, I knew it was important to keep the room focused on the current speaker. So I cried quietly at my table without making a big scene, and it eventually passed.

In the end, when I think about Leigh's last days, I can't ignore her miserable Saturday spent in bed or the grim Sunday spent unconscious in the ICU. I know, however, that the days leading up to that weekend were her true last days. The ones we look back on and know that she spent every day of her life making the world a better place. Whether she was encouraging victims of violence not to be victims within themselves, or teaching students how to live healthy lives, or coaching athletes to achieve more than anyone thought they could, or bridging the gap between misunderstood cultures, Leigh made every day count for herself and for others.

Leigh's words from December 11, 2012:

Chris and I are hosting two amazing and beautiful women from Pakistan for a week. They have become close friends of mine in a short time. We love to talk about our differences and then marvel and laugh when we realize how very much alike we are! They have strengthened my belief that things such as race, ethnicity, country and religion should not define a person or be used to determine if someone is good or not. The heart of a person is what matters. I have made two lifelong friends, Samina and Muzzana, who have beautiful, loving and generous hearts!

.   .   .   .   .

On December 17, 2012, I started a new calendar. This calendar counts the days, weeks, months, and now years since Leigh died. This calendar has been filled with firsts. My first run, the group effort that is becoming an annual affair; and my first race, The Race for RARE. The first Christmas, which was almost unbearable, as it came along while the ink was still drying on my new calendar. Just one week later, at midnight on New Year's Eve, I struggled when my new calendar crossed paths with the traditional one. How could I let one calendar flip over to a new year when the other one had just been handed to me? I wasn't ready for 2013. I wanted to hang onto 2012 a little longer, but that's the way calendars work. They keep moving at a steady, exact pace, regardless of what we do or how we feel about it.

There were many first birthdays, anniversaries, holidays, and vacations. Each of these was difficult in its own way. We made the best of them, showing each other love and support while quietly recognizing the immense absence we felt. There was a first birth, that of a first grandchild, followed almost immediately by another loss within a family that wasn't prepared but somehow managed to work through it, as the baby did not survive.

Year one was also filled with something else, though. I very clearly remember my first laugh, which came sooner than I had expected. Julie, Graig, and I were looking through old pictures, picking out the ones to be used in the slideshow at the visitation on day 3 of the new calendar. We proved that regardless of how fresh the feelings of pain and emptiness were, we were still Cooper siblings, able to laugh at each other in ridiculous old photos. I didn't realize it at the time, but that laughter was the beginning of a renewed relationship with both my brother and my sister. I've grown closer to both of them in a way I never knew was possible before. I also felt a shift in my relationship with my parents, who have always supported me and encouraged me. I found myself, especially in the early months, being the supporter, encouraging them to refill their pools of strength when it seemed as if there were only a few drops left.

Friendship, love, support, and concern came from unexpected places, from everyone and everywhere. I realized just how much I love working at my school, with amazing co-workers who made returning to work in January easier than I expected. My friendships at work have grown, both in number and in quality. I've also reconnected with old friends and learned that others with their own grief calendars can be valuable models for how to navigate this unknown territory.

Year one is over, but this calendar will continue. There will be more firsts – graduations, weddings, more grandchildren, and other firsts that I can't imagine. My goal is to fill this calendar with memories of Leigh while creating new memories based on the happiness and strength we continue to find. And this won't be my last calendar. In fact, I've already started a new one, one that took me by surprise and is bright and colorful, bringing me joy and comfort when I needed it most. I will gladly find the strength to face the challenges I'm confronted with in order to keep this calendar going.

As for December 17th, I have a challege for anyone reading this. Hug your loved ones this day. Encourage someone this day. Make someone laugh this day. Find the strength you didn't know you had this day. Overcome an obstacle this day. Exercise this day. Show the world your beauty, inside and out, this day.   Teach someone something valuable this day. Clean until there is not a speck of dirt to be found this day. Go to a drive-thru and order a large Coke with a bendy straw this day. Leigh did all of these things every day.

If you can manage to complete most of these tasks in one day, you will be late everywhere you go, which is also something Leigh did most days. Do these things not just to honor a great woman on the anniversary of her death, but also to add more greatness to your own life.

JULIE

Dare to Dream

"Julie – You've worked so hard. I'm so glad to see that it is
all paying off. End your incredible season with a BANG!
Run hard! I love you – Leigh"

Leigh wrote this on the back of a "Dare to Dream" plaque she
gave me the night before my Southern Conference cross-country meet
my final year at Appalachian State University. I might have been her
first true coaching experience (experiment??). After battling with
Achilles tendonitis for the third time during cross-country of my
freshman year at ASU, I decided to give up on running. Over the course
of those next three years, I took in all that college had to offer; in other
words, I ate and drank – a lot. I gained about twenty pounds.

I got inspired to run again after seeing Leigh's amazing
transformation her final year at ASU. She had finally gained control
over her eating disorder and won all three distance events in track that
spring at the Southern Conference meet. She was the first person I told
that I wanted to run again the next year and was, naturally, the one I
went to to whip me back in shape. Coach Weaver had a team meeting in
May for all those who would be on the cross-country team the next year.
Leigh was supposed to let Coach know that I wanted to run again and
let him know that I would be attending that meeting. In true "Leigh"
form, she forgot. While Coach was scanning the room as the meeting
started, his eyes fell on me and he had a confused look on his face.

"Julie??"

Sigh..."Yes, Coach, it's me. Leigh was supposed to tell you I
wanted to run again and ask if it was okay for me to come to this
meeting. I'm guessing she forgot."

"Haha – I guess she did forget, but it's okay – you're welcome
here." He went around the room and had everyone give a goal for what

they wanted to accomplish that upcoming season. Most gave goals of what time they wanted to run by the end of the season.

When it came to me, I said "Well, since it's been so long since I ran, I really don't know what times to compare to or what times I might be able to achieve. But I know that I want to be a scorer, so my goal is to be top seven on the team." Coach said that while that was an admirable goal, I was basically saying that I intended to run faster than half of the girls sitting at this table, and they've all been running consistently every year. I replied that I realized that's what I was saying and that I didn't mean any disrespect to the girls currently on the team, but that was my goal nonetheless.

Leigh wrote out a workout schedule for me for the entire summer, and many times she did the workouts with me. I lost all the extra weight I had gained, and I felt like I was in incredible shape. The true test came at the first meet of the season. It was just a dual meet against a small, nearby college, so the meet was mainly for Coach to see what his girls could do. Leigh was there to cheer me on, of course. When I got to the starting line, I had a small moment of panic when I realized I hadn't decided on strategy for this race. Do I go out easy and see how I feel, maybe run with the middle of the pack? Or do I just go out with the leaders (who I knew would be Carrie and Nicole) and see how long I could hang on? At the last second before the gun went off, I decided that I had nothing to lose; no one had any expectations of me, so why not go for it and see what happens? For the first time in my life, I started a race with the leaders. Carrie, Nicole, and I were comfortably in the lead for the entire race. Much to my and everyone's surprise, I didn't "die." I held on and finished the race in 2nd place, between Carrie and Nicole.

Leigh wasn't able to come to the Conference meet at the end of the season. She was so upset that she wasn't able to be there to see me finish off what had been an incredible season for me. As instructed, I called her as soon as the race was over. "What do you want to know first?" I asked, "my time, my place on the team, or my place overall?"

"I don't care about time, what was your place on the team?"

"Second," I said, "behind Carrie." I heard a little squeal.

"Awesome," she said, "now how about your place overall?" I paused for a few moments for dramatic effect.

"Second!!!!! I got second overall, too!!!!"

This time she screamed. This was definitely the proudest I had ever been of myself, and it was all thanks to Leigh, in my opinion. I give her full credit for what I accomplished that year. I finished out the year also running Indoor and Outdoor Track, and also did very well in those seasons. When the local paper interviewed Coach Weaver about Carrie, Nicole, and me after that cross-country season, he said about me, "To be out of cross-country for two to three years and come back in and do so well tells about the maturity one gains. Julie trained well over the summer and prepared herself for a successful season."

There is no reason my body should have been able to accomplish what I did. I had always been a decent runner but never one who could be a "top" runner in college. But especially after three years of doing virtually no running and doing too much eating and drinking, I definitely should not have been able to do what I did. But I knew Leigh believed in me and apparently that was enough.

Leigh went on to create an amazing legacy for herself as an outstanding coach and motivator. Everyone she came in contact with was motivated and inspired by her. Everyone she had a conversation with about fitness, exercise, or whatever it is they asked her opinion or advice on, came away from the conversation believing in themselves and fully believing in her motto that "you're stronger than you think." Her intent in wanting to write a book, as I understand it, was to inspire people and help them find their inner strength. I wonder, though, if she realized the impact she was already making on so many peoples' lives, well before her death and certainly before the finishing of this book. I also wonder if she could ever have predicted the impact her words and her story and her strength would have on so many people after her death.

It certainly made me take a closer look at how I was living my life, and I chose to make some changes. I never loved living in Boone. Nothing against Boone; it is a charming town where my daughters and I made some amazing friends. It just wasn't for me. Leigh loved everything about Boone: the weather, the small-town feel, the snow days. I knew I didn't belong there, but Leigh made it hard to leave. She was definitely the glue holding our family close together. She was usually the one who would start the texts to all of us, suggesting we get together for a family dinner; sometimes because it was someone's birthday, or maybe a big event like the Super Bowl, but sometimes it was just because it had been two weeks since we'd had a family dinner, and she just wanted to see everyone. And the dinners were so fun with much laughter. How could anyone leave something like that? When she died, I thought about how she lived her life; she had no regrets. She was exactly where she wanted to be, with the man she had wanted to be with since college, doing exactly the job that she wanted. I knew I didn't have that. I hated the weather, I prefer more of a big-city feel, I knew there was very little chance of my finding someone to date there, and I knew that the girls could have better opportunities in school and sports if we moved to a bigger city. I knew that I needed to follow her example and live my life to its fullest. It took about a year for me to come to this decision and act on it, but in November of 2013, eleven months after she died, I started a job in Charlotte and lived first with my aunt and uncle in Rock Hill, and then we moved into our new house in Fort Mill, SC, in December.

The girls were upset at first about leaving their friends, but they quickly made new friends and came to love their new school here in Fort Mill. They are both thriving. My younger daughter, Regan Leigh, has really embraced the fact that she is named after Leigh. She has taken an interest in running and quickly realized that she is good at it. In several of her classes this year, she has had to write a story about her life and her goals, and in each one, she has mentioned Leigh and mentioned how they share a love of running, and she has used Leigh's motto "You're stronger than you think" in her writings.

Leigh has always been a huge fan and supporter of her nieces and nephews. She was clearly the "favorite aunt." It makes me so sad that she is no longer here to see how well her nieces and nephews are doing. I know how much she would love to be on the sidelines cheering at Riley's soccer games, or yelling for Regan as she runs cross-country and track. But at least I have the comfort of knowing she is still with them in spirit, that she still has such a strong effect on my 13-year old that Regan is choosing to pursue the same sport as Leigh. Regan even said that as she's running and starting to get tired, she thinks of Leigh, and she tells herself "You're stronger than you think," and that helps her to push through that run or that race.

In July 2015, the last of the Coopers left Boone when Holley moved away. I feel guilty sometimes, like we all abandoned Leigh. She is the only Cooper left in Boone. But she is in the place that she loved, overlooking the school that she gave so much of her life to. And I know she would want all of us to be happy and would want us to do what was best for us and our families. I know she would be the first to encourage us to leave and follow our dreams, as we did. I love it here in Fort Mill and know this was a good move for us. I have a good job, I have made some great friends, and the girls have made many friends and are doing so well in school and in their sports. No, I haven't started dating yet, but I am still hopeful that it will happen.

I still feel like I need her, though. I sometimes feel like I'm floundering and that I'm not "getting anywhere." When my extremely compassionate daughter Riley asks me daily how my day was or how I'm doing and my response is always "It was fine" or "I'm fine," I can see the concern in her eyes. Fine isn't good enough for her. She wants her mom to be happy. I'm obviously not doing a good job of convincing my girls that everything is okay. I need Leigh's advice. I need her to do like she did that summer in college: make a plan for me, map it out, write it down, and then be by my side, cheering me on as I accomplish whatever it is I set out to accomplish. I just still don't feel like I'm living my full life. Leigh truly led a life with no regrets, no enemies, no resentments. She attracted people to her – drew them close. I feel like I push people away, never truly letting anyone in. The pain of not having her here to help me push through this is unbearable. But I will push through – I have to. I can't allow myself to be swallowed whole by my sadness because I feel that would be letting Leigh down.

Twenty-five years after giving me the Dare to Dream plaque, I

289

still believe its words because Leigh gave it to me, so that must mean she believed it. The plaque read:

"Choose a wish, find a dream,
pick a wishing star;
let your hopes and spirits soar,
high and free and far.
Reach for the unreachable,
stretch to touch the sky;
know no dream you treasure
is too far away or high.
Believe in the impossible,
then work and try and do
for only those who dare to dream,
can make a dream come true."

Author Unknown

LOUISE

Thinking of Leigh

When I think of Leigh:

I remember the beautiful 9-pound, 3-ounce baby who started her life by arriving ten days late and kept the tradition by being late the rest of her life. The one who started my journey as a mother.

I smile at the memories of her childhood:

The toddler who didn't talk until she was well over two years old. We had a Spanish-speaking nanny in Pamana who spoke only Spanish to Leigh - and Leigh's first real word was not Mama or Daddy, but "cucaracha." We worried about her speech - but anyone who knew her later in life would find that worry absolutely ludicrous.

The toddler who showed her "love" for her cousin by biting him several times a day - the same cousin who spoke such touching words at her memorial service that he obviously didn't remember those youthful injuries.

The child who was very stubborn and would resist all of my efforts to be "the boss" of her. Later in life, this stubbornness, this tenacity, saved her life.

The gymnast who became a gym rat, loving every minute working to improve. The first time we realized how determined she would be as an athlete.

The student of mine who loved having her mom as her teacher. One day in class, when I said they would work with a partner, she rolled her eyes sideways to let me know that she wanted to work with Jorge, her current crush. I picked up on it right away. She loved that I was involved with all that was happening in her life as a young adolescent.

A hint that she would always want me involved in her life, as a friend and confidant.

The teenager who stuggled with a demon she couldn't face - her weight. But when the time came, she recognized that she couldn't let that demon control her life, and she took control. A life-changing decision, in her eyes.

The college student who rejoiced when we decided to move to Boone where she was going to college. "Yea! I'll have a place to do my laundry!" Although that was her initial reaction to the news, she loved the opportunity to see her younger sister and brother grow up—an opportunity she totally embraced when she came "home" or attended their sports events.

The "victim" of a brutal kidnapping and assault who was determined to be a survivor, not a victim. I remember the first time I fussed at her, months after her kidnapping. We both cried and embraced - thankful that life was returning to normal and that I could take off the kid gloves.

The sister who loved her siblings with all her heart:

She and Julie, so close in age, seemed to have their differences but were fiercely loyal to each other. In high school, they were lab partners and their teacher was amazed at how well they got along. When Leigh showed up with a black eye one day - given to her by Julie in a fight over which radio station to listen to - they didn't have the heart to admit their fight and destroy their teacher's admiration of their relationship. Throughout their lives, they communicated with a slight glance, each knowing exactly the other's thoughts. Usually a result of laughing in sync at something I said or did.

She and Holley, separated in years and temperament from being friends growing up, but becoming close friends as adults. Finding the same joy in running that brought them close, as they used their runs to make up for lost time and lost closeness. Coaching lacrosse together and sharing the same goals and the same coaching strategies that focused on making each player feel important and loved. Not knowing what lay ahead for Holley, but we all know without a doubt that Leigh would have supported her fully.

She and Graig, though ten years apart, had a special bond. Maybe it started out that Leigh was his second mother, helping me daily with keeping him in check. But a bond that grew over the years into a deep friendship. Always there to cheer him on: his wrestling achievements, his stuggles to gain custody of his son, his disappointments in life. She always believed in him and her pride in him never wavered from the day he was born. There is a great sadness that she does not know the happiness he has found in his life with Debbie but a belief that maybe she does.
.
I feel pride at the young woman she became:

The wife of a special son-in-law, a young woman who had found the perfect match and loved being married. She and Chris were so happy together, despite their meager beginnings as young college students. It was such fun being around them - Chris making jokes and Leigh laughing her head off. The shared joys of their children, their home, their families. The one who brought Chris into our lives forever.

The mother of a son who proved the be the "perfect" son. She loved Jake with all her heart, and he grew into such a strong young man - one who faced adversity as she did and showed us all how to face life without her. He knows what he wants and works hard to make his life one she would be proud of. Just as his mother did, he lets his family know how important they are in his life.

The mother of a beautiful young daughter - the spitting image of Leigh as a child. You know how mothers always say, "One of these days, you will have a daughter like you and you'll see how it is." I got my wish with Haleigh - she was the high-spirited and determined image of her mother. Still is, as she is making her way through loss and uncertainty with a strength we didn't know she had.

The crazy Aunt Leigh, who adored Riley, Cade, Regan, Coen, and Findley. She gave them a sense of adventure and fun and made each feel special. Whether it was showing up at their sports activities, playing games with them, or just making them laugh - she showed them the joy of family.

The daughter every parent would treasure. Was it the fear she once faced of dying at a young age? Was it the responsibility of being the first child? Whatever it was, Leigh always wanted to be close to us, to be involved in our daily lives, to bring laughter to our hearts, and to assure us that she would take care of us in our old age.

Strange how life changes things. Now it is my turn to become like my daughter - to be a person who can face a tragedy and move forward through life. It has been over three years, and yet I still wake each morning and wonder where I will find the strength to face the day with the heavy sadness that still lives within me, the guilt I feel that I am experiencing the years she will never have. So the path I have chosen has been to remember all that she believed so strongly in and draw upon her life lessons.

When facing adversity, use the support of family and friends to give you strength:

A major factor in Leigh's recovery from her kidnapping was the outpouring of concern from the people in our community and the many friends who reached out to support her. Her ordeal was a very public matter, and everyone knew that she had been assaulted. When young women are victims of sexual assault, they often feel guilt or shame, and they don't want others to know. Leigh had no choice in this, as her assault was highly publicized. As her college coach expressed it, "Leigh absolutely refused to let this ruin her life." She was very proud of these words, as it was a testament to her inner strength. But she would be the first to say that this inner strength came from the support she received from others, and she always encouraged people to reach out to their friends, teachers, parents, counselors, or even strangers when facing adversity.

Our support came before we even returned home from Johnson City that cold, dismal morning. My sister, Jane, came back with us to be at my side throughout the next few days of planning the unimaginable: burying a child. Friends showed up at our house to help us make our way through the haze that enveloped us: bringing food and reminding us to eat, taking phone calls, greeting visitors, helping with grandchildren, and most importantly, being there to let us know how much they cared. Our family members began making their way to Boone from all parts of the country, trips that were difficult for most. Four separate schools worked together to have a dinner for out-of-town guests on the day of the memorial service. And most touching, the policemen who helped direct traffic during our trip to the cemetery wiped their tears as we passed by.

The outpouring of support continued for months after her death. As we returned to work, our co-workers reached out to us to help us through the difficult days. My teacher friends, especially Sandra, Erin, Brooke, and Erika, opened their hearts to me when I needed to talk or cry; my principal, Mr. Griffin, made sure I had help in the classroom; and my students showed compassion not often found in young teenagers.

Friends who saw us around town openly cried with us to show us how much they cared.

And our family: How Julie met me every day after school to walk and talk, knowing that I found it painful to walk alone with my thoughts. How Holley let me unburden my grief on her, willing to listen in her quiet manner any time I felt overwhelmed. How Graig offered to move back to North Carolina to help us though our suffering, despite his love of life in San Francisco. And our precious grandchildren, who gave us reason to hold our heads up and be the grandparents they needed.

My sister Jane who wrote me a letter each day for two years.

Our extended families who gave us opportunities to continue our traditions without Leigh.

Make choices that will help you to move forward:

Our plan – our dream – had been to spend our retirement on

Cooper Ridge. We tried, we truly tried, to continue our family traditions, but each gathering was a painful reminder of Leigh's absence. We no longer had weekly dinners together. Chris and Haleigh eventually left to look for peace away from the many memories that enveloped them each day. Julie moved off the mountain to escape the winters, and Holley made plans to look for opportunities elsewhere upon finishing her teacher certification program. Claude spent many lonely days on Cooper Ridge, and we knew it was time to make a change.

As much as Leigh loved our life, I know she would have encouraged each of us to follow our dream - to find a life that would help us heal. This life for us has been at Clemson with friends we have known for years. We are at peace here with people who know our grief and are helping us live with it, whether it's encouraging us to become involved in causes where we can help others, including us in fun outings that give us reason to laugh, or simply providing a listening ear when we need to talk.

We are finding our strong and it's going to be the hardest thing we've ever had to do. We look at our family and friends and know all the rewards are worth it. We won't stop trying.

APPENDIX

REMEMBRANCES:

For additional insight on the impact that Leigh had on those with whom she worked and played, I have included several personal notes we received shortly after her death.

The Rock, Watauga High School

Dec 17, 2012

David Honea (former Watauga High assistant coach; from his blog a day or two after Leigh died)

I can't really imagine what it must be like to be at Watauga High School today. It is disorienting trying to process the stunning news about Coach Wallace from my home in Wilkesboro, in a place where no one else knows who she is. Most of you knew of her as a teacher and a parent of a classmate and track teammate, and probably as someone who was still a very good runner. The most important thing that some runners and parents might not have known is that she was Coach Holley Quick's sister, so please keep Haleigh, Holley, and the rest of their family in your prayers.

Many of our most recent runners may also not know that, to the extent that it is possible in a program that has thrived for so long with so many different coaches and with so many great athletes, Leigh Wallace probably contributed more than anyone to the historic success of Watauga running. For people around the state, Coach Wallace is still very much one of the first people they think of when thinking about Watauga running, but some of our runners were just starting kindergarten when she left coaching cross-country and track. A person is much more than a list of facts, especially someone who continues to have such a lasting impact on so many people she coached.   But because numbers about running are what I do and what I can retreat to, I wanted to tell you in concrete terms some of what she was a part of.

In the 10 years from 1994 to 2003, the Watauga girls won the state cross country championship once, finished second three times, and third three times (plus one year when they were fourth but only five points from winning.) They had an individual state champ and 14 all-state finishers, with at least one individual in the top ten at the state meet in nine out of ten years. In the six years starting in 1994, the Watauga boys won three state championships and finished second the other three years. In the three runner-up years, once they lost the state championship on a tiebreaker, and the other two years they scored 47 and 64 points. Individually the boys produced two state champions and two Foot Locker national qualifiers (with three different runners accounting for those honors) and had 11 all-state runners in six years.

With the exception of the pre-1980 days when most schools did not sponsor cross-country, it is the best six-year stretch by one boys' team in North Carolina history.

In track, Coach Wallace worked with the three girls' state championship teams from 1995 to 1997, and her distance runners provided most of the points for the boys' state runner-up team in 2000. Individually Watauga won eight state titles outdoors, plus a state record in the 4×800 in 2000. The girls also had a pair of outdoor individual titles and two 4 x 800 state championships. Indoors, six different boys won seven individual state titles between 1995 and 2000.

Beginning in the mid-90's when I was a coach at NC State, multiple Watauga runners competed for the Wolfpack. At least a couple of others ran for UNC, and there were many other former runners attending those schools that were not competing collegiately. It was a running joke among NC State runners that you could never go anywhere with a Watauga native without having five more show up out of nowhere. That is a testament to the community they built on those Watauga teams, and a legacy for Coach Wallace that will last for decades to come.

The Bob Cherry Family

Like so many others, our family is devastated by Leigh's death. So typically, she touched various members of our family in different ways

For Kelly and me, she was a permanent gym fixture for years. Whether it was taking her spin class, "competing" (haha) with her in Crossfit, or just watching her intensity, intently and methodically move from one piece of machinery to another like there was nothing in the world that could stop her ... she was such an inspiration and a pleasure to be around! Just watching Leigh go full throttle on everything she did always served as a big kick in the pants for those of us around her who would have killed to possess a fraction of her determination!

For Michael, he was one of so many cross-country and track kids she coached at the high school. And he certainly wasn't one of the elite runners! Rather he was a true back-of-the-packer for his first couple of years, though from the way Leigh treated him, you would have never known that – you would have thought he was a star, same as all the rest! I have such a vivid memory of their end-of-year Senior dinner, where each of the coaches got up and voiced their memories and funny stories about each graduating runner. First came Coach Mac, then Coach Don Wood, who both said a few very nice things about Michael and the improvements he had made over the year, etc. - very nice and very short and sweet. Then came Coach Leigh who (of course) had prepared a full page handwritten monologue about each and every Senior! It clearly had taken her hours and hours of thought and preparation, and her memories of each of the kids were sometimes more detailed than even the parents probably remembered! Each remembrance was packed full of positive thoughts, pats on the back, and inspiration going forward, and they were anything but short, though certainly very sweet. It was Leigh at her finest – she touched each and every one of those kids that night with her thoughtfulness and encouragement and gave them the best send-off anyone could ever imagine. It was the most awesome display of how much she cared about them and how much she had tuned in to every one of them, not just the super talented kids, but the whole team! She was really something else!

So we send our thoughts and prayers your way to help you heal from this terrible tragedy, a life taken way too soon. She will literally be missed by the whole community; she touched so many. However, I hope you can take some comfort in knowing that Leigh clearly lived more in her 43 years than most of us can even fathom for our entire lifetime; she was a force and such a beautiful person! Leigh made such a mark on the world in her short time here!

John Weaver (Head Track and Cross-country Coach, Appalachian State University)

December 19, 2012

I am sitting in Orlando reflecting on the occurrences of this week with the passing of Leigh. I can only imagine the anguish, grief and severe loss that you must feel, knowing how tough it is to think about for all of us. It was difficult for me to be away and not be able to get back to Boone for the ceremonies for Leigh. In my moments of solitude, there was so much time spent trying to figure out why and attempting to recover from the shock. I am sure you are still trying to sort things out. I did a lot of reflecting, remembering and ultimately, feeling grateful and blessed that she was a part of my life.

Leigh was such an exceptional person. If you were around her, you were touched by her. She had a zest for life and all who were in it around her. It is difficult to imagine not having her among us. Yet, she will always be with us. There are so many stories, so many times, so many things that come with knowing Leigh that will never fade and never be less special for those who lived them with her. To say she was special is not enough for those of us whose lives were enriched by her friendship and love, she was so much more.

Leigh's bold spirit, survivorship instincts, and unsurpassed determination helped her make it through her most life-threatening moments many years ago.   There are so many who still receive inspiration and courage from her actions those days. After that, she took her own life to another level of excellence and so many have benefited from her courage, will and resourcefulness. It is still ongoing and will forever be a human achievement legacy.

I look back at her exploits as an athlete in our program. Being one of only two women to win the 10K, 5K and 3K in the conference championship.   Her complete involvement, determination and discipline to put herself at the top of the list against her peers. Always a gracious sportswoman whether she was winning, which she did often, or not winning, which she used to motivate her in her next racing

303

challenges. Such an outstanding team spirit and presence.

She brought that great persona to her coaching and guided so many athletes to their highest levels. I know my sons, Chase and Jay, who are in Oregon right now, loved her as their coach. There are so many athletes who were touched by her. Probably the greatest legacy a coach can have is the love and gratitude of his or her athletes. Winning is not everything, but she brought achievement, character, discipline and the winning feeling to all her athletes.

Please forgive me for not being at the ceremonies, but please accept that she was constantly on my mind and will forever be a most positive, endearing and inspirational part of my life today and forever.

Erinn Struss (Former Watauga High runner)

I've been looking for a card for two weeks, and it'll take another five for this to arrive. I'm in the middle-of-nowhere Bulgaria teaching with a State Department program.

I'm sorry.

It was through Leigh and Coach Mac that I found a home in running - a home that doesn't care how shy I am, and a home that moves with me from Madrid to San Francisco to Bulgaria. Leigh, Julie, and Holley were role models for me when I was an awkward adolescent and in bad need of folks to look up to. I can't put into words the long-term difference this has made and continues to make today.

My sophomore year of high school, the year we won State, I remember a run on Watauga River Road with the cross-country team. It was a there-and-back run; Leigh had passed me once, gone far, far ahead, and was on the return leg. She slowed down to talk to me - we chatted about breakfast cereals (no joke). What we talked about wasn't important; what mattered was the energy she imparted. I felt on top of the world for days just because she slowed down her run to talk to me. I still feel special for having encountered such a powerful individual.

Thank you.

Barbara Daye (Former Associate Vice Chancellor for Student Development, Dean of Students Emeritus, Appalachian State University)

A picture comes to mind – an early memory ('89 or '90). I call Leigh's name at the Big Apple Road Race to come forward for her award. She ran forward to receive the award and ran back to her family, all of you sitting in the grass.

Leigh's family – the importance too significant to measure. I believe she learned courage and strength from you, Louise and Claude. You supported her, and with her loving and devoted Chris, gave her the strength to become the amazing person she was.

I grieve with all of you and we all struggle with losing Leigh. A pebble drops in a pond. The ripples spread and spread. That was Leigh's impact and now our loss.

She chose "not to follow a path" but to go forward and "blaze a trail" for others to follow.

I hope we can, in perhaps a small way, live up to her example. She will always live in my heart.

Shane Austin (Former Watauga High runner)

To my extended running family!

I am so sorry to hear about your loss. It was my loss as well and thousands of others are feeling the same. Leigh was my coach for three amazing years!! I say "my" because she treated us uniquely and cared for each soul like a parent would. I will never forget her and her family; also how you are supposed to honk the horn when you see a fellow runner on the road, a single toot – toot, not a Mack truch TOOOOT – TOOOOT. Please show Chris and Holley this card. Chris, I always had great respect for you as a person! And Holley, I got to run with you for one amazing year. I always looked up to you!!

Mark Hurst (Former Director of Curriculum, Watauga County Schools)

Please know how sorry I am for your loss. Leigh was a wonderful woman who had so many special attributes and who touched so many lives in such a positive way. I know she developed many of those attributes throughout her life but I also know that she learned many of them as well from two wonderful parents.

I have a number of fond memories of Leigh; most revolving around her incredible athletic skills and coaching accomplishments. However, one of these I remember most is her leadership in making positive changes to the healthful living curriculum. Many of us saw the need to incorporate more drug education and life skills training in that course but, as you know, change can be hard.

Leigh saw the need for such changes and, thanks in large part to her leadership, such positive changes were made in that curriculum. That is just one of the many ways she positively impacted our youth.

Please know that you are in all my prayers. It is my hope and prayer that, in time, some of the hurt and pain will subside and leave you with the opportunity to remember and celebrate all the wonderful times you had with Leigh.

Anita Kitchens (parent of four Watauga High student athletes)

I can't even begin to express how I feel - Joe called - and told me, saying "It just can't be - I don't know if it's true" - at the same time Steve called from California - our whole family was shocked, saddened.

My prayer is that God sends you comfort in knowing how powerful Leigh was in reaching, in touching, so many students.   She made them realize that "coming in 4th and getting one point was important - and everyone's contribution mattered.   And there were so many of these moments.

Even though physically she will be in another place - her spirit will remain - her passion, her caring, her strength, and her integrity.

Mrs Cooper, you are the backbone of Green Valley School and the work you do there is so good.   Just know that my thoughts and prayers are with you.   With love and compassion.

Louise Moore (parent of a Watauga High runner)

So many people I know will be sharing "Leigh" stories with you, but I just had to share mine as well. Years ago, she helped coach the WHS cross-country team when my daughter, Kellen, was on the team. One day I went to pick Kellen up after practice out at Bass Lake. As I walked down unnoticed, Leigh had all the girls seated on the bank. She was telling them the importance of watching out for anything harmful to their bodies, particularly drugs, tobacco, and alcohol. They were absolutely mesmerized by her words – clinging to every word she said. I remember thinking that we parents could have been saying the very same things, and the words would likely be falling on deaf ears! But she truly did have their respect and love. What a gift she had! I am so thankful for her influence on so many lives, including my daughter's.

Please know we all share your grief. She will be missed by so many.

My heartfelt prayers and much love to you and your family.

Wendy Smith (parent of WHS runners)

Leigh touched our lives in so many ways over the years .... at Hardin Park, at WHS, at the Wellness Center. She lived fully, generously, and passionately. Our whole family grieves her loss, your loss.

Isaac commented that Leigh was the only high school coach who liked him. She inspired Matthew in cross-country after bad experiences in basketball. Leigh was a role model for Ruth, who has become a strong, competent young woman. We will forever be grateful that Leigh invested in our children and sent them a strong message that they matter.

Many nights at the Wellness Center, Leigh and I would be the only ones still in the locker room. She supported me when I was alone in Boone, and she reminded me that families are to be treasured. Thank you for sharing her with us and with the entire community.

Thank you for your sweet note. My heart aches for you and your husband; Chris, Jake, and Haleigh; and your entire family. As you requested and know, I have been praying for you all daily and throughout the night when I awaken, and various times during the day. I will continue to pray for you all.

I am sorry that I will not be at Blowing Rock to support Chris, but I know that our friends there will not let him down. I also know that you have a loving community of support. I'm grateful. If ever you need another ear or someone to cry with, please call or email me.

Please know how much Leigh and her family matter to us and how much we appreciate her presence in our lives.

I pray that God will somehow bring you healing and make your pain bearable, that you will feel his presence in the people of the community who surround you, and that you will find some peace during this time of sorrow.

Love to you.

Donna Breitenstein (Director, North Carolina Comprehensive School Health Training Center)

I am sad to think of the Boone community without Leigh Wallace in it. Your daughter, sister, wife, and mother was such a gift to us all. I knew Leigh as a dedicated student, a compelling guest speaker in my classes, an inspirational role model for student teachers in Health Education, and a devoted adjunct faculty member for future teachers.

When grading her students' last set of lesson plans and final exam, I realized with even more certainty that she taught Appalachian State University students the content and skills they will need to deliver meaningful instruction in Health. Her assignments were practical and meaningful. On the back of her final exam, one student wrote, *Thank you so much for being such a great and inspirational teacher. This was my first education class and by far my favorite this semester. The lessons that I have learned in this class I hope to take with me when I graduate and become a teacher.*

As you begin a new year, please know that we share your sadness but also your belief that Leigh truly made a difference in the lives of her students, colleagues, and friends.

Wishing you peace and comfort.

Whitney Woods Schutz (former WHS runner)

I met Leigh when I was a Freshman in high school; she was my cross-country coach. I was extremely successful in cross-country and at my first meet I came in third on the team. Later that year I would be named all-state in cross-country with a 6th place finish at the state championship meet; the team went on to win the meet. Running gave me friends and confidence; it made me different because I was good. It is safe to say my love for running began with the first step. In track that spring I was named all-state again in the 3200 meters when I came in 3rd place; our team went on to win yet another state championship.

My running career went on this way until my Junior year in cross-country. For some reason I had lost my confidence. I have always been an emotional runner and I could not find any reason to believe in myself. What followed was disappointment after disappointment. I would finish races sometimes being 8th on the team. At regional and state meets, a team is only allowed seven runners and everyone brings their seven best; I was 8th on the team. I was embarrassed; I had been known in high school as a good runner and I was struggling with who I was. In a sense, not being good made me like everyone else; I wasn't special or different.

One day Leigh asked me to run with her. I remember thinking 'This is where she tells me I am not going to run in the state meet.' We spent the whole run just talking, none of which I remember. What I do remember is getting done and her looking directly in my eyes and telling me she believed in me; I was going to run at State. I had lost my spirit for a bit but she knew it was not gone forever. To be so young with no belief or confidence in yourself and have someone you respect tell you they believe in you, well, words cannot describe what that meant to me. I ran State and finished 74th. Leigh's whole family was there: her mother and father, her two sisters, Julie and Holley, and her brother, Graig. Running was a family sport. I walked off crying, and for the millionth time that season, I was embarrassed. Leigh walked up to me and told me to forget the past, mistakes make us human, and to look towards the future; track was just around the corner.

Track did begin that following spring. Fellow runner and friend, Marina Chase, and I decided early in the season that we wanted to be first and second in the 3200 meters at the state meet. I had no reason to believe in myself, but I forgot the past and looked toward the future as I had been instructed. I think in the beginning Marina and I were joking but, by God, Leigh was not going to let us forget our goal. During hard workouts she would run with us, talking effortlessly while Marina and I struggled to breathe, pushing us to run harder. After three months of practice it was time for the state meet and we accomplished our goal. Marina came in second and I was first. We made a goal, worked hard, and achieved it. During the season a friend and teammate, Joe Lion, lost his mother to a long battle with cancer. It was during this time, while at a gas station in Wilkesboro, NC, Leigh told us she was pregnant. She would give birth months later to Haleigh, her second child and only daughter. The entire team came to the hospital after cross-country practice to visit her - only hours after she had given birth.

During the summer before my senior year I attended the Appalachian State University running camp. I was in the top group and Leigh was our coach. Whenever the team was in the van driving to practice and we pulled up next to another van, Leigh would crank up the music and yell "Insta-fun!" At this point we would all begin dancing just to show everyone we were the funniest team in camp.

I ran in college at Western Carolina University, but I did not achieve the success I had while in high school. Leigh had set the bar really high, and my college coach did not understand my emotional side like Leigh had. In addition, Leigh brought our team together; she fostered teamwork just by being who she was; I was never on a team like I had been in high school. To put it simply, running in college just wasn't as much fun.

Through the years (2005-2012) I saw Leigh at weddings, in town and at their house. At the end of 2005 Leigh's brother, Graig, brought his newborn son, Findley, and wife home for a visit. We played pool, drank beer, and caught up on life at the Cooper house while Findley slept. I asked Leigh a hundred questions and she answered them all openly and honestly as she had her whole life. The last time I saw Leigh was at Mellow Mushroom on Wednesday, August 1, 2012, nearly 20 years after our first meeting and just three days after getting engaged. She had met my fiancee at a fellow high school runner's wedding the year before; we had been seated at the same table. Chris and she looked exhausted because they had just gotten back from their yearly family reunion at the beach, but she would not have missed this wedding no matter how inconvenient it may have been. Brian and I had only been together for eight days and Leigh said to me "You look so beautiful and happy, Whitney."

I looked at Brian and said "I am." Once again, she was able to read me like a book.

When Leigh heard of our engagement at Mellow Mushroom, she instantly looked at Brian and said, "Do you know what you're getting into?" We all laughed and spent the next five minutes making fun of me and talking about the wedding.

I learned of Leigh's illness via Facebook. I called Graig on Saturday night to see how everything was going and then on Sunday; we never did get in touch. On Monday morning my mother called me to tell me about her death.

I came home to attend Leigh's funeral. I wanted to see the family that had touched my life in so many ways. My mother decided she wanted to say goodbye to Leigh in person and asked me to go with her. I said I would but I wasn't ready to see her family yet; I was scared. As I sat in the parking lot of the funeral home, waiting for my mother, hiding, I saw Claude come out and head towards our car. He came up to the passenger window and waved at me. As I opened the car and stepped out, he hugged me and said "Why don't you come inside?"

I responded with "Because I'm not dressed properly" and looked down at my jeans with holes in them.

While still hugging me, he said "We don't care about that; come inside and see the family" and he led me inside.

Once in the door, Julie came to me, hugged me and said "Do you want me to walk up with you to see Leigh?" I nodded and she led me, with her arm around my shoulders, to see Leigh.

315

We were stopped halfway by Louise, who told me "You were one of her success stories."

I got to Leigh, looked at her, and said to myself "You did it; you lived a life that moved and inspired hundreds. You lived so that you will never be forgotten." I told her I loved her and I would remember everything I learned through her words and life. When I got home afterwards, I thought about the experience while Brian held me. What moved me most was how the family, in the midst of tragedy and heartbreak, was more concerned about me than themselves. It should have been me comforting them, but I was unable to find my words. The Coopers were truly selfless by their very nature.

After Leigh's memorial service over 30 former Watauga High School runners whom Leigh had coached gathered at my house. We drank beer, told funny stories, and watched the highlight videos from 1994-1998 together. There was talk of dancing to Billy Idol as we had while in high school. Once again Leigh had brought us all together for the first time since high school, and it felt as if no time had passed even though it had been nearly 14 years.

Leigh was who she was because of the family that surrounded her. Each member aided in making Leigh the person she had become. Louise, who taught me in 7th grade, still is a person whom I admire, consider a mentor, and truly believe her guidance and belief in me steered my life in the direction it is today. By signing me up to compete in a county-wide middle school race in 7th grade, she made me realize I could run. I still run to this day. She will be there for others even if it is at detriment to her own self. Graig has her humor, her ability to listen and to give inspiring advice. Holley, the quietest of the bunch, has the ability to put you at ease just by being in her presence. Julie had the strength to guide me when I felt lost to say goodbye. Claude made me feel safe when I was scared.

I knew Leigh as a coach, sister, hero, runner and friend. When I think back on my experiences with Leigh, I remember the stories above. She taught me to forget the past; it can't be changed. Look to the future. She taught me to have fun so others will always want to be around me. She taught me to take love seriously and remember to include those who matter, not only in my life, but in the life of others. I learned to

316

make a goal, work hard, and achieve it. If I fail, try again and again until I succeed. She taught me to be honest and to only give out compliments when they are truly deserved; that way people will remember them, as I have. She taught me to believe in myself. But the thing I learned most from Leigh stems from her actions and not from her words.

During my senior year, after a run, Joe Lion informed me that he and his brother, Todd, were going to Leigh's house for dinner.

I asked him why and he told me "Because one year ago my mother died."

I apologized; I hadn't remembered and he responded with "Nobody has; it feels like everyone has forgotten but Leigh."

From that day I vowed never to have someone feel as if everyone had forgotten. Even if I may not have known the person who died personally, I would never forget what that person meant to them. I would call them, take them out for a beer, do whatever they needed so they knew I cared about them, their life, and their loved one.

Pioneer Booster Club: Establishes Leigh Cooper Wallace Memorial Scholarship

As a teacher, coach, and mother, Leigh Cooper Wallace's spirit, inspiration, and memory continue on in the hearts of her children, students and athletes – those she dedicated herself to most passionately. It is they, along with the staff and faculty of Watauga High School to whom Leigh imparted the values of good decision-making, working hard to achieve goals and overcome adversity, and truly living life to the fullest every day.

Leigh Cooper Wallace graduated from Appalachian State University in 1992 with a degree in Exercise Science. She was a standout distance runner for ASU. Leigh also coached winning track and cross-country teams at Watauga High School for over ten years. She helped establish women's lacrosse as a varsity sport at Watauga High School and was the first head coach in this sport. She was inducted into the Watauga County Sports Hall of Fame in 2006. She taught healthful living and physical education at Watauga High School from 1998-2012.

"She had this way about her . . . of being vulnerable, humble, strong and focused – that invited those around her to be unabashadly human, joyfully alive and relentless in their pursuit to achieve personal greatness. She will be missed."

Accomplishments:

The impact that Leigh has had on others has been recognized in many ways, some while she was living, some after her passing. Included here are a few of Leigh's triumphs and recognitions.

1990 – All-Southern-Conference, Cross-country.

1991 – All-Southern-Conference, Cross-country.

1992 – Southern Conference Champion, Indoor Track 5,000 meters.

Southern Conference Champion, Outdoor Track 10,000 meters.

Southern Conference Champion, Outdoor Track 5,000 meters.

Southern Conference Champion, Outdoor Track 3,000 meters.

1993 - 1st Place, Summer Breeze 5,000 meters, Charlotte, NC.

1993 - 1st Place, Rhododendron Run 10,000 meters, Bakersville, NC.

1994 - 1st Place, Winthrop Eagle 8,000 meters, Rock Hill, SC.

1994 – Nominee, Young Adult Leadership Award, Women's Forum of NC.

1995 – Guest on Leeza Gibbons TV Program, Los Angeles, CA.

2004 - 1st Place, The Bear 5,000 meters, Grandfather Mountain, NC.

2005 - 1st Place, Valle Crucis River Run 5,000 meters, Valle Crucis, NC.

2005 – Inducted into Watauga County Sports Hall of Fame, Boone, NC.

2008 – Featured in Oxygen Channel TV Series, *Captured.*

2011 – Featured in Investigative Discovery Channel TV Series, *Sins and Secrets.*

2013 – Leigh Cooper Wallace Making a Difference Award established, Girls on The Run of High Country.

2013 – Recognized as 2013 Woman of Vision, Appalachian Women's Fund, Boone, NC.

2013 – Leigh Cooper Wallace Memorial Scholarship established, Watauga High School, Boone, NC.

2016 – Appalachian State University Sports Hall of Fame announcement:

LEIGH COOPER WALLACE (Women's Cross Country/Track and Field – 1988-1992):

Was a six-time all-Southern Conference performer and four-time conference champion as a standout distance runner...four conference titles all came as a senior - 5,000 meters (indoors) and 3,000, 5,000 and 10,000 meters (outdoors)...is one of only two athletes in SoCon history to win all three distance races (3,000, 5,000 and 10,000 meters) at one conference championship meet (joining App State teammate Whitney Ball)...named all-SoCon as a junior and senior in cross country, placing third at the conference championship as a senior in 1991...in her four years at Appalachian State, she helped the Mountaineers capture all 12 SoCon cross country, indoor track and field and outdoor track and field team championships...served as an inspiration for the entire campus community as the survivor of a kidnapping and sexual assault while a student at App State in 1989...regularly shared her story at Appalachian State's annual Walk for Awareness, which promotes campus safety, commemorates lives lost to violence and supports victims and survivors of violent crimes... went on to be a longtime teacher and coach at nearby Watauga High School and helped the Pioneers' cross country and track and field teams to numerous conference, regional and state championships in her 10-plus years as a coach...was inducted into the Watauga County Sports Hall of Fame in 2005...died after a brief and sudden illness in 2012 at the age of 43.

ACKNOWLEDGMENTS

This is Leigh's story, and I wanted her to tell it. Unfortunately, it didn't work out that way. Even though Leigh died, the story survived thanks to Louise, who not only encouraged me to keep it alive but contributed significantly to the telling of it. I'm grateful to all the other family contributors as well as to the extended family for their support and encouragement.

I also thank all the non-family who contributed to her story: the athletes, students, parents of students and athletes, co-workers, and others who shared their experiences with Leigh.

And I am thankful for the editing work done by my friends Chris Benson and Jimmy Addison. I always believed this would be a powerful story, and through their efforts, they've given me added confidence that we are doing it the right way.

We will always treasure the love and support our family received from our friends in Boone and Watauga County in the days and years following Leigh's death. Your compassion makes us strong.

And finally, Louise and I are so grateful to all our Clemson friends who have supported us and allowed us to begin a new life after the one we loved so much came to an end. You've enabled us to live and love and laugh again.

Made in the USA
Middletown, DE
09 April 2025